WRITER: **JONATHAN HICKMAN**

ARTIST: **MIKE DEODATO**

COLOR ARTIST: **FRANK MARTIN** WITH **RAIN BEREDO** (#12)

LETTERER: **VC'S JOE CARAMAGNA**

COVER ART: **MIKE DEODATO** WITH **RAIN BEREDO** (#7), **MARTE GRACIA** (#8) & **LAURA MARTIN** (#9-12)

ASSISTANT EDITOR: **JAKE THOMAS**

EDITORS: **TOM BREVOORT** WITH **LAUREN SANKOVITCH**

COLLECTION EDITOR: **JENNIFER GRÜNWALD**
ASSISTANT EDITOR: **SARAH BRUNSTAD**
ASSOCIATE MANAGING EDITOR: **ALEX STARBUCK**
EDITOR, SPECIAL PROJECTS: **MARK D. BEAZLEY**
SENIOR EDITOR, SPECIAL PROJECTS: **JEFF YOUNGQUIST**
SVP PRINT, SALES & MARKETING: **DAVID GABRIEL**
BOOK DESIGN: **JEFF POWELL**

EDITOR IN CHIEF: **AXEL ALONSO**
CHIEF CREATIVE OFFICER: **JOE QUESADA**
PUBLISHER: **DAN BUCKLEY**
EXECUTIVE PRODUCER: **ALAN FINE**

NEW AVENGERS VOL. 2: INFINITY. Contains material originally published in magazine form as NEW AVENGERS #7-12. First printing 2014. ISBN# 978-0-7851-6662-7. Published by MARVEL WORLDWIDE, INC., a subsidiary of MARVEL ENTERTAINMENT, LLC. OFFICE OF PUBLICATION: 135 West 50th Street, New York, NY 10020. Copyright © 2013 and 2014 Marvel Characters, Inc. All rights reserved. All characters featured in this issue and the distinctive names and likenesses thereof, and all related indicia are trademarks of Marvel Characters, Inc. No similarity between any of the names, characters, persons, and/or institutions in this magazine with those of any living or dead person or institution is intended, and any such similarity which may exist is purely coincidental. **Printed in the U.S.A.** ALAN FINE, EVP - Office of the President, Marvel Worldwide, Inc. and EVP & CMO Marvel Characters B.V.; DAN BUCKLEY, Publisher & President - Print, Animation & Digital Divisions; JOE QUESADA, Chief Creative Officer; TOM BREVOORT, SVP of Publishing; DAVID BOGART, SVP of Operations & Procurement, Publishing; C.B. CEBULSKI, SVP of Creator & Content Development; DAVID GABRIEL, SVP Print, Sales & Marketing; JIM O'KEEFE, VP of Operations & Logistics; DAN CARR, Executive Director of Publishing Technology; SUSAN CRESPI, Editorial Operations Manager; ALEX MORALES, Publishing Operations Manager; STAN LEE, Chairman Emeritus. For information regarding advertising in Marvel Comics or on Marvel.com, please contact Niza Disla, Director of Marvel Partnerships, at ndisla@marvel.com. For Marvel subscription inquiries, please call 800-217-9158. **Manufactured between 7/18/2014 and 8/25/2014 by R.R. DONNELLEY, INC., SALEM, VA, USA.**

10 9 8 7 6 5 4 3 2 1

PREVIOUSLY IN NEW AVENGERS

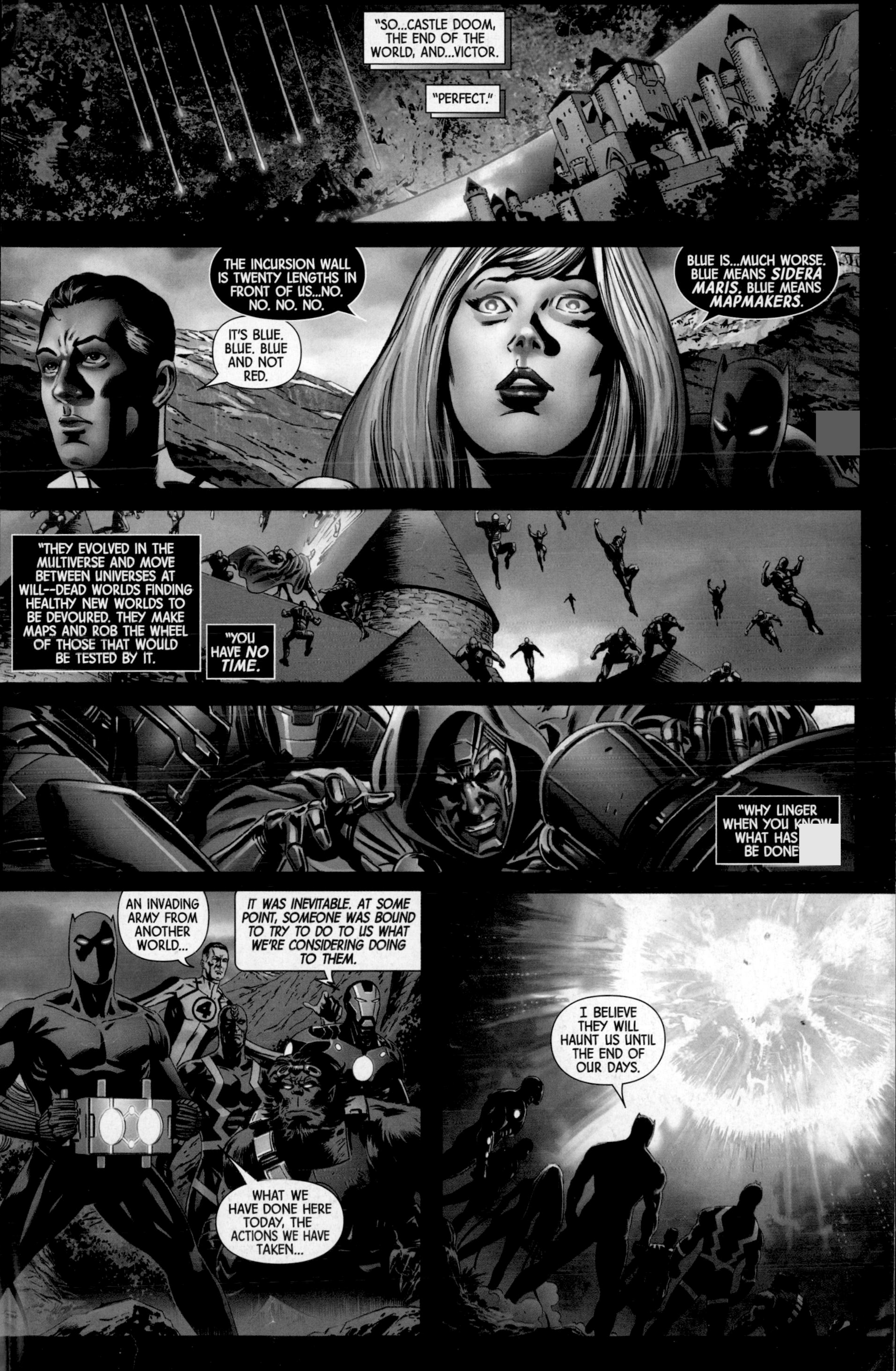
"SO...CASTLE DOOM, THE END OF THE WORLD, AND...VICTOR.
"PERFECT."
THE INCURSION WALL IS TWENTY LENGTHS IN FRONT OF US...NO. NO. NO. NO.
IT'S BLUE. BLUE. BLUE AND NOT RED.
BLUE IS...MUCH WORSE. BLUE MEANS *SIDERA MARIS.* BLUE MEANS *MAPMAKERS.*
"THEY EVOLVED IN THE MULTIVERSE AND MOVE BETWEEN UNIVERSES AT WILL--DEAD WORLDS FINDING HEALTHY NEW WORLDS TO BE DEVOURED. THEY MAKE MAPS AND ROB THE WHEEL OF THOSE THAT WOULD BE TESTED BY IT.
"YOU HAVE *NO TIME.*
"WHY LINGER WHEN YOU KN
WHAT HAS
BE DONE
AN INVADING ARMY FROM ANOTHER WORLD...
IT WAS INEVITABLE. AT SOME POINT, SOMEONE WAS BOUND TO TRY TO DO TO US WHAT WE'RE CONSIDERING DOING TO THEM.
WHAT WE HAVE DONE HERE TODAY, THE ACTIONS WE HAVE TAKEN...
I BELIEVE THEY WILL HAUNT US UNTIL THE END OF OUR DAYS.

"THRONES"

THE ILLUMINATI

BLACK BOLT
Celestial Messiah

NAMOR
Imperius Rex

REED RICHARDS
Universal Builder

IRON MAN
Master of Machines

BEAST
Mutant Genius

DOCTOR STRANGE
Sorcerer Supreme

BLACK PANTHER
King of the Dead

ONE
MONTH
LATER...

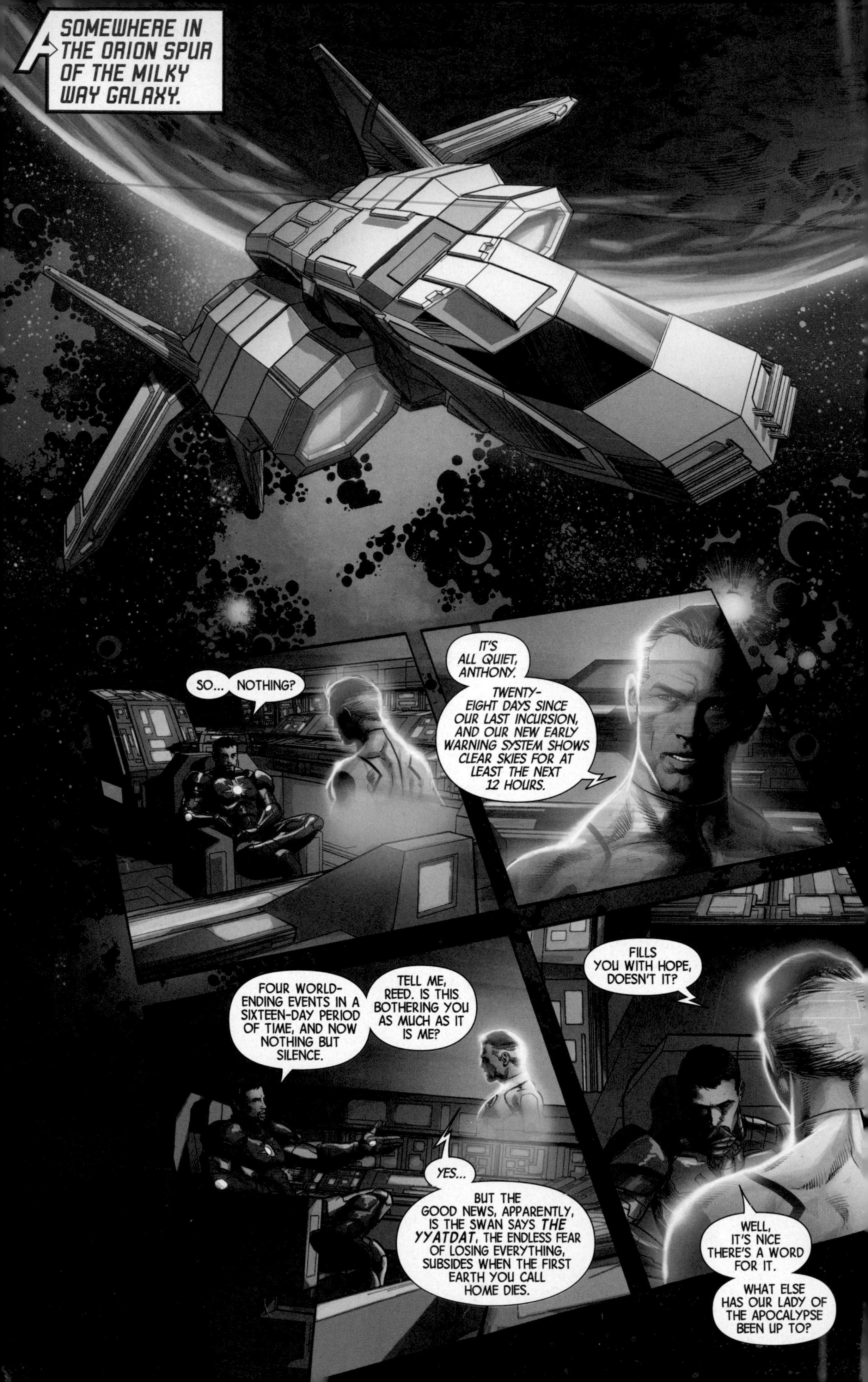
SOMEWHERE IN THE ORION SPUR OF THE MILKY WAY GALAXY.
SO... NOTHING?
IT'S ALL QUIET, ANTHONY.
TWENTY-EIGHT DAYS SINCE OUR LAST INCURSION, AND OUR NEW EARLY WARNING SYSTEM SHOWS CLEAR SKIES FOR AT LEAST THE NEXT 12 HOURS.
FOUR WORLD-ENDING EVENTS IN A SIXTEEN-DAY PERIOD OF TIME, AND NOW NOTHING BUT SILENCE.
TELL ME, REED. IS THIS BOTHERING YOU AS MUCH AS IT IS ME?
YES...
BUT THE GOOD NEWS, APPARENTLY, IS THE SWAN SAYS THE YYATDAT, THE ENDLESS FEAR OF LOSING EVERYTHING, SUBSIDES WHEN THE FIRST EARTH YOU CALL HOME DIES.
FILLS YOU WITH HOPE, DOESN'T IT?
WELL, IT'S NICE THERE'S A WORD FOR IT.
WHAT ELSE HAS OUR LADY OF THE APOCALYPSE BEEN UP TO?

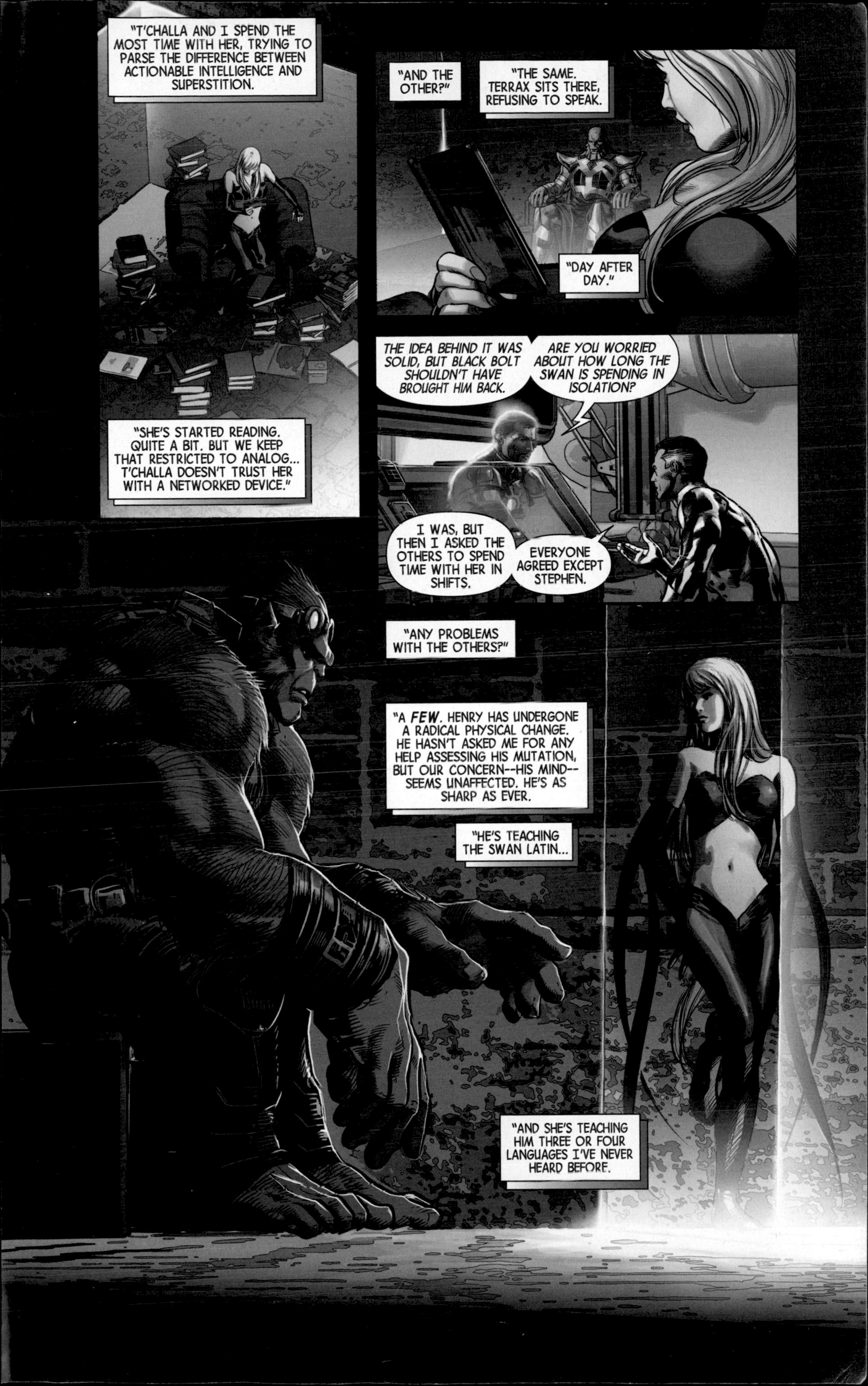
"T'CHALLA AND I SPEND THE MOST TIME WITH HER, TRYING TO PARSE THE DIFFERENCE BETWEEN ACTIONABLE INTELLIGENCE AND SUPERSTITION.
"SHE'S STARTED READING. QUITE A BIT. BUT WE KEEP THAT RESTRICTED TO ANALOG... T'CHALLA DOESN'T TRUST HER WITH A NETWORKED DEVICE."
"AND THE OTHER?"
"THE SAME. TERRAX SITS THERE, REFUSING TO SPEAK.
"DAY AFTER DAY."
THE IDEA BEHIND IT WAS SOLID, BUT BLACK BOLT SHOULDN'T HAVE BROUGHT HIM BACK.
ARE YOU WORRIED ABOUT HOW LONG THE SWAN IS SPENDING IN ISOLATION?
I WAS, BUT THEN I ASKED THE OTHERS TO SPEND TIME WITH HER IN SHIFTS.
EVERYONE AGREED EXCEPT STEPHEN.
"ANY PROBLEMS WITH THE OTHERS?"
"A FEW. HENRY HAS UNDERGONE A RADICAL PHYSICAL CHANGE. HE HASN'T ASKED ME FOR ANY HELP ASSESSING HIS MUTATION, BUT OUR CONCERN--HIS MIND--SEEMS UNAFFECTED. HE'S AS SHARP AS EVER.
"HE'S TEACHING THE SWAN LATIN...
"AND SHE'S TEACHING HIM THREE OR FOUR LANGUAGES I'VE NEVER HEARD BEFORE.

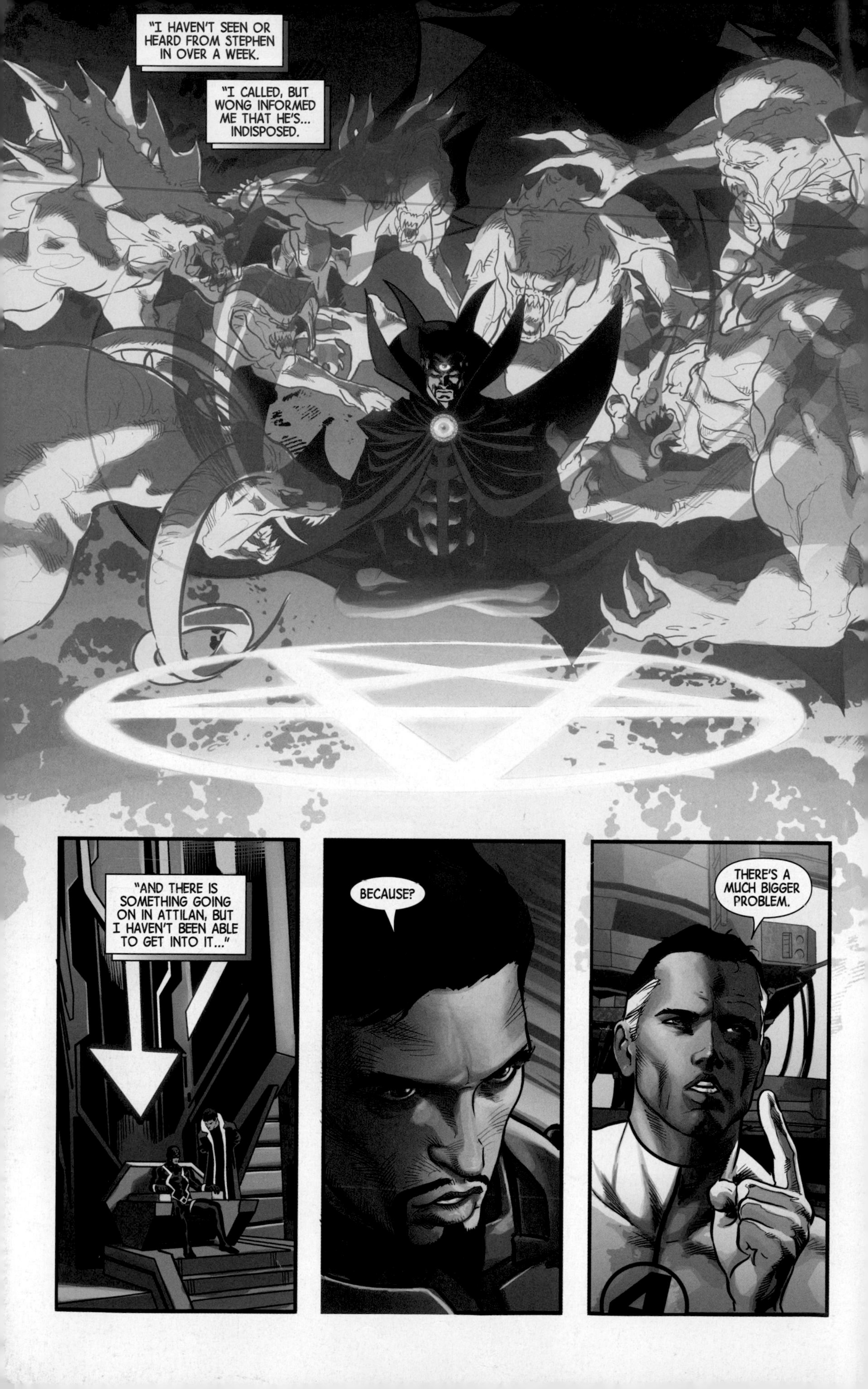
"I HAVEN'T SEEN OR HEARD FROM STEPHEN IN OVER A WEEK.
"I CALLED, BUT WONG INFORMED ME THAT HE'S... INDISPOSED.
"AND THERE IS SOMETHING GOING ON IN ATTILAN, BUT I HAVEN'T BEEN ABLE TO GET INTO IT..."
BECAUSE?
THERE'S A MUCH BIGGER PROBLEM.

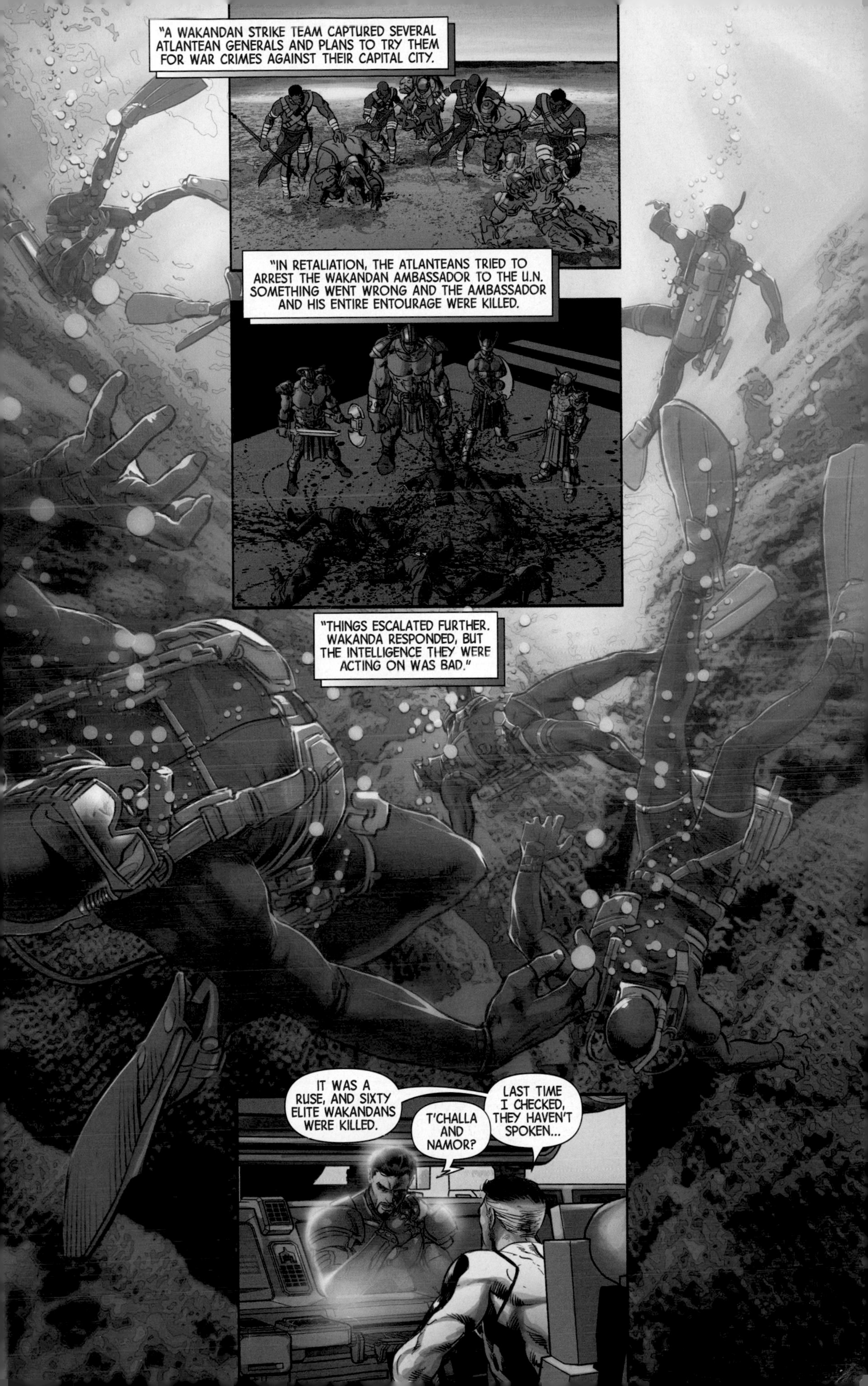
"A WAKANDAN STRIKE TEAM CAPTURED SEVERAL ATLANTEAN GENERALS AND PLANS TO TRY THEM FOR WAR CRIMES AGAINST THEIR CAPITAL CITY.
"IN RETALIATION, THE ATLANTEANS TRIED TO ARREST THE WAKANDAN AMBASSADOR TO THE U.N. SOMETHING WENT WRONG AND THE AMBASSADOR AND HIS ENTIRE ENTOURAGE WERE KILLED.
"THINGS ESCALATED FURTHER. WAKANDA RESPONDED, BUT THE INTELLIGENCE THEY WERE ACTING ON WAS BAD."
IT WAS A RUSE, AND SIXTY ELITE WAKANDANS WERE KILLED.
T'CHALLA AND NAMOR?
LAST TIME I CHECKED, THEY HAVEN'T SPOKEN...

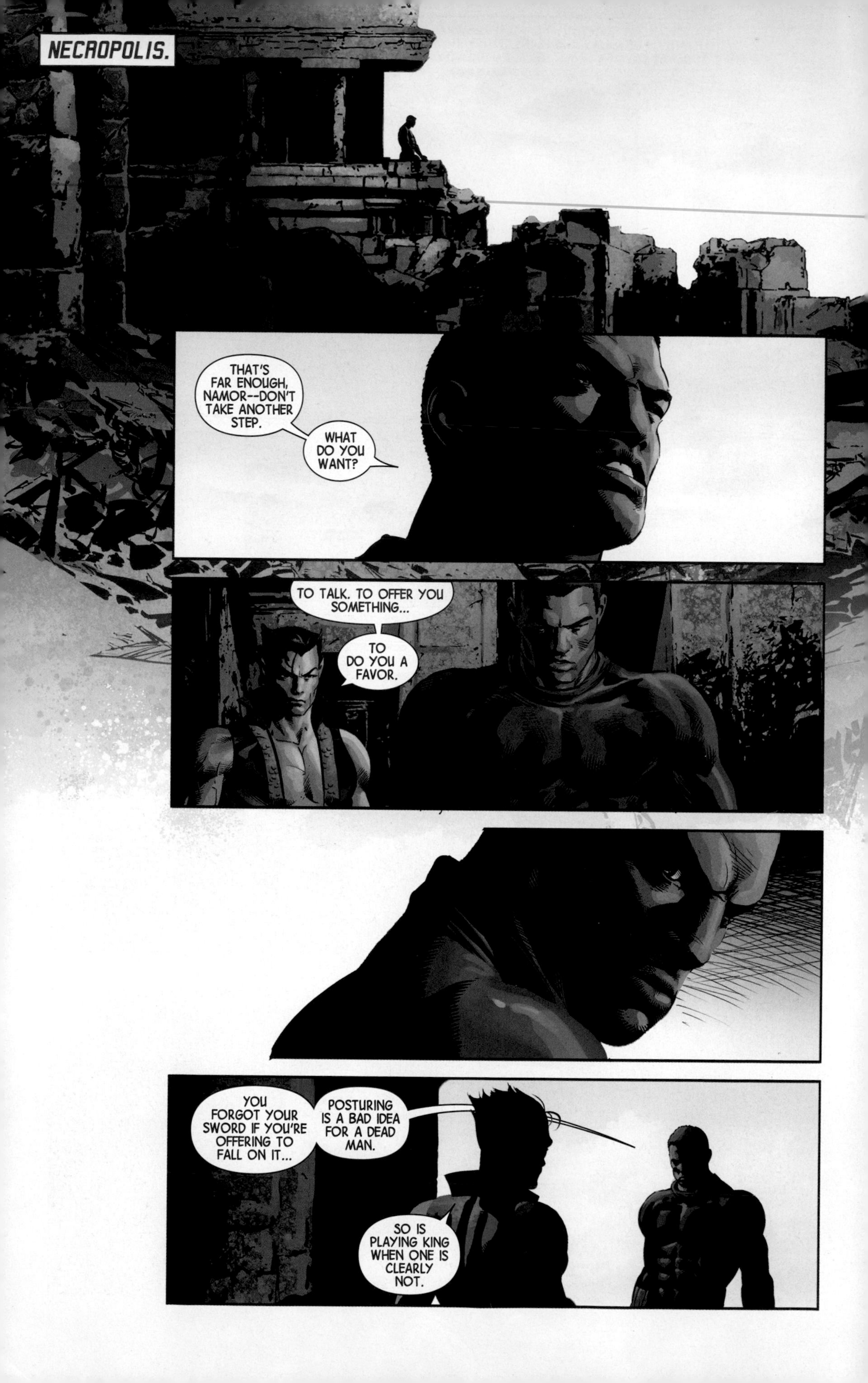
NECROPOLIS.
THAT'S FAR ENOUGH, NAMOR--DON'T TAKE ANOTHER STEP.
WHAT DO YOU WANT?
TO TALK. TO OFFER YOU SOMETHING...
TO DO YOU A FAVOR.
YOU FORGOT YOUR SWORD IF YOU'RE OFFERING TO FALL ON IT...
POSTURING IS A BAD IDEA FOR A DEAD MAN.
SO IS PLAYING KING WHEN ONE IS CLEARLY NOT.

I WANT YOU TO LISTEN TO ME.

WAKANDA CANNOT WIN A WAR WITH ATLANTIS.

I THINK YOU'RE OVERESTIMATING THE STRENGTH OF ATLANTIS AND ANY...PERCEIVED WEAKNESSES OF WAKANDA.

NAMOR, YOU'RE WRONG.

AH, THE FABLED TECHNOLOGICAL SUPERIORITY OF THE WAKANDAN PEOPLE. THE GREAT NATION THAT HAS NEVER FALLEN...

AND MEN CALL ME ARROGANT.

T'CHALLA, YOUR PROBLEM IS NOT RESOURCES, TACTICS, OR EVEN YOUR PEOPLE'S ARMY...

IT'S THE PEOPLE.

MANY DO NOT CARE FOR THE PRETENDER WHO KEEPS WAKANDA'S THRONE WARM...

THE QUEEN--YOUR SISTER--HAS ENEMIES. THESE ENEMIES WHISPER... AND WOULD LIKE TO SEE HER FALL.

HOW DO YOU THINK WE SO EASILY DISPATCHED YOUR ELITE WARRIORS?

HOW DO YOU THINK WE KNEW THEY WERE COMING?

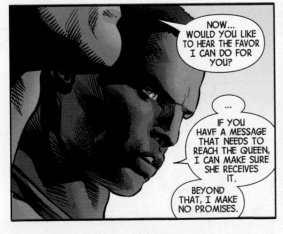

NOW... WOULD YOU LIKE TO HEAR THE FAVOR I CAN DO FOR YOU?

...

IF YOU HAVE A MESSAGE THAT NEEDS TO REACH THE QUEEN, I CAN MAKE SURE SHE RECEIVES IT.

BEYOND THAT, I MAKE NO PROMISES.

VERY WELL...

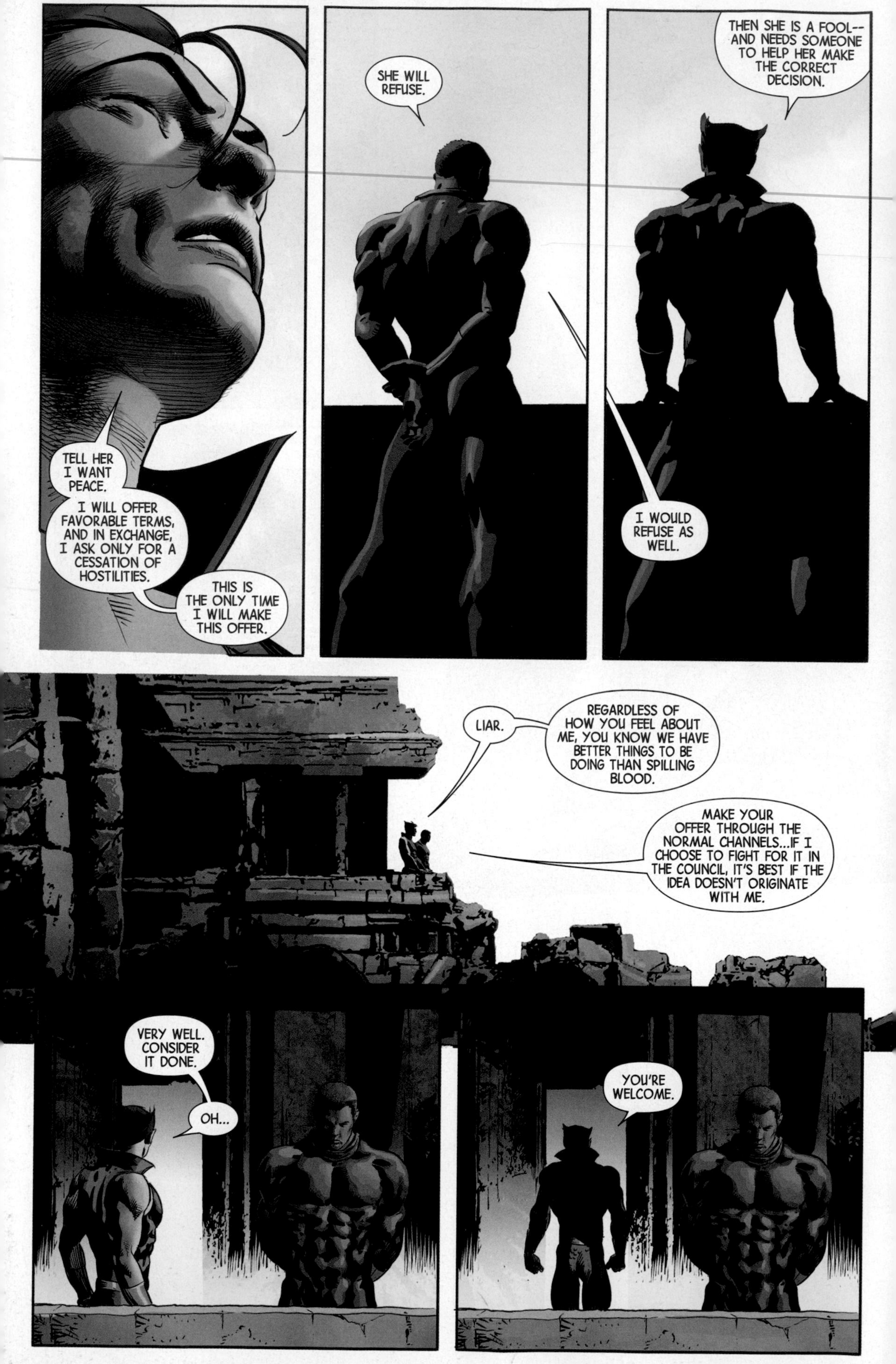

TELL HER I WANT PEACE.
I WILL OFFER FAVORABLE TERMS, AND IN EXCHANGE, I ASK ONLY FOR A CESSATION OF HOSTILITIES.
THIS IS THE ONLY TIME I WILL MAKE THIS OFFER.
SHE WILL REFUSE.
THEN SHE IS A FOOL-- AND NEEDS SOMEONE TO HELP HER MAKE THE CORRECT DECISION.
I WOULD REFUSE AS WELL.
LIAR.
REGARDLESS OF HOW YOU FEEL ABOUT ME, YOU KNOW WE HAVE BETTER THINGS TO BE DOING THAN SPILLING BLOOD.
MAKE YOUR OFFER THROUGH THE NORMAL CHANNELS...IF I CHOOSE TO FIGHT FOR IT IN THE COUNCIL, IT'S BEST IF THE IDEA DOESN'T ORIGINATE WITH ME.
VERY WELL. CONSIDER IT DONE.
OH...
YOU'RE WELCOME.

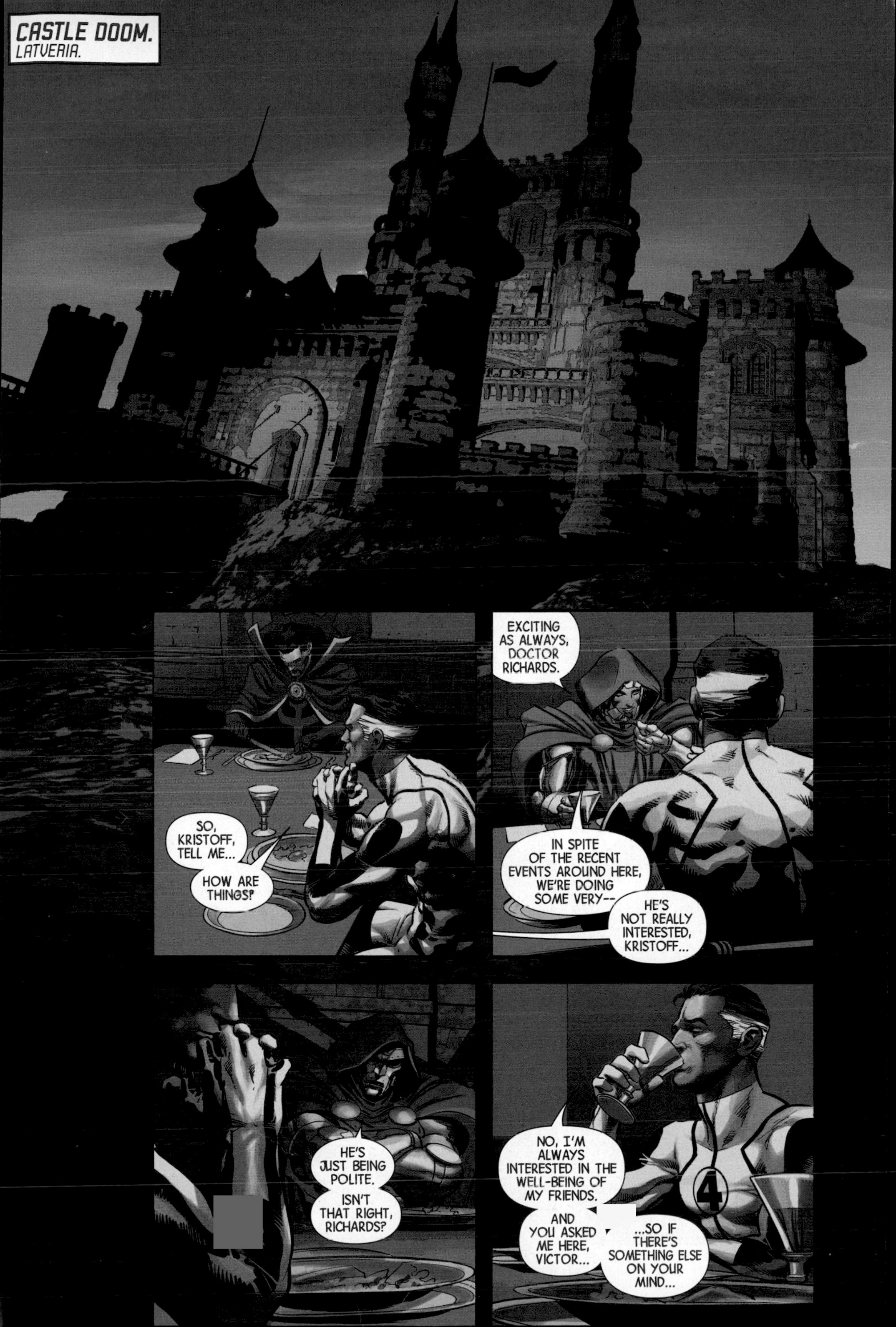
CASTLE DOOM.
LATVERIA.
SO, KRISTOFF, TELL ME...
HOW ARE THINGS?
EXCITING AS ALWAYS, DOCTOR RICHARDS.
IN SPITE OF THE RECENT EVENTS AROUND HERE, WE'RE DOING SOME VERY--
HE'S NOT REALLY INTERESTED, KRISTOFF...
HE'S JUST BEING POLITE.
ISN'T THAT RIGHT, RICHARDS?
NO, I'M ALWAYS INTERESTED IN THE WELL-BEING OF MY FRIENDS.
AND YOU ASKED ME HERE, VICTOR...
...SO IF THERE'S SOMETHING ELSE ON YOUR MIND...

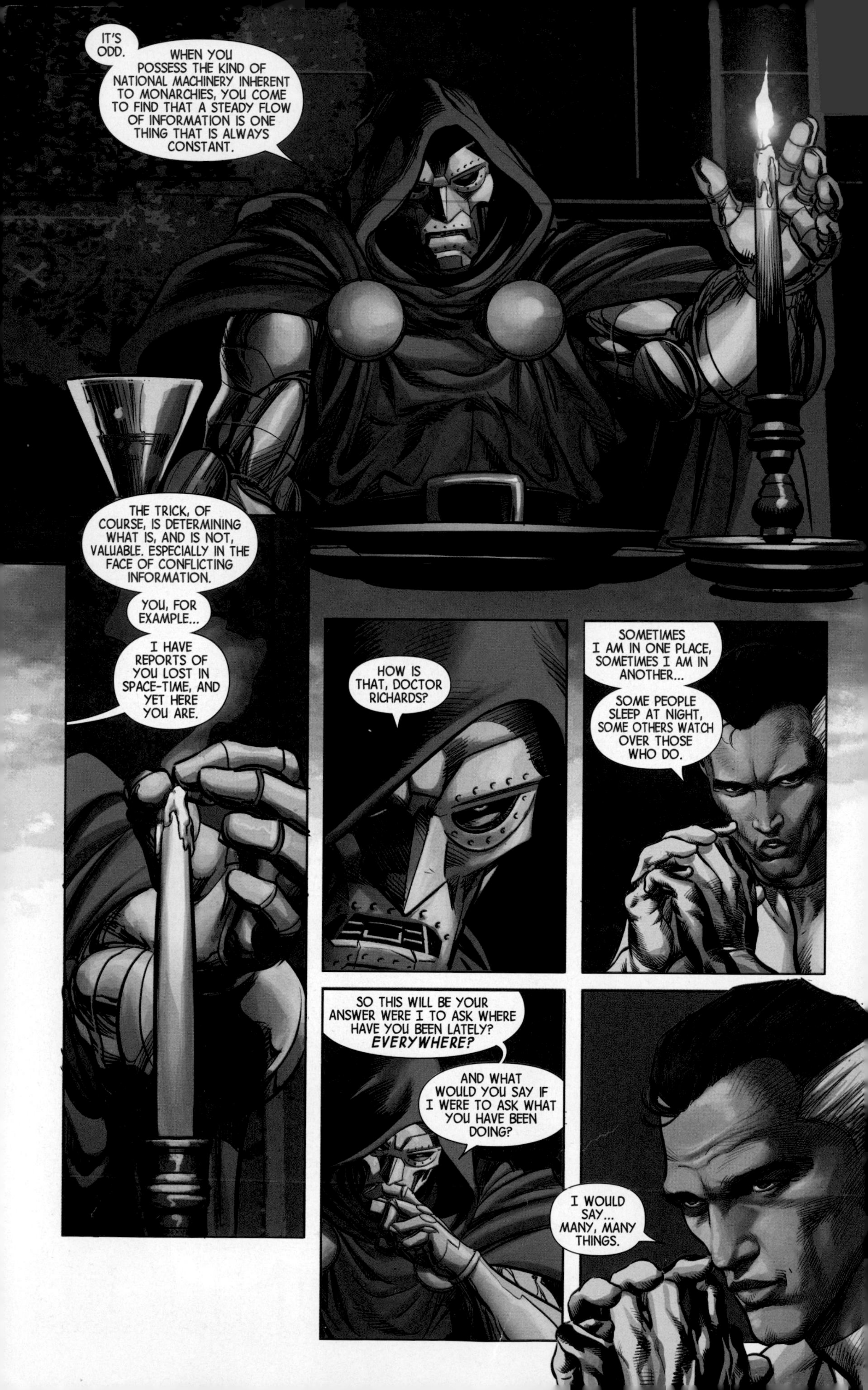
IT'S ODD.
WHEN YOU POSSESS THE KIND OF NATIONAL MACHINERY INHERENT TO MONARCHIES, YOU COME TO FIND THAT A STEADY FLOW OF INFORMATION IS ONE THING THAT IS ALWAYS CONSTANT.
THE TRICK, OF COURSE, IS DETERMINING WHAT IS, AND IS NOT, VALUABLE. ESPECIALLY IN THE FACE OF CONFLICTING INFORMATION.
YOU, FOR EXAMPLE...
I HAVE REPORTS OF YOU LOST IN SPACE-TIME, AND YET HERE YOU ARE.
HOW IS THAT, DOCTOR RICHARDS?
SOMETIMES I AM IN ONE PLACE, SOMETIMES I AM IN ANOTHER...
SOME PEOPLE SLEEP AT NIGHT, SOME OTHERS WATCH OVER THOSE WHO DO.
SO THIS WILL BE YOUR ANSWER WERE I TO ASK WHERE HAVE YOU BEEN LATELY? *EVERYWHERE?*
AND WHAT WOULD YOU SAY IF I WERE TO ASK WHAT YOU HAVE BEEN DOING?
I WOULD SAY... MANY, MANY THINGS.

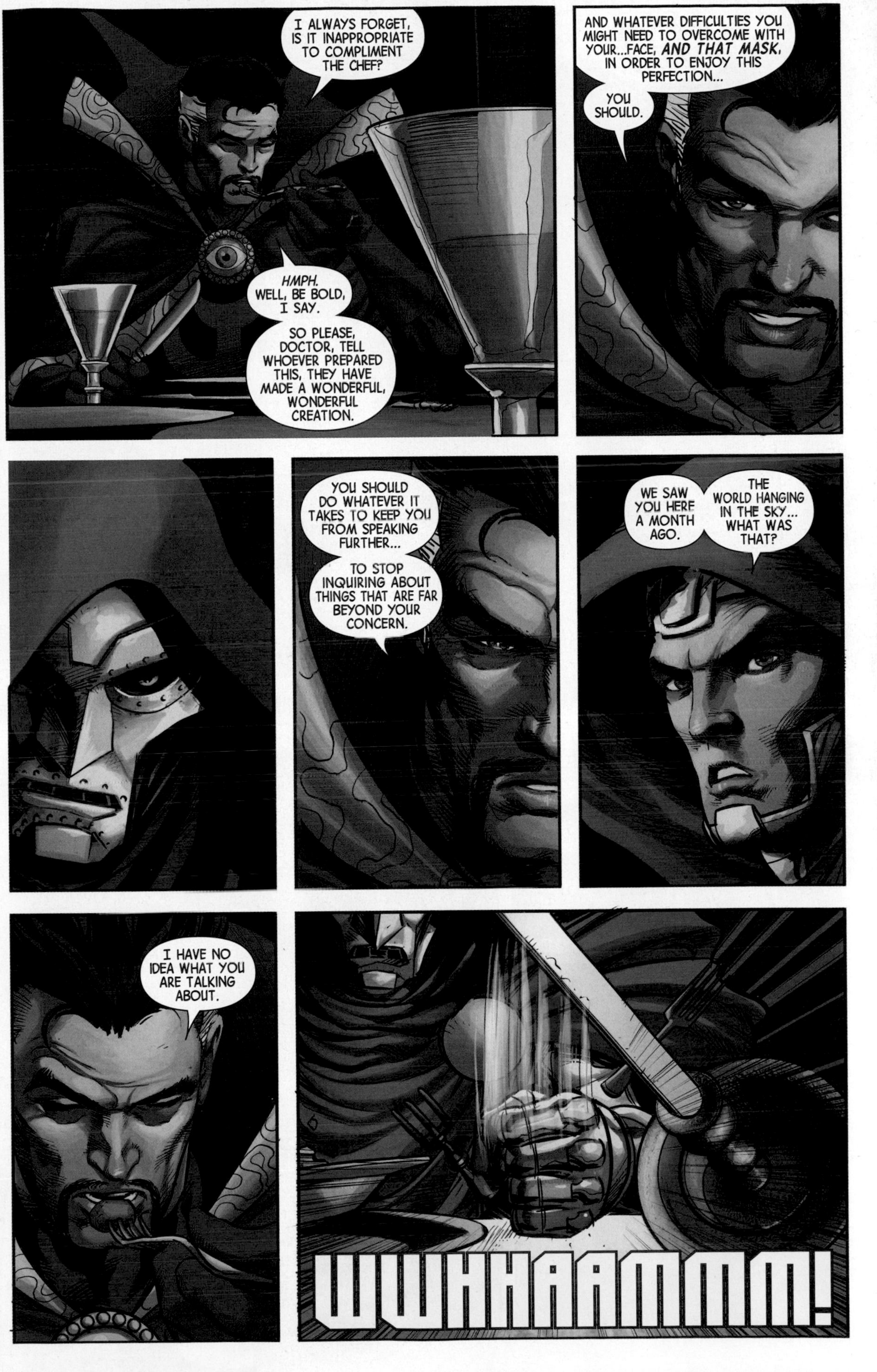
I ALWAYS FORGET, IS IT INAPPROPRIATE TO COMPLIMENT THE CHEF?
HMPH. WELL, BE BOLD, I SAY.
SO PLEASE, DOCTOR, TELL WHOEVER PREPARED THIS, THEY HAVE MADE A WONDERFUL, WONDERFUL CREATION.
AND WHATEVER DIFFICULTIES YOU MIGHT NEED TO OVERCOME WITH YOUR...FACE, AND THAT MASK, IN ORDER TO ENJOY THIS PERFECTION...
YOU SHOULD.
YOU SHOULD DO WHATEVER IT TAKES TO KEEP YOU FROM SPEAKING FURTHER...
TO STOP INQUIRING ABOUT THINGS THAT ARE FAR BEYOND YOUR CONCERN.
WE SAW YOU HERE A MONTH AGO.
THE WORLD HANGING IN THE SKY... WHAT WAS THAT?
I HAVE NO IDEA WHAT YOU ARE TALKING ABOUT.
WWHHAAMMMM!

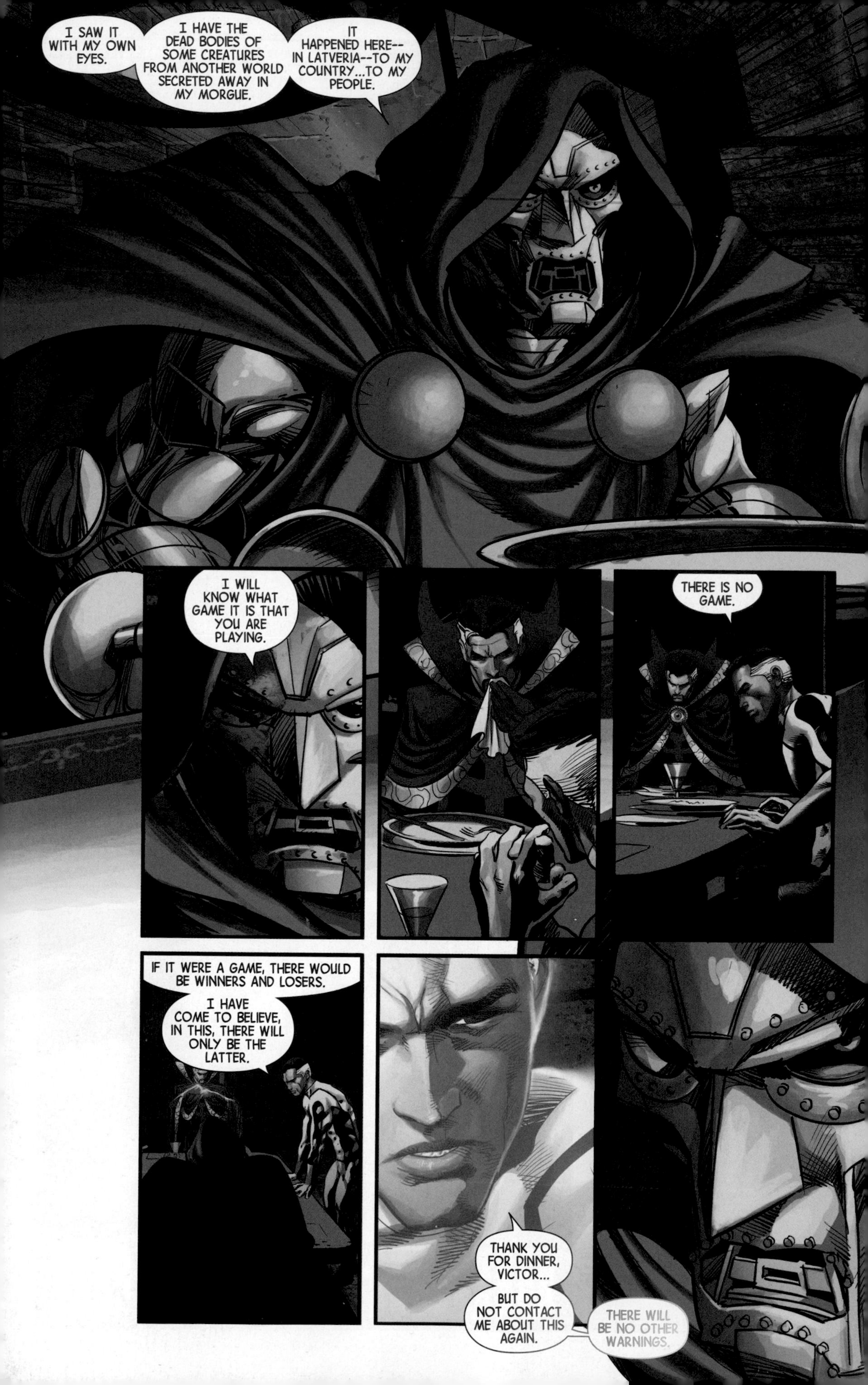
I SAW IT WITH MY OWN EYES.
I HAVE THE DEAD BODIES OF SOME CREATURES FROM ANOTHER WORLD SECRETED AWAY IN MY MORGUE.
IT HAPPENED HERE-- IN LATVERIA--TO MY COUNTRY...TO MY PEOPLE.
I WILL KNOW WHAT GAME IT IS THAT YOU ARE PLAYING.
THERE IS NO GAME.
IF IT WERE A GAME, THERE WOULD BE WINNERS AND LOSERS.
I HAVE COME TO BELIEVE, IN THIS, THERE WILL ONLY BE THE LATTER.
THANK YOU FOR DINNER, VICTOR...
BUT DO NOT CONTACT ME ABOUT THIS AGAIN.
THERE WILL BE NO OTHER WARNINGS.

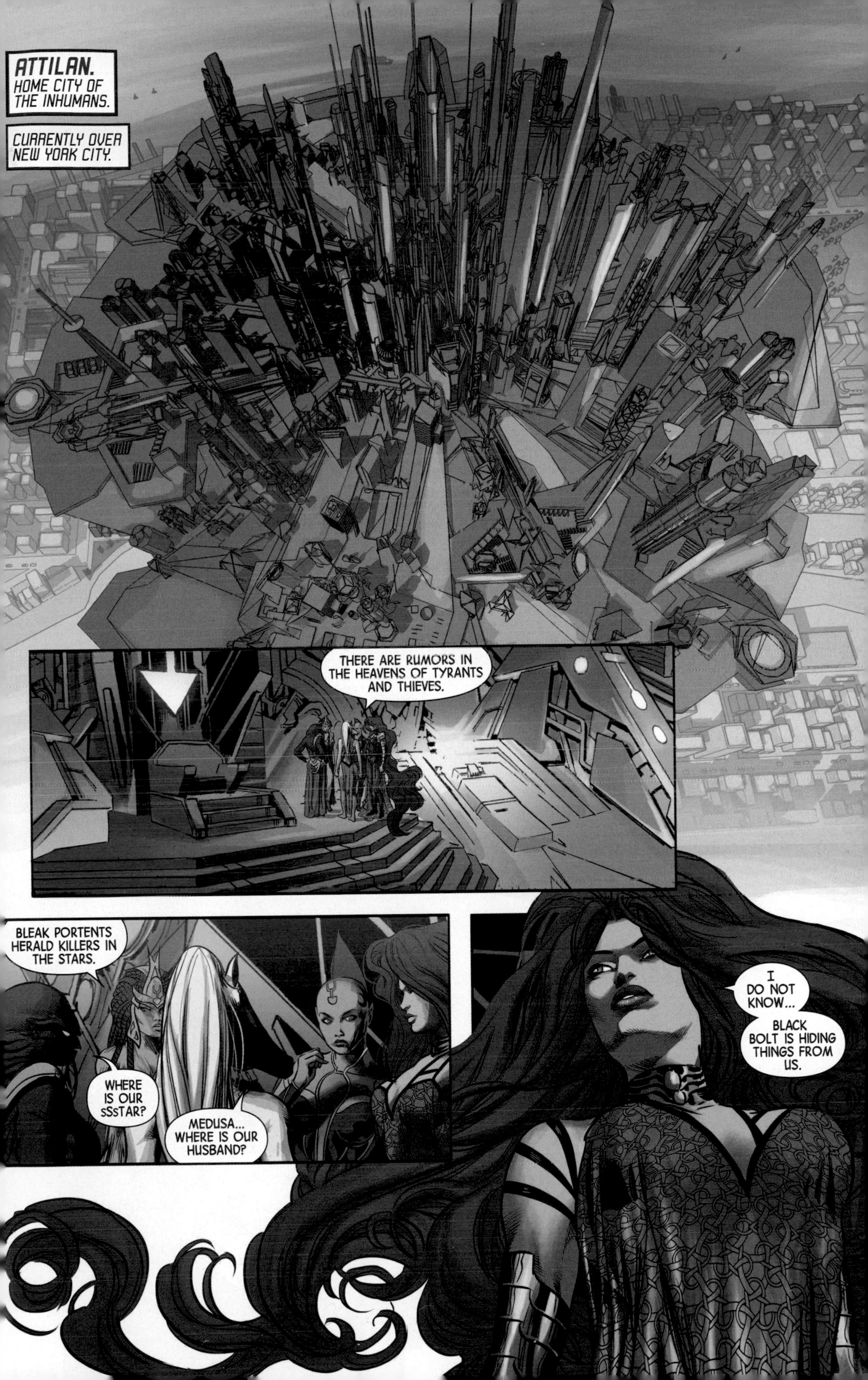
ATTILAN.
HOME CITY OF THE INHUMANS.
CURRENTLY OVER NEW YORK CITY.
THERE ARE RUMORS IN THE HEAVENS OF TYRANTS AND THIEVES.
BLEAK PORTENTS HERALD KILLERS IN THE STARS.
WHERE IS OUR sSsTAR?
MEDUSA... WHERE IS OUR HUSBAND?
I DO NOT KNOW...
BLACK BOLT IS HIDING THINGS FROM US.

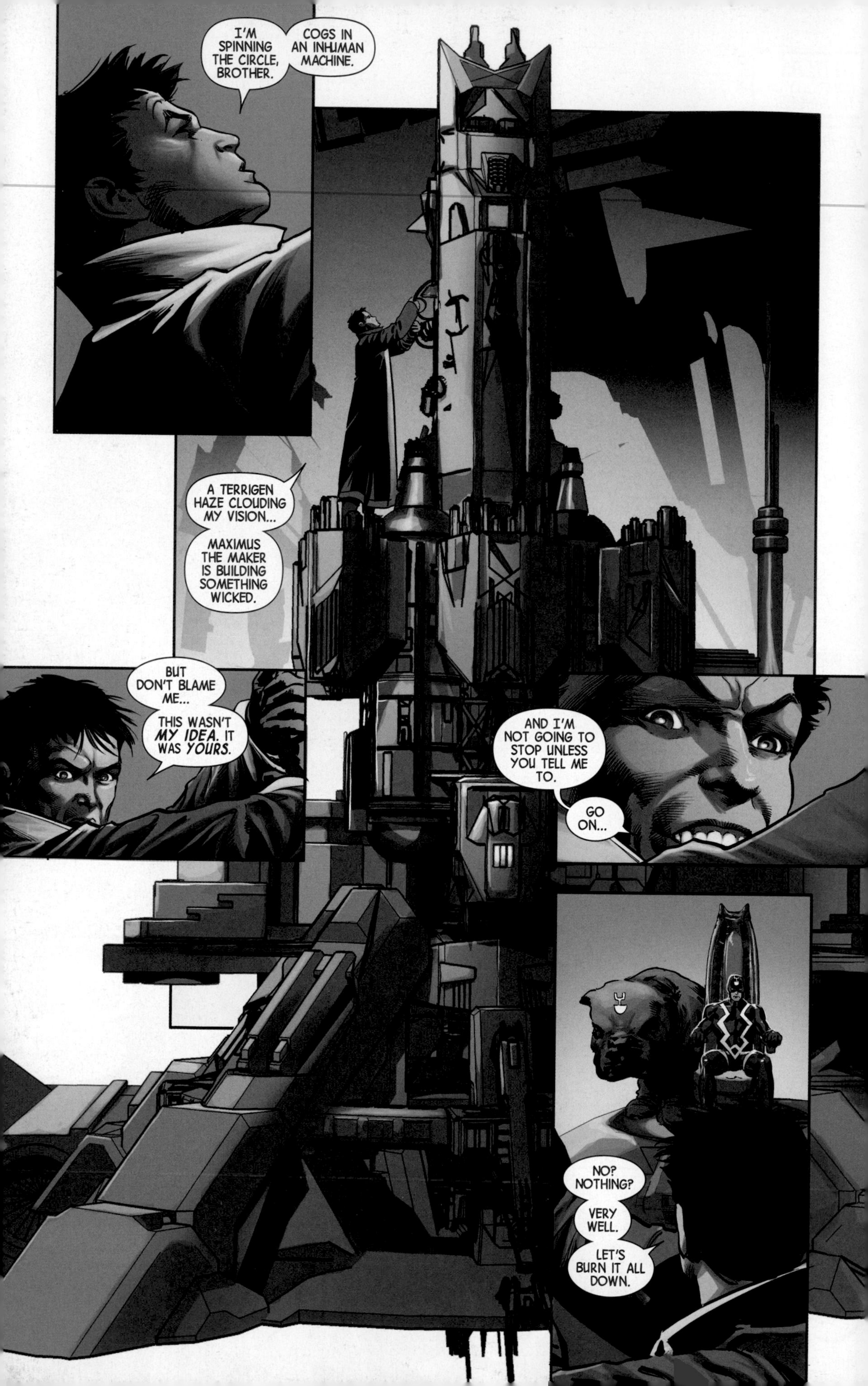
I'M SPINNING THE CIRCLE, BROTHER.
COGS IN AN INHUMAN MACHINE.
A TERRIGEN HAZE CLOUDING MY VISION...
MAXIMUS THE MAKER IS BUILDING SOMETHING WICKED.
BUT DON'T BLAME ME...
THIS WASN'T *MY IDEA*. IT WAS *YOURS*.
AND I'M NOT GOING TO STOP UNLESS YOU TELL ME TO.
GO ON...
NO? NOTHING?
VERY WELL.
LET'S BURN IT ALL DOWN.

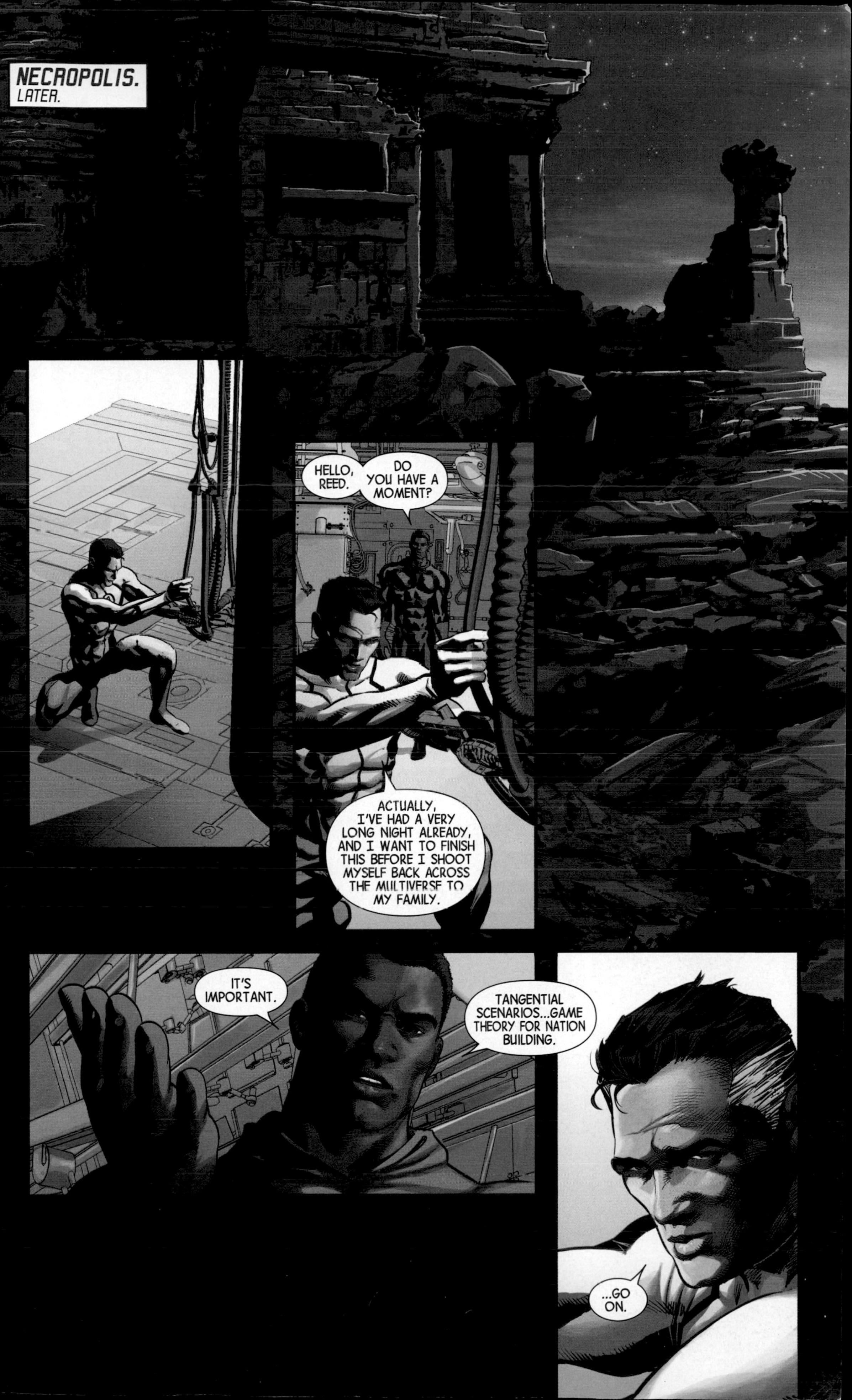
NECROPOLIS.
LATER.
HELLO, REED.
DO YOU HAVE A MOMENT?
ACTUALLY, I'VE HAD A VERY LONG NIGHT ALREADY, AND I WANT TO FINISH THIS BEFORE I SHOOT MYSELF BACK ACROSS THE MULTIVERSE TO MY FAMILY.
IT'S IMPORTANT.
TANGENTIAL SCENARIOS...GAME THEORY FOR NATION BUILDING.
...GO ON.

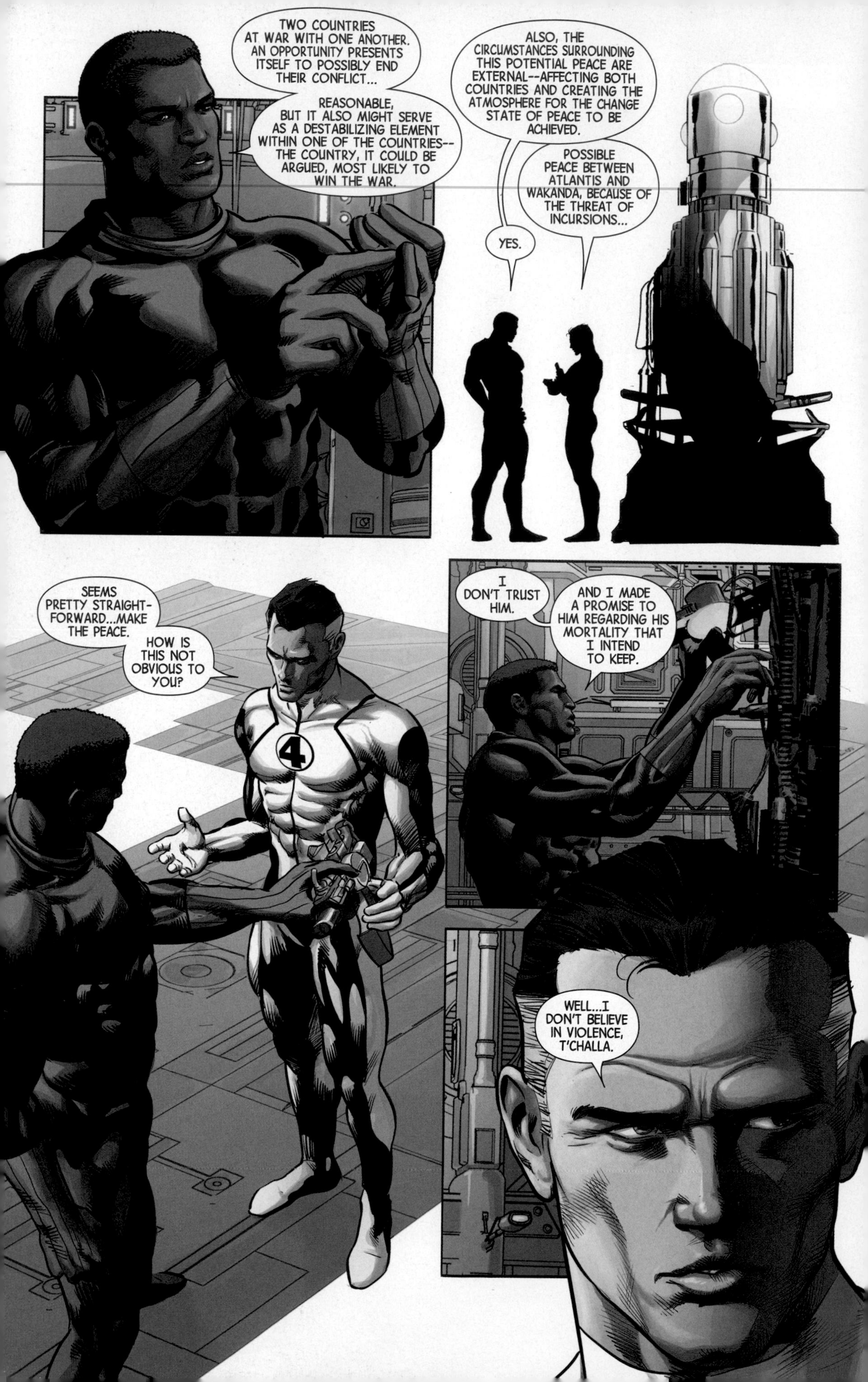
TWO COUNTRIES AT WAR WITH ONE ANOTHER. AN OPPORTUNITY PRESENTS ITSELF TO POSSIBLY END THEIR CONFLICT...
REASONABLE, BUT IT ALSO MIGHT SERVE AS A DESTABILIZING ELEMENT WITHIN ONE OF THE COUNTRIES-- THE COUNTRY, IT COULD BE ARGUED, MOST LIKELY TO WIN THE WAR.
ALSO, THE CIRCUMSTANCES SURROUNDING THIS POTENTIAL PEACE ARE EXTERNAL--AFFECTING BOTH COUNTRIES AND CREATING THE ATMOSPHERE FOR THE CHANGE STATE OF PEACE TO BE ACHIEVED.
POSSIBLE PEACE BETWEEN ATLANTIS AND WAKANDA, BECAUSE OF THE THREAT OF INCURSIONS...
YES.
SEEMS PRETTY STRAIGHT-FORWARD...MAKE THE PEACE.
HOW IS THIS NOT OBVIOUS TO YOU?
I DON'T TRUST HIM.
AND I MADE A PROMISE TO HIM REGARDING HIS MORTALITY THAT I INTEND TO KEEP.
WELL...I DON'T BELIEVE IN VIOLENCE, T'CHALLA.

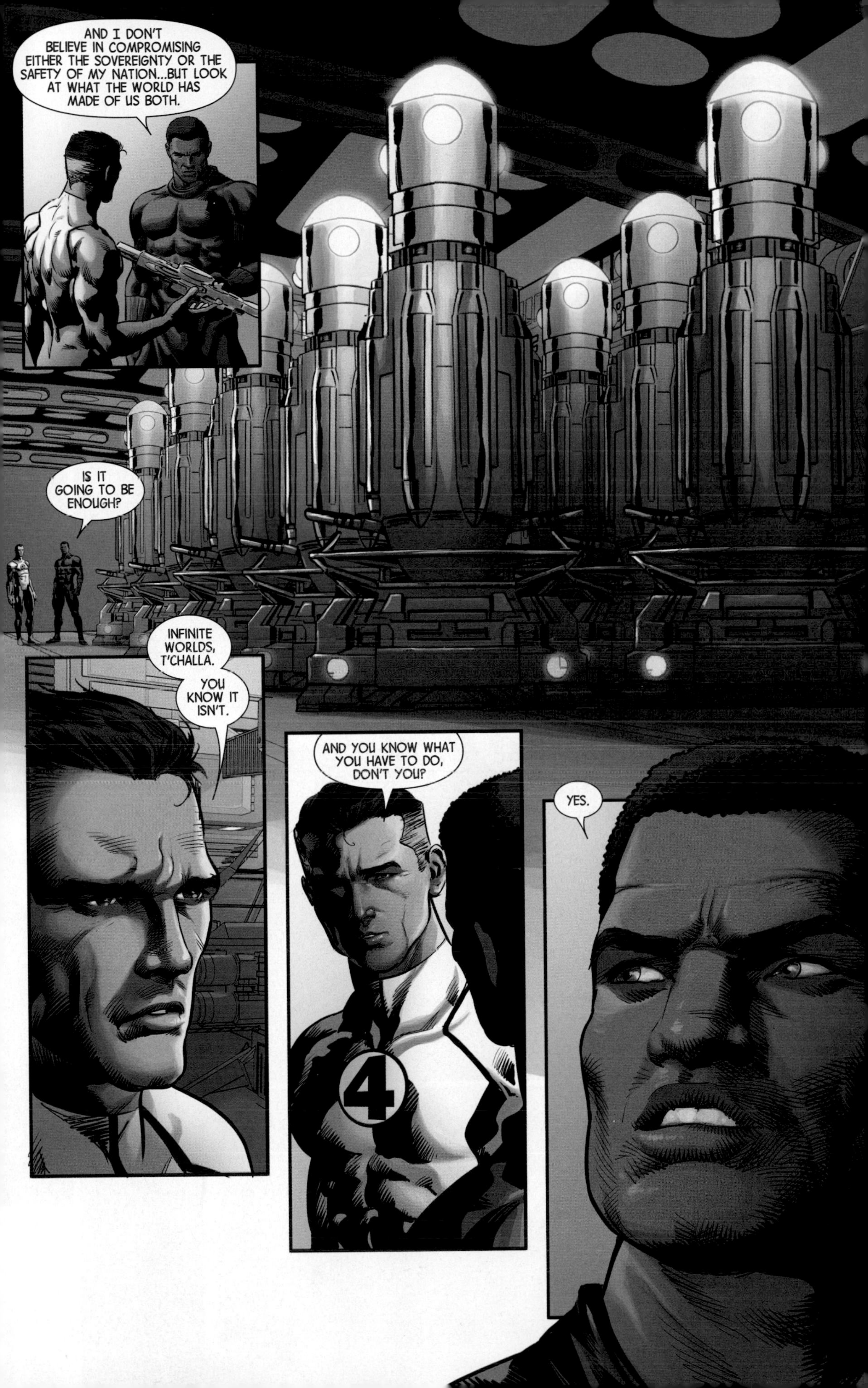
AND I DON'T BELIEVE IN COMPROMISING EITHER THE SOVEREIGNTY OR THE SAFETY OF MY NATION...BUT LOOK AT WHAT THE WORLD HAS MADE OF US BOTH.
IS IT GOING TO BE ENOUGH?
INFINITE WORLDS, T'CHALLA.
YOU KNOW IT ISN'T.
AND YOU KNOW WHAT YOU HAVE TO DO, DON'T YOU?
YES.

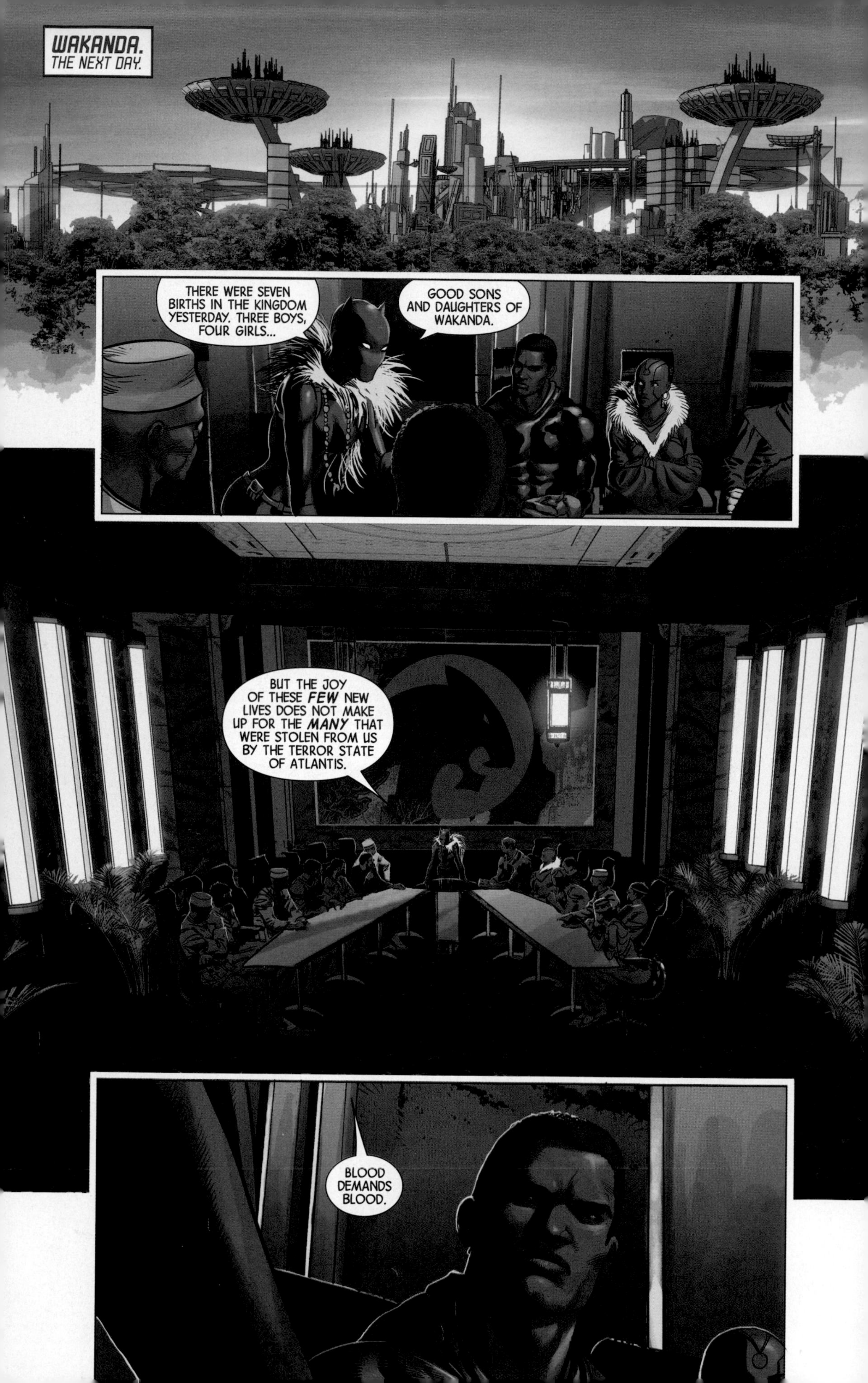
WAKANDA.
THE NEXT DAY.
THERE WERE SEVEN BIRTHS IN THE KINGDOM YESTERDAY. THREE BOYS, FOUR GIRLS...
GOOD SONS AND DAUGHTERS OF WAKANDA.
BUT THE JOY OF THESE FEW NEW LIVES DOES NOT MAKE UP FOR THE MANY THAT WERE STOLEN FROM US BY THE TERROR STATE OF ATLANTIS.
BLOOD DEMANDS BLOOD.

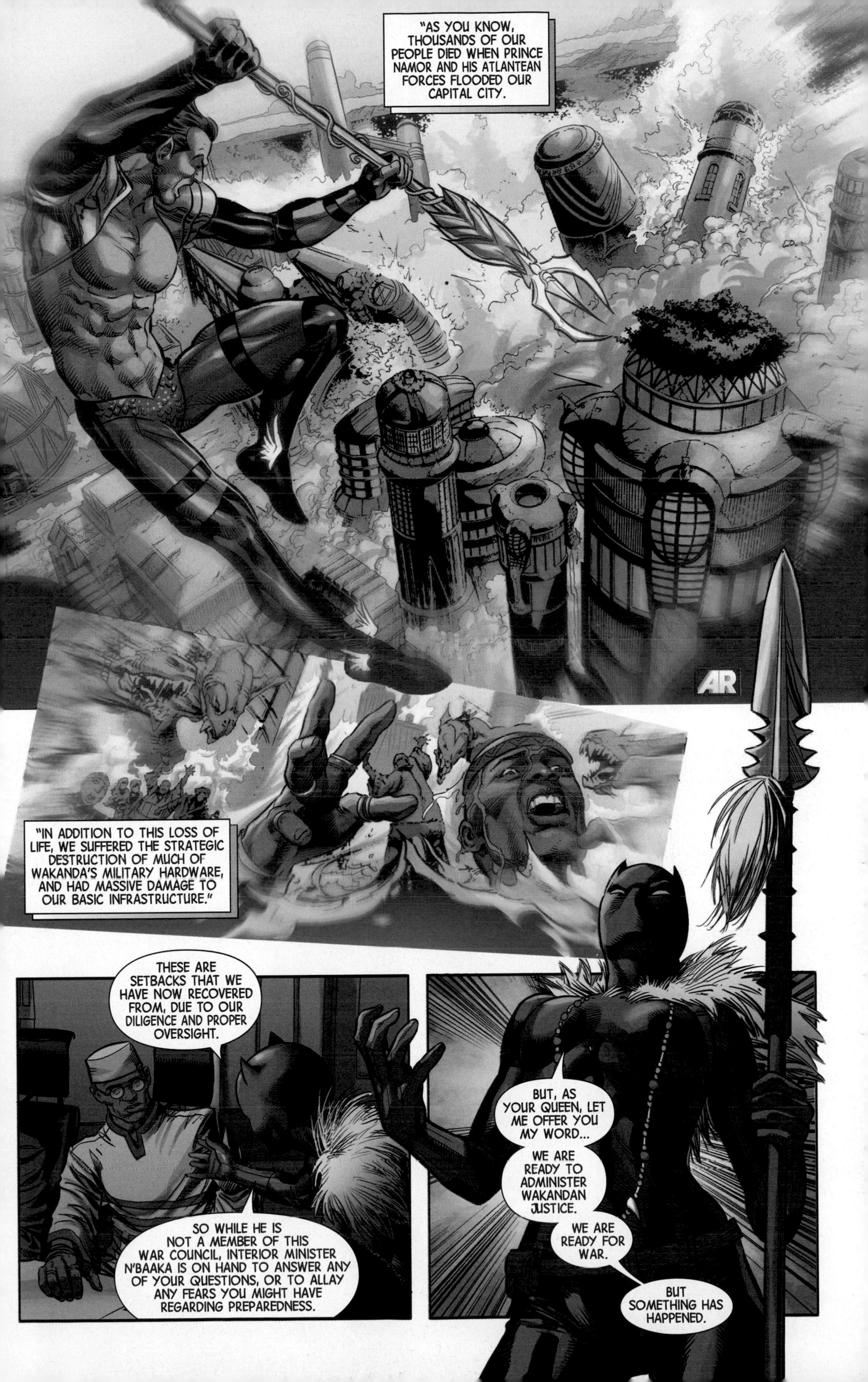
"AS YOU KNOW, THOUSANDS OF OUR PEOPLE DIED WHEN PRINCE NAMOR AND HIS ATLANTEAN FORCES FLOODED OUR CAPITAL CITY.
AR
"IN ADDITION TO THIS LOSS OF LIFE, WE SUFFERED THE STRATEGIC DESTRUCTION OF MUCH OF WAKANDA'S MILITARY HARDWARE, AND HAD MASSIVE DAMAGE TO OUR BASIC INFRASTRUCTURE."
THESE ARE SETBACKS THAT WE HAVE NOW RECOVERED FROM, DUE TO OUR DILIGENCE AND PROPER OVERSIGHT.
SO WHILE HE IS NOT A MEMBER OF THIS WAR COUNCIL, INTERIOR MINISTER N'BAAKA IS ON HAND TO ANSWER ANY OF YOUR QUESTIONS, OR TO ALLAY ANY FEARS YOU MIGHT HAVE REGARDING PREPAREDNESS.
BUT, AS YOUR QUEEN, LET ME OFFER YOU MY WORD...
WE ARE READY TO ADMINISTER WAKANDAN JUSTICE.
WE ARE READY FOR WAR.
BUT SOMETHING HAS HAPPENED.

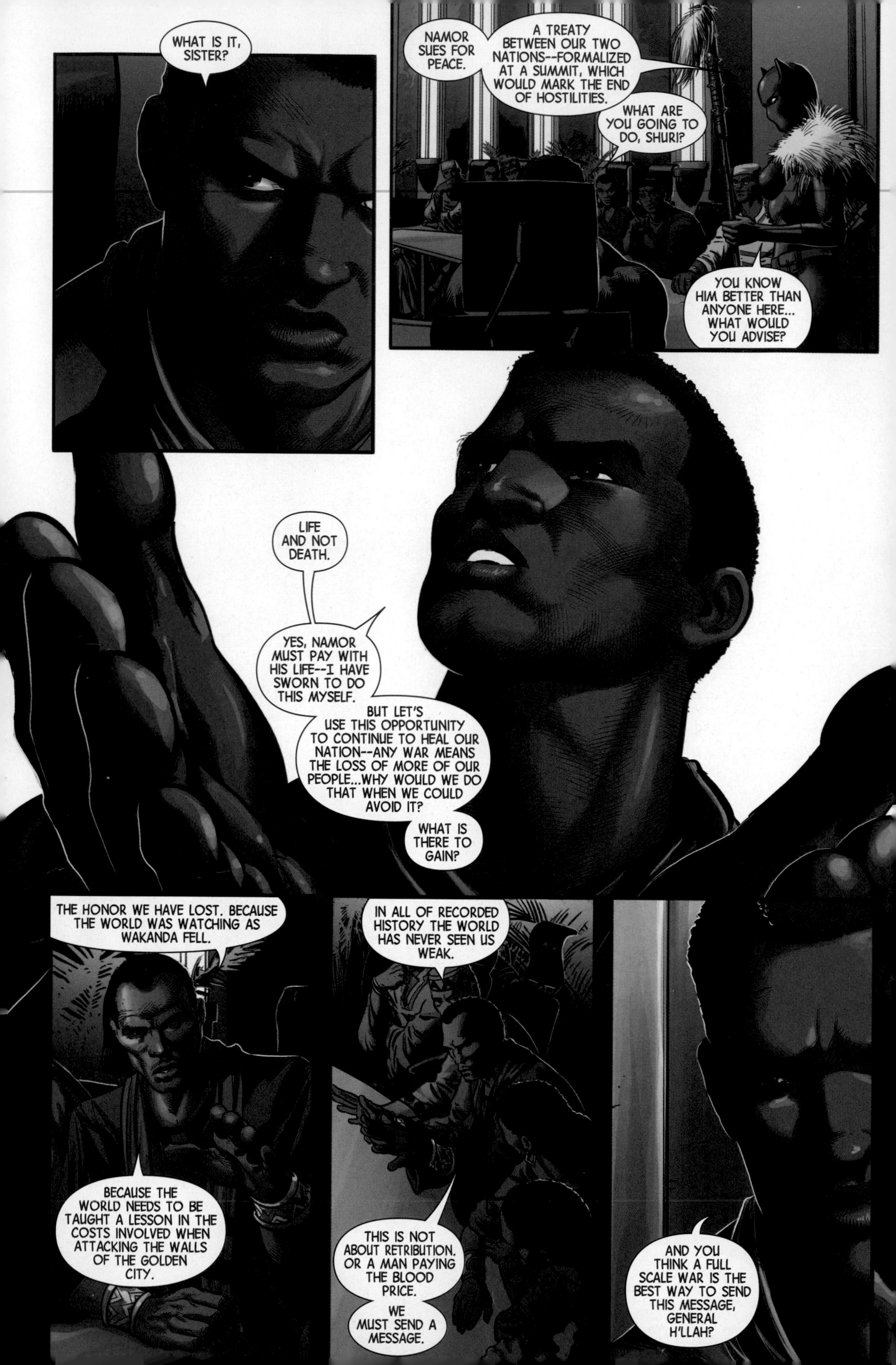
WHAT IS IT, SISTER?
NAMOR SUES FOR PEACE.
A TREATY BETWEEN OUR TWO NATIONS--FORMALIZED AT A SUMMIT, WHICH WOULD MARK THE END OF HOSTILITIES.
WHAT ARE YOU GOING TO DO, SHURI?
YOU KNOW HIM BETTER THAN ANYONE HERE... WHAT WOULD YOU ADVISE?
LIFE AND NOT DEATH.
YES, NAMOR MUST PAY WITH HIS LIFE--I HAVE SWORN TO DO THIS MYSELF.
BUT LET'S USE THIS OPPORTUNITY TO CONTINUE TO HEAL OUR NATION--ANY WAR MEANS THE LOSS OF MORE OF OUR PEOPLE...WHY WOULD WE DO THAT WHEN WE COULD AVOID IT?
WHAT IS THERE TO GAIN?
THE HONOR WE HAVE LOST. BECAUSE THE WORLD WAS WATCHING AS WAKANDA FELL.
BECAUSE THE WORLD NEEDS TO BE TAUGHT A LESSON IN THE COSTS INVOLVED WHEN ATTACKING THE WALLS OF THE GOLDEN CITY.
IN ALL OF RECORDED HISTORY THE WORLD HAS NEVER SEEN US WEAK.
THIS IS NOT ABOUT RETRIBUTION. OR A MAN PAYING THE BLOOD PRICE.
WE MUST SEND A MESSAGE.
AND YOU THINK A FULL SCALE WAR IS THE BEST WAY TO SEND THIS MESSAGE, GENERAL H'LLAH?

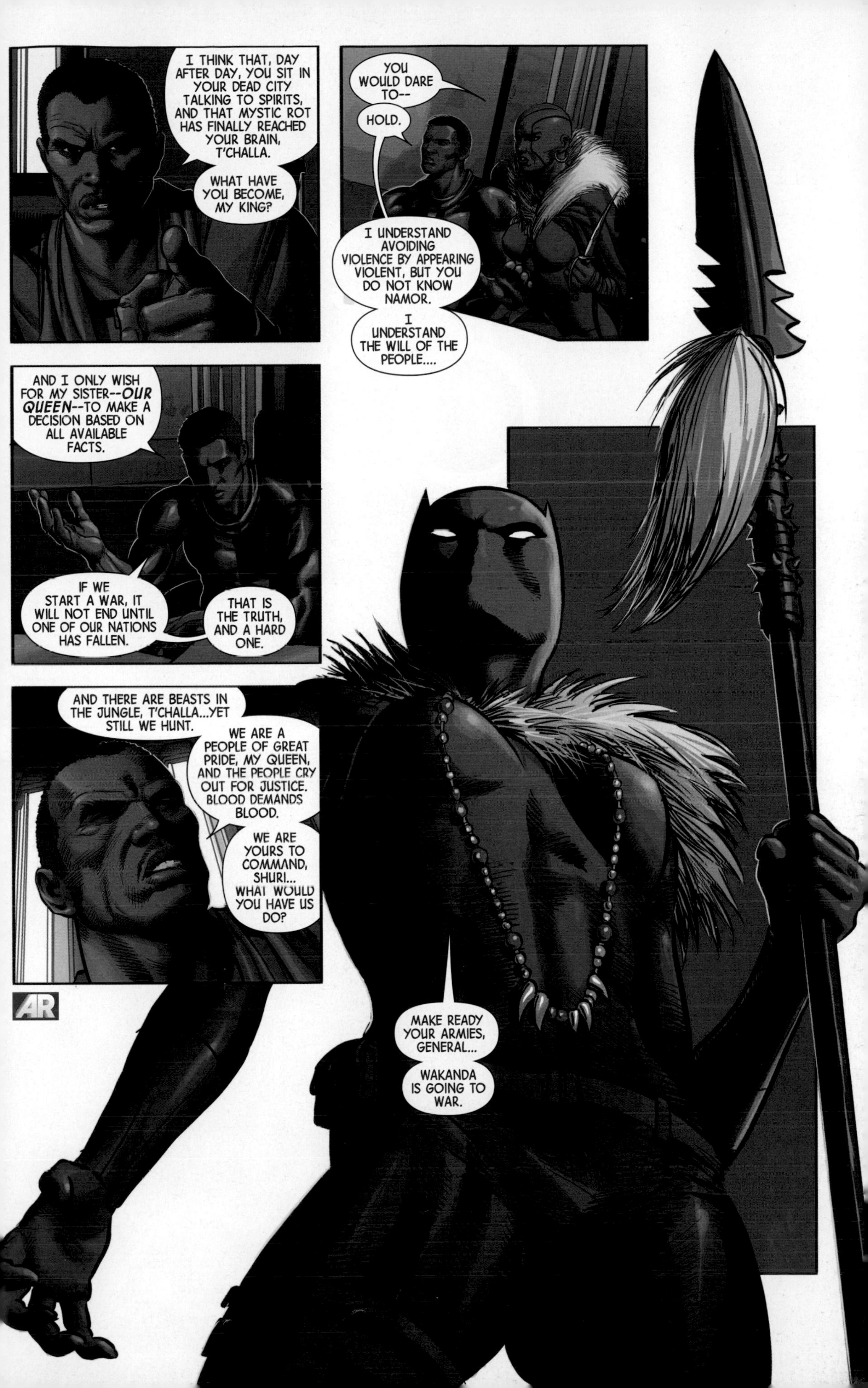
I THINK THAT, DAY AFTER DAY, YOU SIT IN YOUR DEAD CITY TALKING TO SPIRITS, AND THAT MYSTIC ROT HAS FINALLY REACHED YOUR BRAIN, T'CHALLA.
WHAT HAVE YOU BECOME, MY KING?
YOU WOULD DARE TO--
HOLD.
I UNDERSTAND AVOIDING VIOLENCE BY APPEARING VIOLENT, BUT YOU DO NOT KNOW NAMOR.
I UNDERSTAND THE WILL OF THE PEOPLE....
AND I ONLY WISH FOR MY SISTER--*OUR QUEEN*--TO MAKE A DECISION BASED ON ALL AVAILABLE FACTS.
IF WE START A WAR, IT WILL NOT END UNTIL ONE OF OUR NATIONS HAS FALLEN.
THAT IS THE TRUTH, AND A HARD ONE.
AND THERE ARE BEASTS IN THE JUNGLE, T'CHALLA...YET STILL WE HUNT.
WE ARE A PEOPLE OF GREAT PRIDE, MY QUEEN, AND THE PEOPLE CRY OUT FOR JUSTICE. BLOOD DEMANDS BLOOD.
WE ARE YOURS TO COMMAND, SHURI... WHAT WOULD YOU HAVE US DO?
AR
MAKE READY YOUR ARMIES, GENERAL...
WAKANDA IS GOING TO WAR.

"WHAT MAXIMUS MADE"

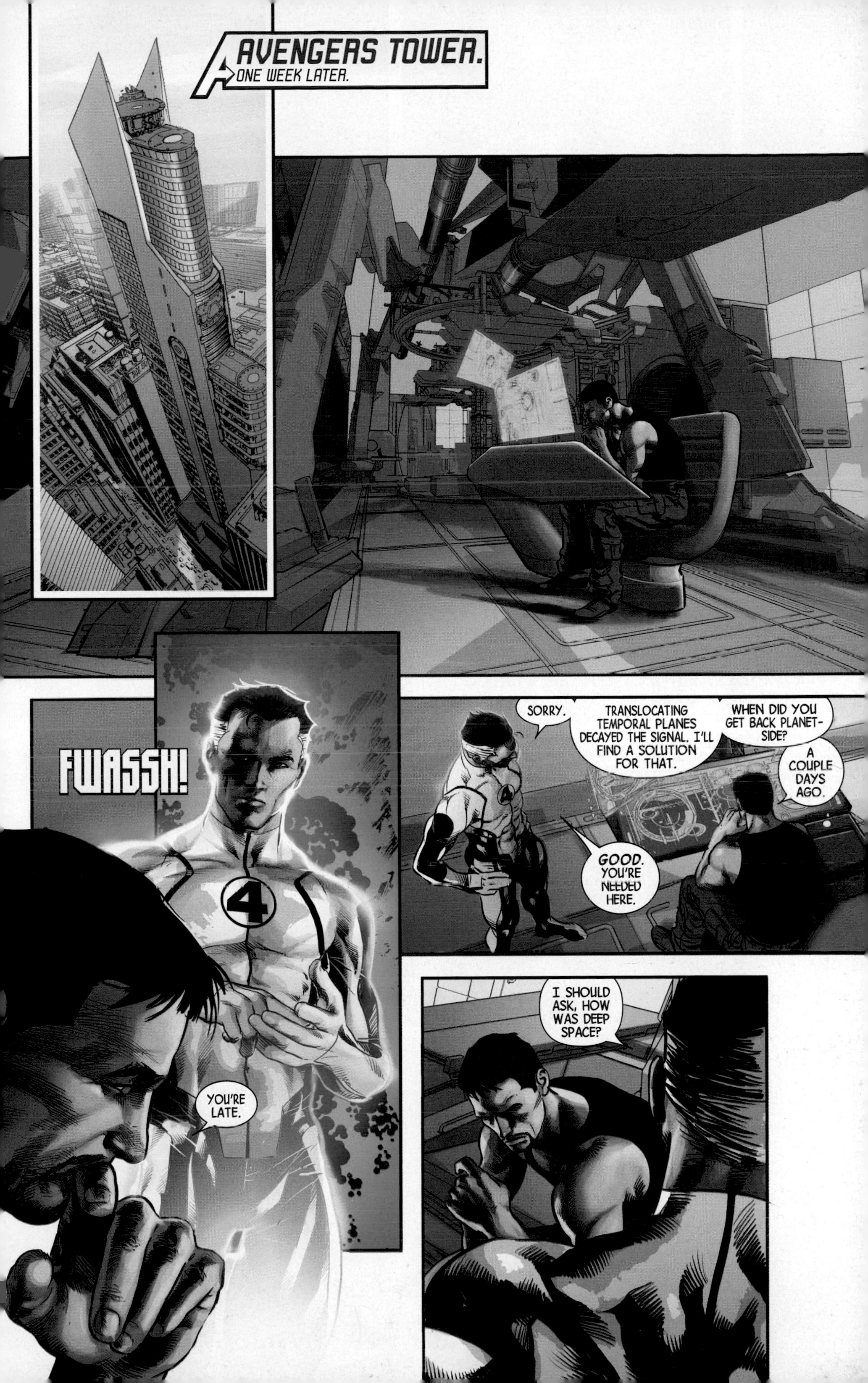
AVENGERS TOWER.
ONE WEEK LATER.
FWASSH!
YOU'RE LATE.
SORRY.
TRANSLOCATING TEMPORAL PLANES DECAYED THE SIGNAL. I'LL FIND A SOLUTION FOR THAT.
WHEN DID YOU GET BACK PLANET-SIDE?
A COUPLE DAYS AGO.
GOOD. YOU'RE NEEDED HERE.
I SHOULD ASK, HOW WAS DEEP SPACE?

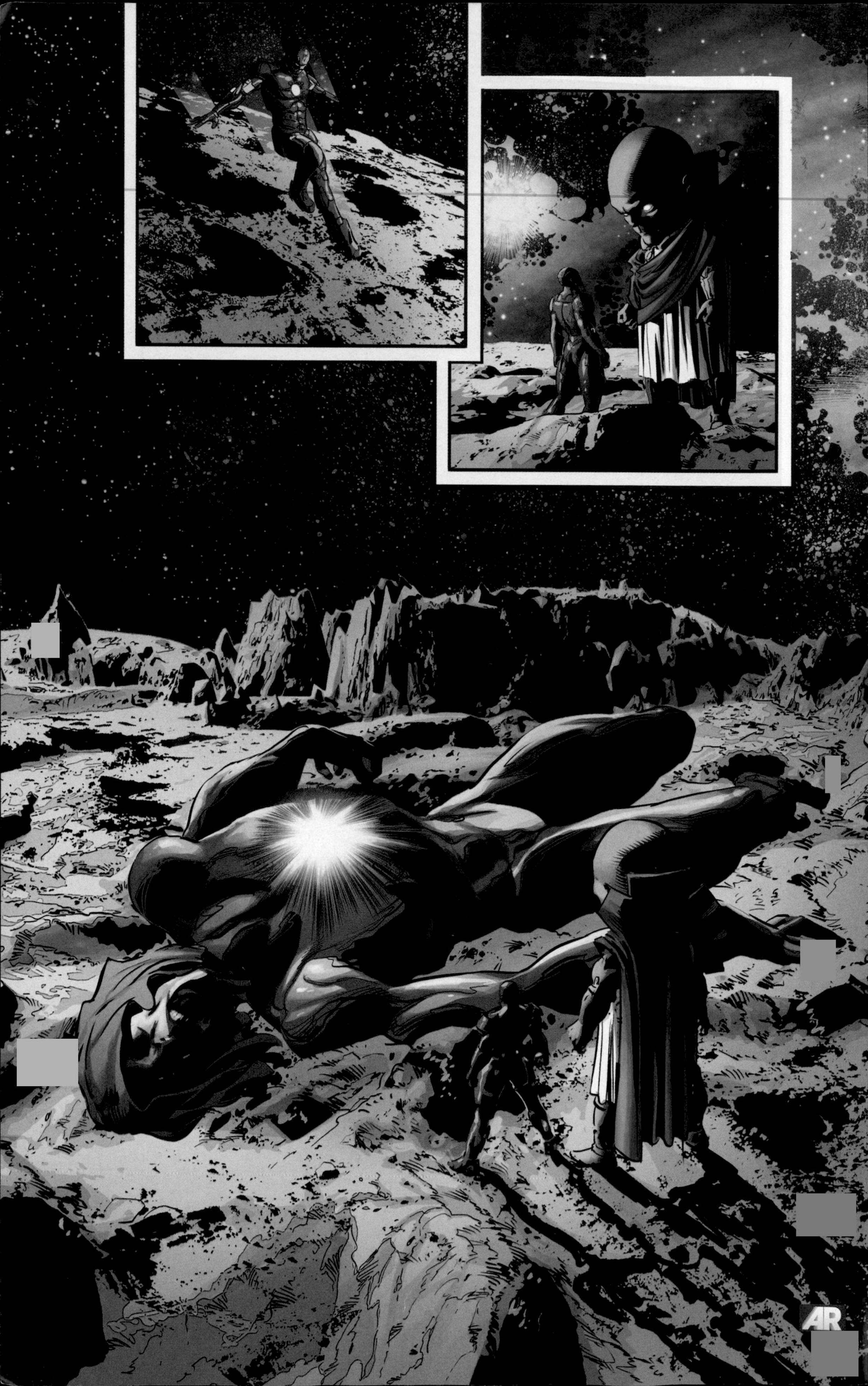

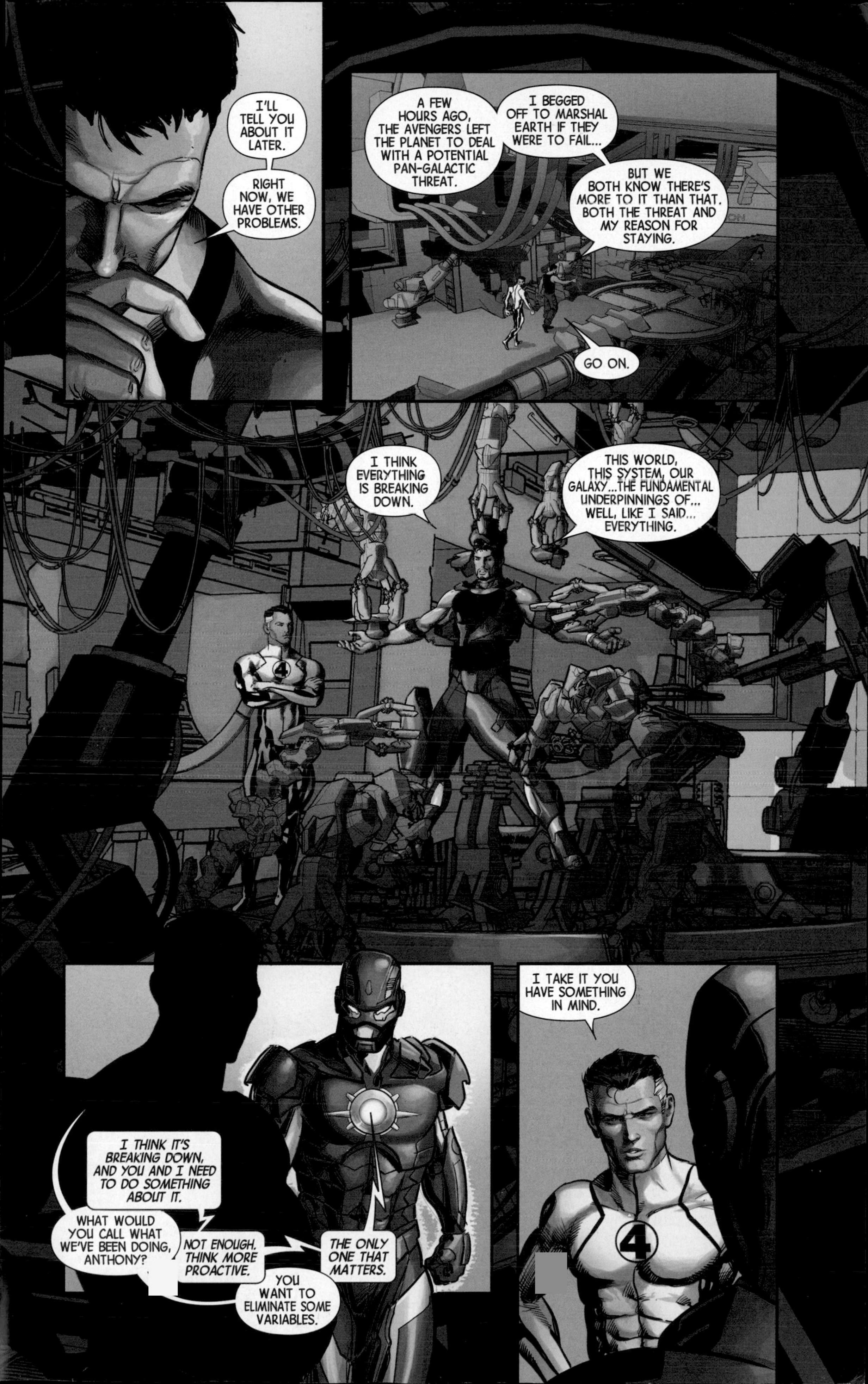
I'LL TELL YOU ABOUT IT LATER.
RIGHT NOW, WE HAVE OTHER PROBLEMS.
A FEW HOURS AGO, THE AVENGERS LEFT THE PLANET TO DEAL WITH A POTENTIAL PAN-GALACTIC THREAT.
I BEGGED OFF TO MARSHAL EARTH IF THEY WERE TO FAIL...
BUT WE BOTH KNOW THERE'S MORE TO IT THAN THAT. BOTH THE THREAT AND MY REASON FOR STAYING.
GO ON.
I THINK EVERYTHING IS BREAKING DOWN.
THIS WORLD, THIS SYSTEM, OUR GALAXY...THE FUNDAMENTAL UNDERPINNINGS OF... WELL, LIKE I SAID... EVERYTHING.
I TAKE IT YOU HAVE SOMETHING IN MIND.
I THINK IT'S BREAKING DOWN, AND YOU AND I NEED TO DO SOMETHING ABOUT IT.
WHAT WOULD YOU CALL WHAT WE'VE BEEN DOING, ANTHONY?
NOT ENOUGH. THINK MORE PROACTIVE.
THE ONLY ONE THAT MATTERS.
YOU WANT TO ELIMINATE SOME VARIABLES.

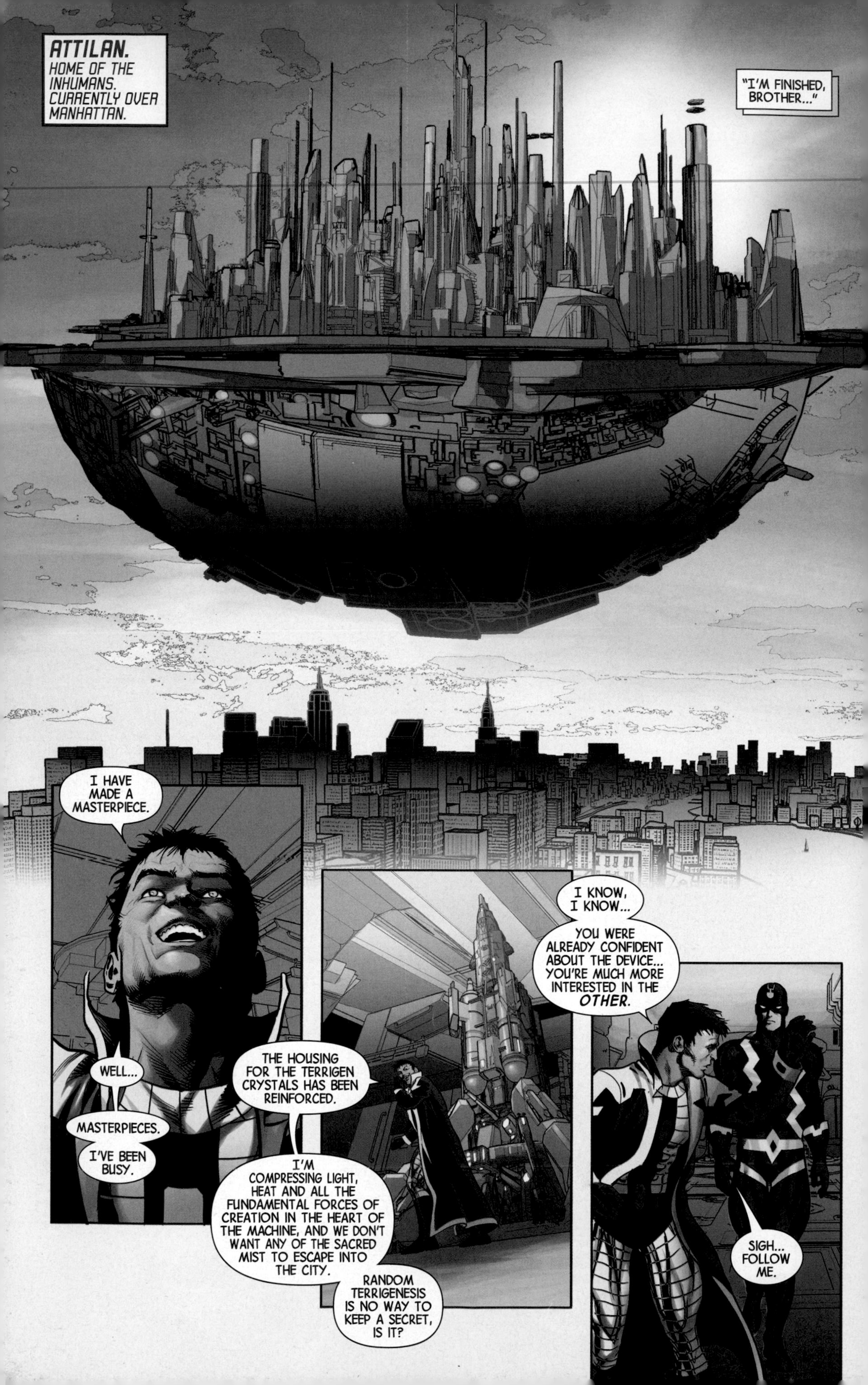
ATTILAN. HOME OF THE INHUMANS. CURRENTLY OVER MANHATTAN.
"I'M FINISHED, BROTHER..."
I HAVE MADE A MASTERPIECE.
WELL...
MASTERPIECES.
I'VE BEEN BUSY.
THE HOUSING FOR THE TERRIGEN CRYSTALS HAS BEEN REINFORCED.
I'M COMPRESSING LIGHT, HEAT AND ALL THE FUNDAMENTAL FORCES OF CREATION IN THE HEART OF THE MACHINE, AND WE DON'T WANT ANY OF THE SACRED MIST TO ESCAPE INTO THE CITY.
RANDOM TERRIGENESIS IS NO WAY TO KEEP A SECRET, IS IT?
I KNOW, I KNOW...
YOU WERE ALREADY CONFIDENT ABOUT THE DEVICE... YOU'RE MUCH MORE INTERESTED IN THE *OTHER*.
SIGH... FOLLOW ME.

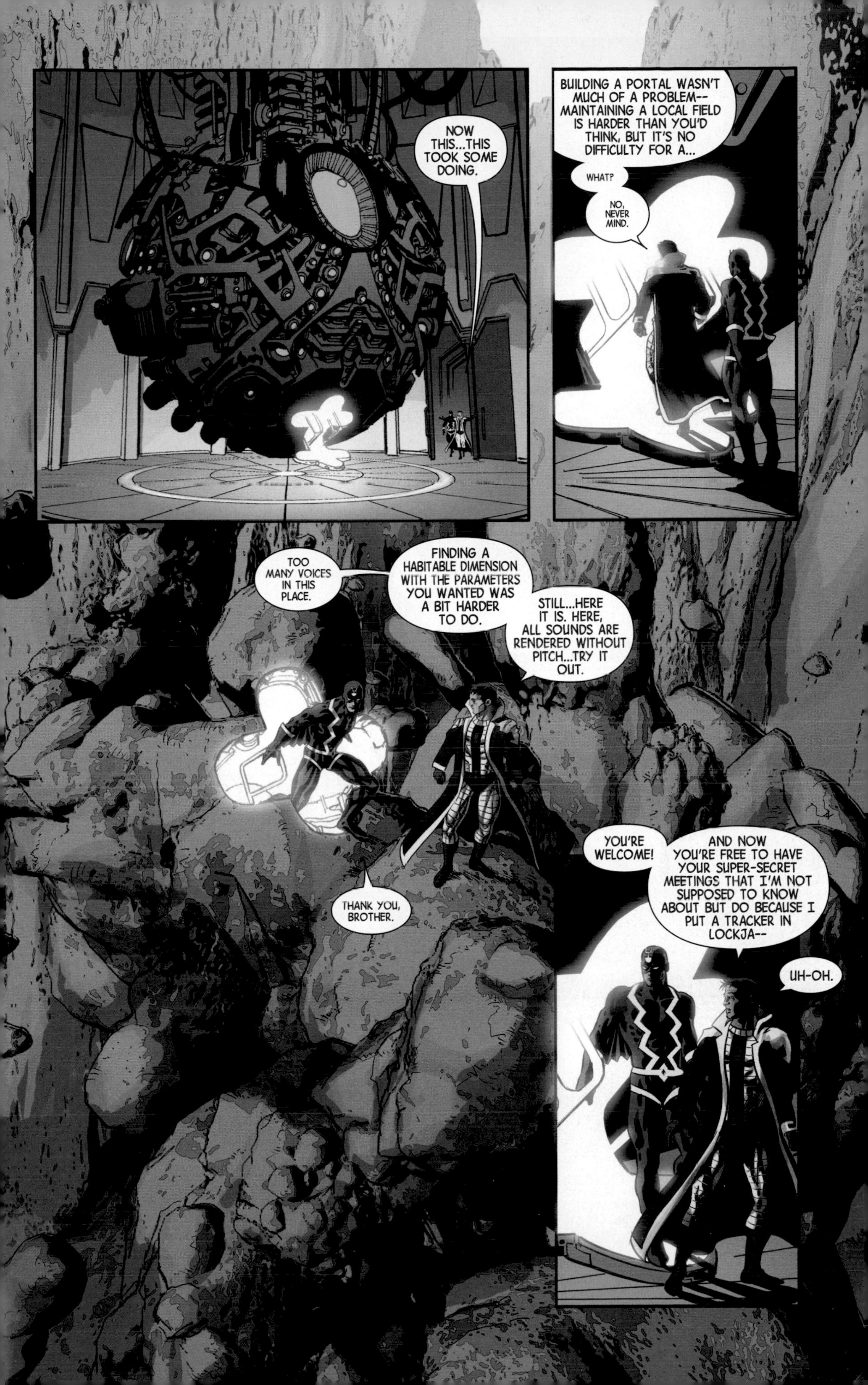
NOW THIS...THIS TOOK SOME DOING.
BUILDING A PORTAL WASN'T MUCH OF A PROBLEM-- MAINTAINING A LOCAL FIELD IS HARDER THAN YOU'D THINK, BUT IT'S NO DIFFICULTY FOR A...
WHAT?
NO, NEVER MIND.
FINDING A HABITABLE DIMENSION WITH THE PARAMETERS YOU WANTED WAS A BIT HARDER TO DO.
TOO MANY VOICES IN THIS PLACE.
STILL...HERE IT IS. HERE, ALL SOUNDS ARE RENDERED WITHOUT PITCH...TRY IT OUT.
THANK YOU, BROTHER.
YOU'RE WELCOME!
AND NOW YOU'RE FREE TO HAVE YOUR SUPER-SECRET MEETINGS THAT I'M NOT SUPPOSED TO KNOW ABOUT BUT DO BECAUSE I PUT A TRACKER IN LOCKJA--
UH-OH.

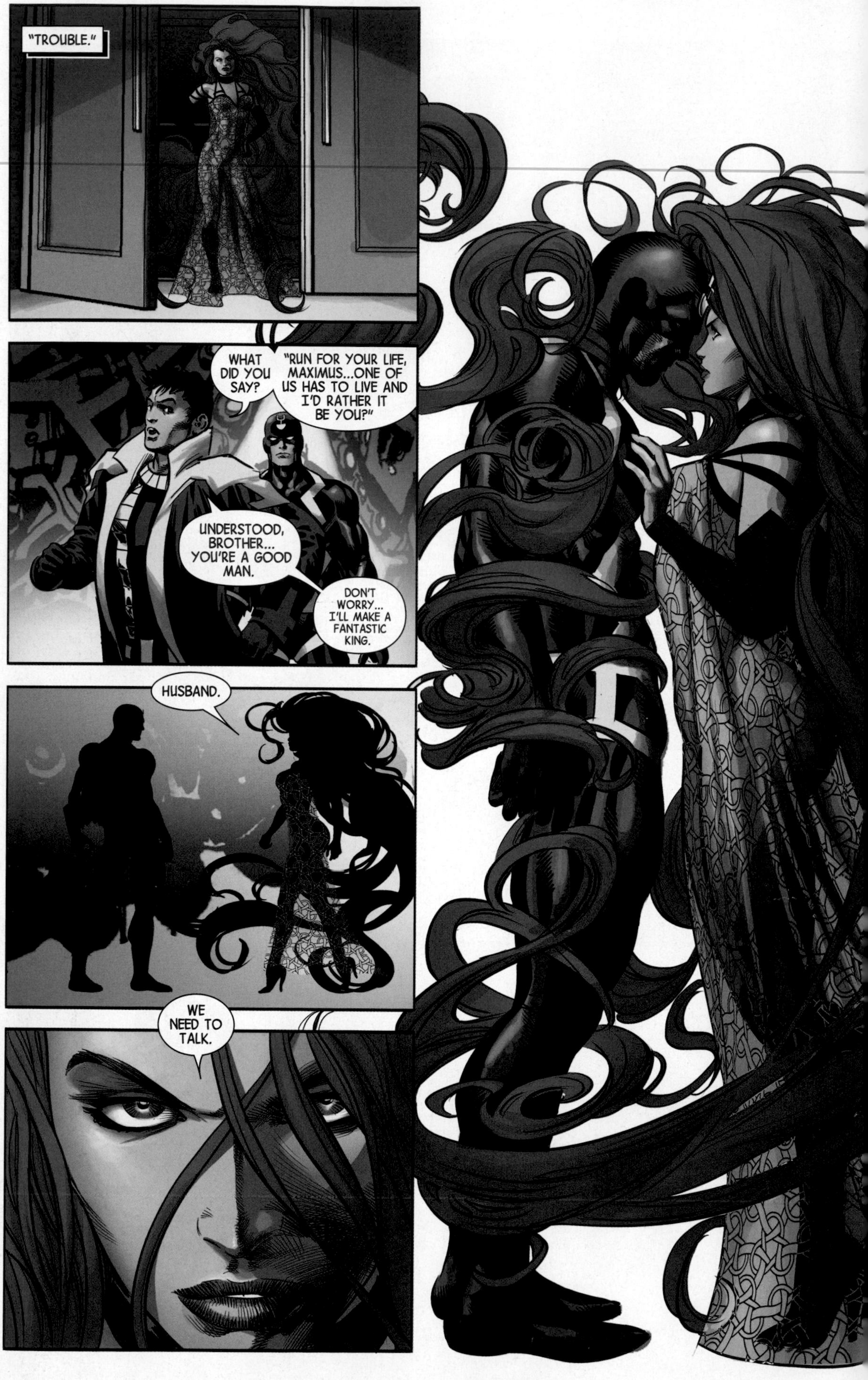
"TROUBLE."
WHAT DID YOU SAY?
"RUN FOR YOUR LIFE, MAXIMUS...ONE OF US HAS TO LIVE AND I'D RATHER IT BE YOU?"
UNDERSTOOD, BROTHER... YOU'RE A GOOD MAN.
DON'T WORRY... I'LL MAKE A FANTASTIC KING.
HUSBAND.
WE NEED TO TALK.

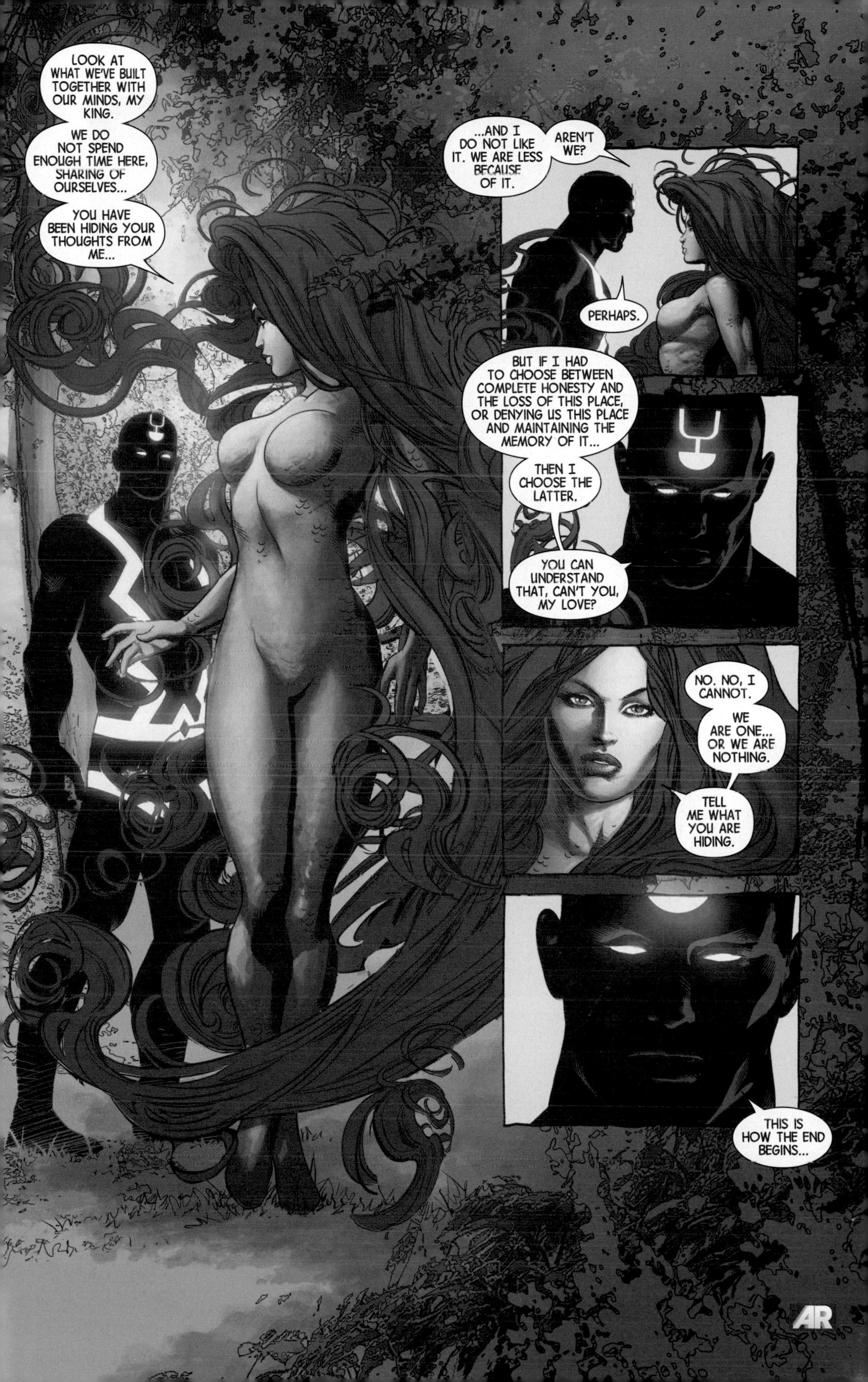
LOOK AT WHAT WE'VE BUILT TOGETHER WITH OUR MINDS, MY KING.
WE DO NOT SPEND ENOUGH TIME HERE, SHARING OF OURSELVES...
YOU HAVE BEEN HIDING YOUR THOUGHTS FROM ME...
...AND I DO NOT LIKE IT. WE ARE LESS BECAUSE OF IT.
AREN'T WE?
PERHAPS.
BUT IF I HAD TO CHOOSE BETWEEN COMPLETE HONESTY AND THE LOSS OF THIS PLACE, OR DENYING US THIS PLACE AND MAINTAINING THE MEMORY OF IT...
THEN I CHOOSE THE LATTER.
YOU CAN UNDERSTAND THAT, CAN'T YOU, MY LOVE?
NO. NO, I CANNOT.
WE ARE ONE... OR WE ARE NOTHING.
TELL ME WHAT YOU ARE HIDING.
THIS IS HOW THE END BEGINS...
AR

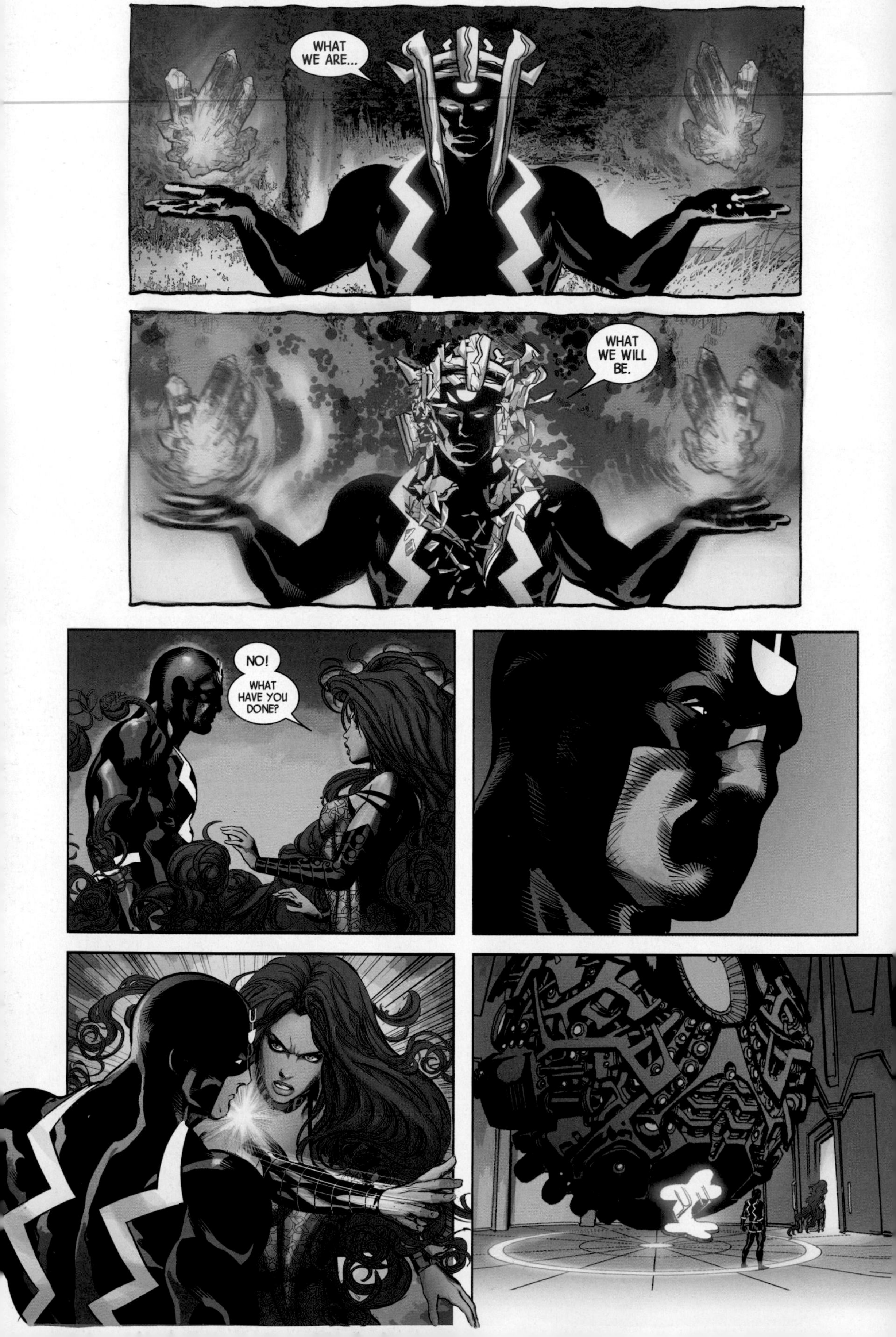
WHAT WE ARE...
WHAT WE WILL BE.
NO! WHAT HAVE YOU DONE?

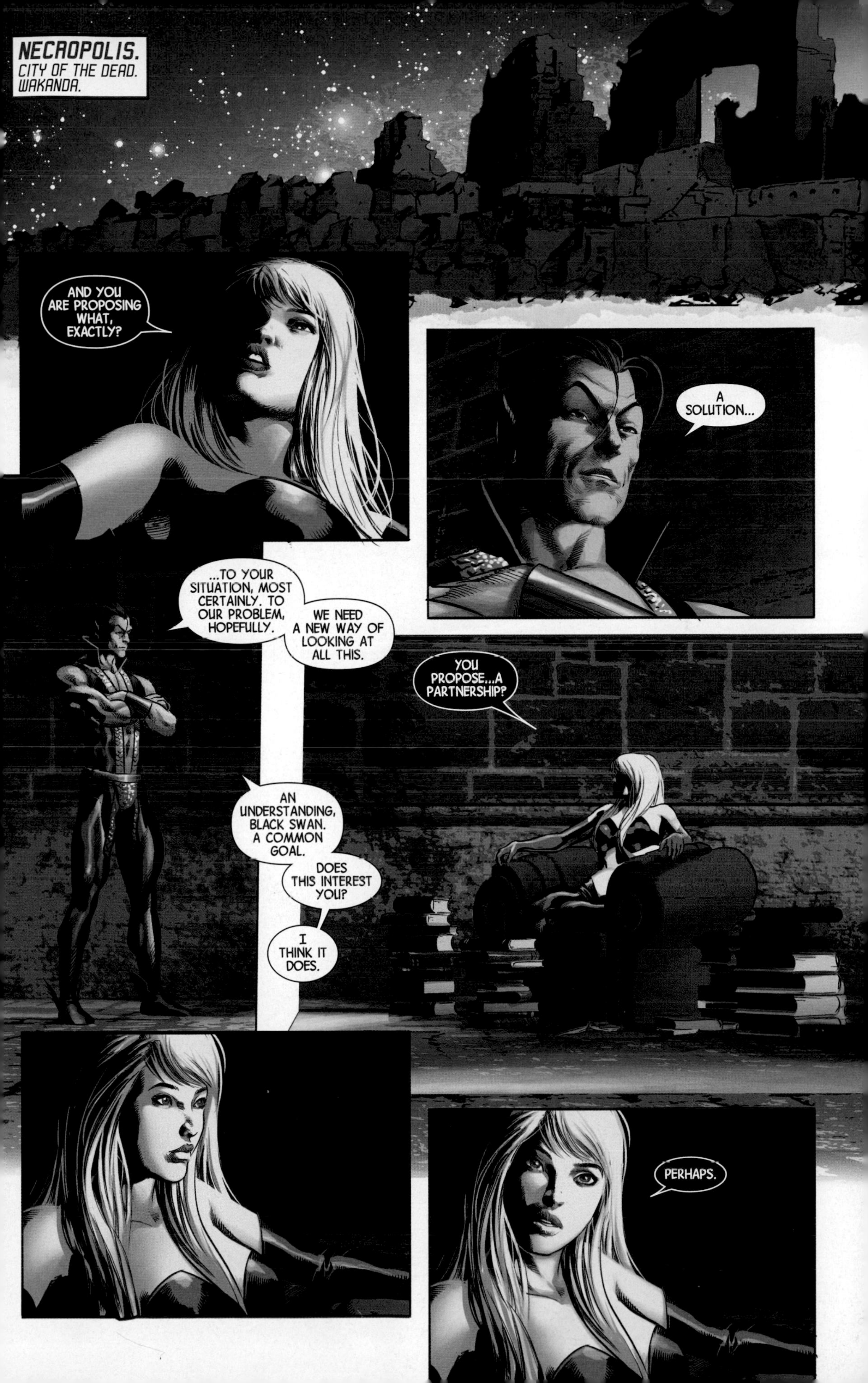
NECROPOLIS.
CITY OF THE DEAD.
WAKANDA.
AND YOU ARE PROPOSING WHAT, EXACTLY?
A SOLUTION...
...TO YOUR SITUATION, MOST CERTAINLY. TO OUR PROBLEM, HOPEFULLY.
WE NEED A NEW WAY OF LOOKING AT ALL THIS.
YOU PROPOSE...A PARTNERSHIP?
AN UNDERSTANDING, BLACK SWAN. A COMMON GOAL.
DOES THIS INTEREST YOU?
I THINK IT DOES.
PERHAPS.

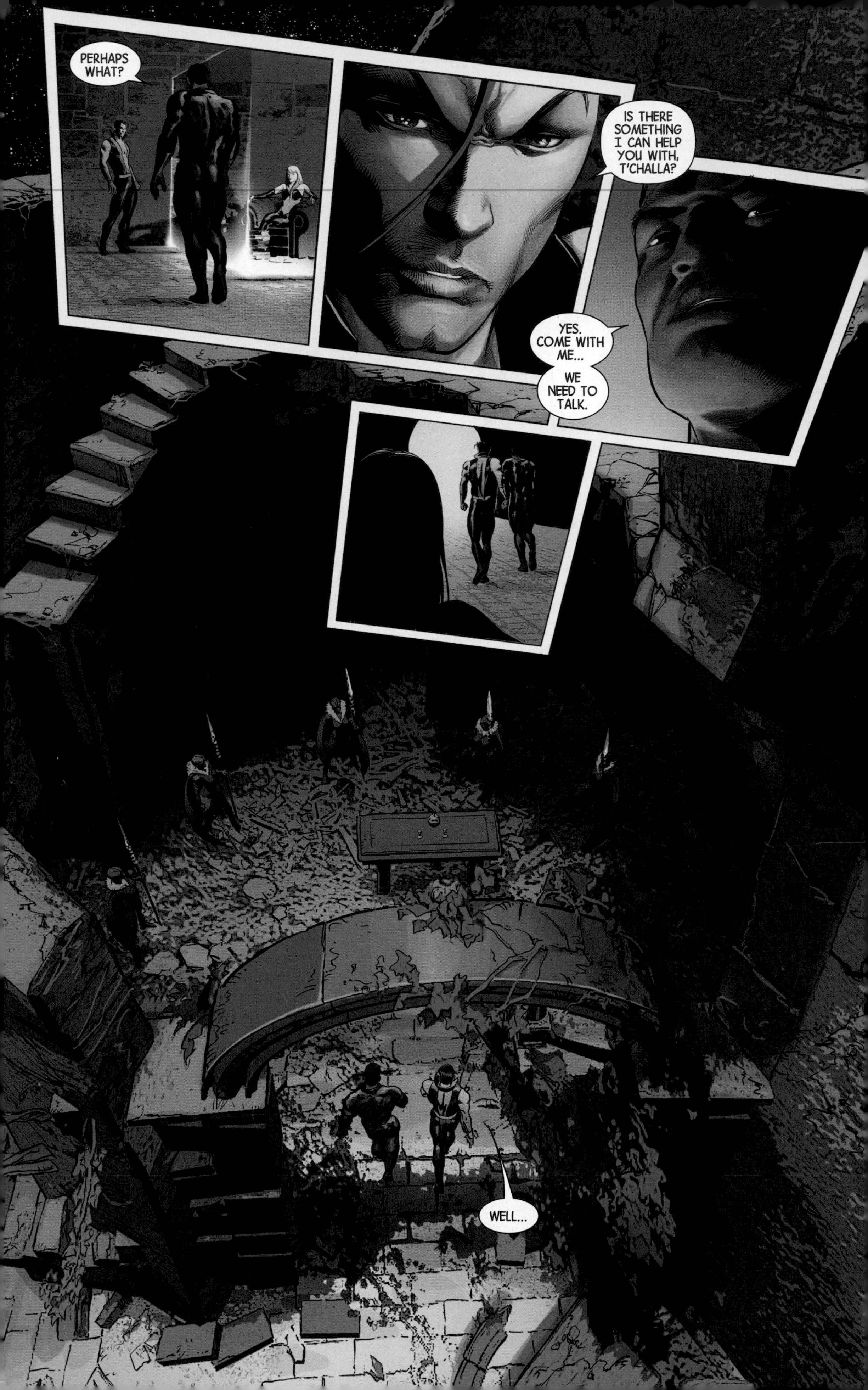
PERHAPS WHAT?
IS THERE SOMETHING I CAN HELP YOU WITH, T'CHALLA?
YES. COME WITH ME...
WE NEED TO TALK.
WELL...

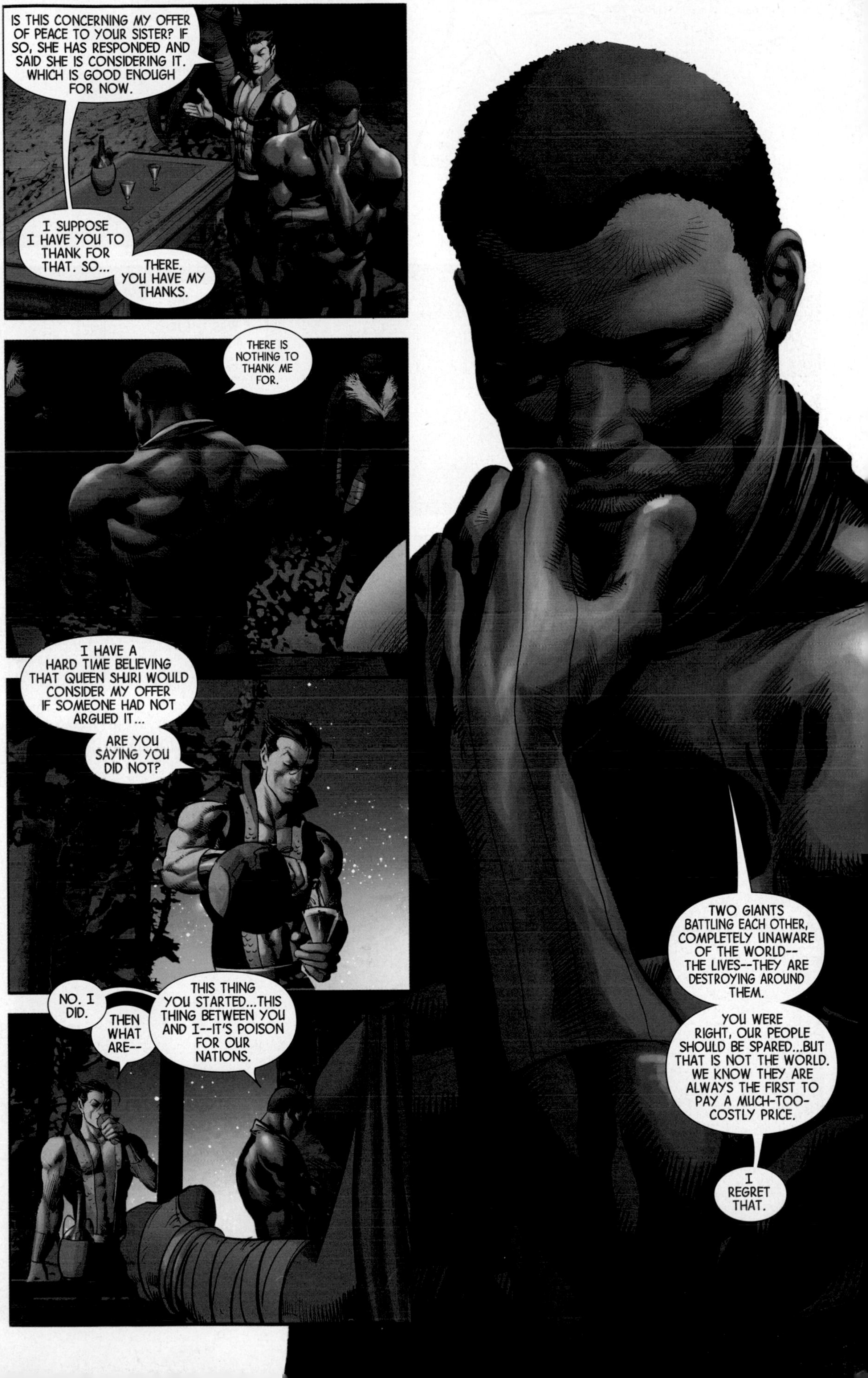
IS THIS CONCERNING MY OFFER OF PEACE TO YOUR SISTER? IF SO, SHE HAS RESPONDED AND SAID SHE IS CONSIDERING IT. WHICH IS GOOD ENOUGH FOR NOW.
I SUPPOSE I HAVE YOU TO THANK FOR THAT. SO...
THERE. YOU HAVE MY THANKS.
THERE IS NOTHING TO THANK ME FOR.
I HAVE A HARD TIME BELIEVING THAT QUEEN SHURI WOULD CONSIDER MY OFFER IF SOMEONE HAD NOT ARGUED IT...
ARE YOU SAYING YOU DID NOT?
NO. I DID.
THEN WHAT ARE--
THIS THING YOU STARTED...THIS THING BETWEEN YOU AND I--IT'S POISON FOR OUR NATIONS.
TWO GIANTS BATTLING EACH OTHER, COMPLETELY UNAWARE OF THE WORLD-- THE LIVES--THEY ARE DESTROYING AROUND THEM.
YOU WERE RIGHT, OUR PEOPLE SHOULD BE SPARED...BUT THAT IS NOT THE WORLD. WE KNOW THEY ARE ALWAYS THE FIRST TO PAY A MUCH-TOO-COSTLY PRICE.
I REGRET THAT.

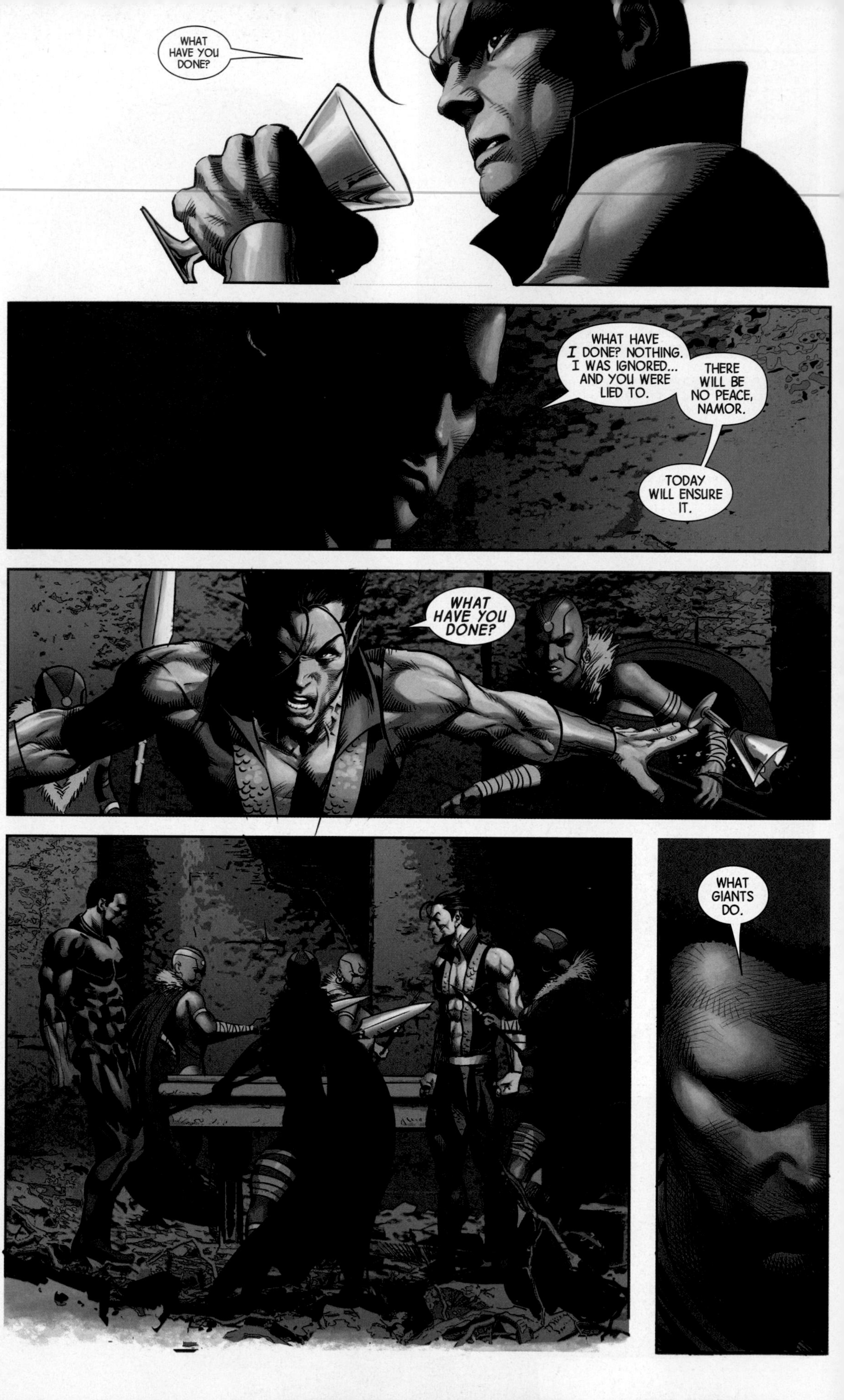
WHAT HAVE YOU DONE?
WHAT HAVE I DONE? NOTHING. I WAS IGNORED... AND YOU WERE LIED TO.
THERE WILL BE NO PEACE, NAMOR.
TODAY WILL ENSURE IT.
WHAT HAVE YOU DONE?
WHAT GIANTS DO.

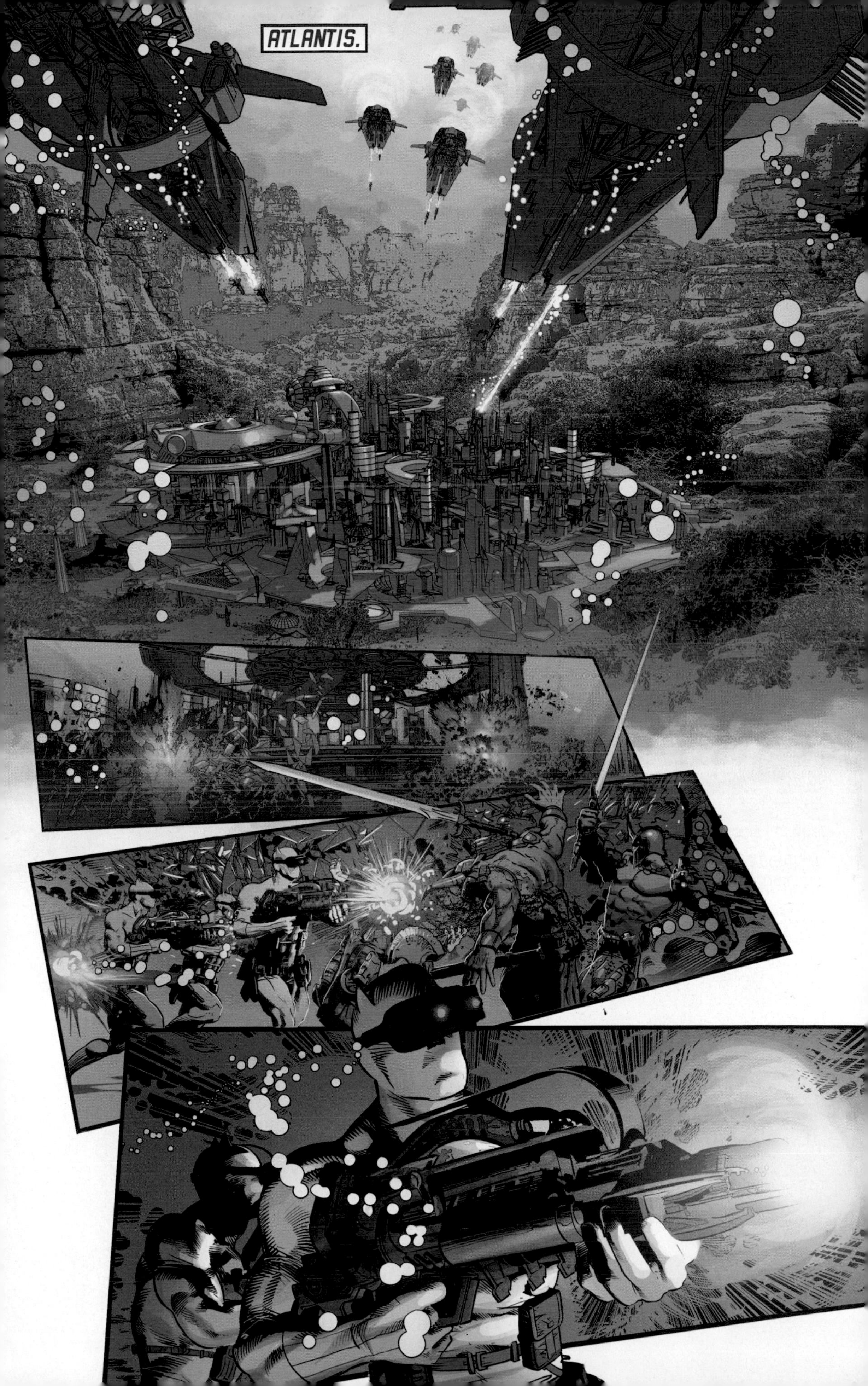
ATLANTIS.

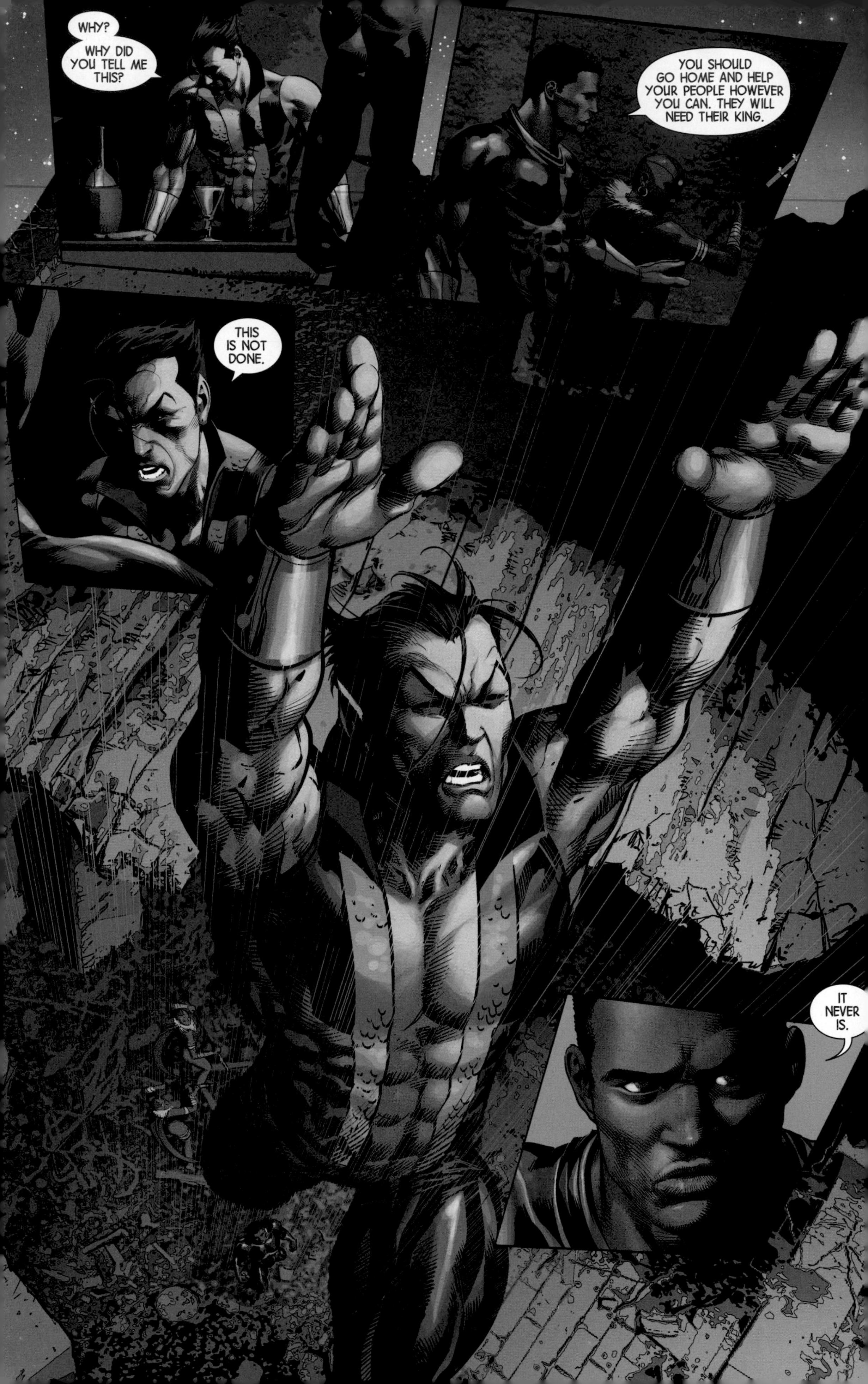
WHY?
WHY DID YOU TELL ME THIS?
YOU SHOULD GO HOME AND HELP YOUR PEOPLE HOWEVER YOU CAN. THEY WILL NEED THEIR KING.
THIS IS NOT DONE.
IT NEVER IS.

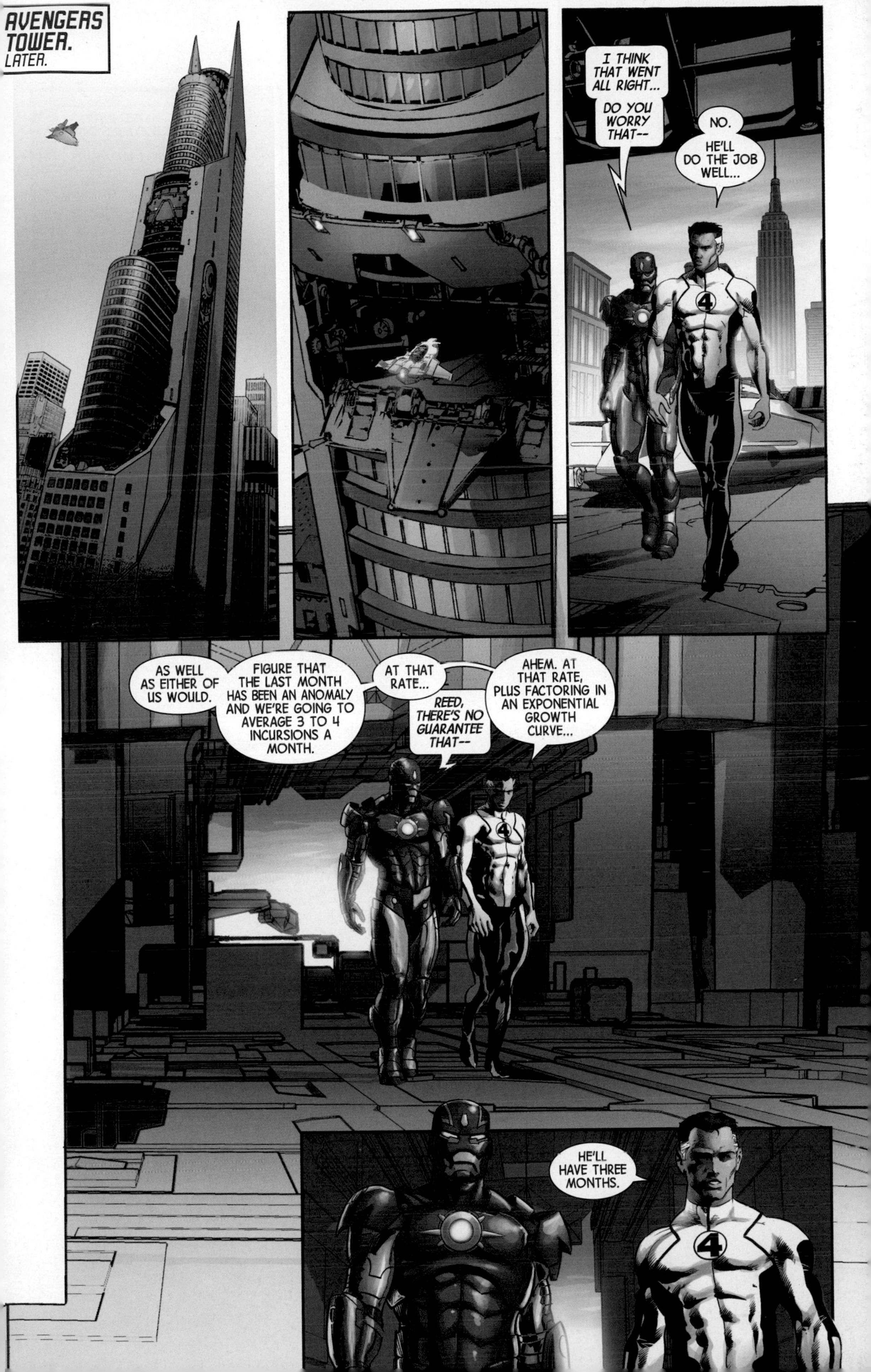
AVENGERS TOWER. LATER.
I THINK THAT WENT ALL RIGHT... DO YOU WORRY THAT--
NO. HE'LL DO THE JOB WELL...
AS WELL AS EITHER OF US WOULD.
FIGURE THAT THE LAST MONTH HAS BEEN AN ANOMALY AND WE'RE GOING TO AVERAGE 3 TO 4 INCURSIONS A MONTH.
AT THAT RATE...
REED, THERE'S NO GUARANTEE THAT--
AHEM. AT THAT RATE, PLUS FACTORING IN AN EXPONENTIAL GROWTH CURVE...
HE'LL HAVE THREE MONTHS.

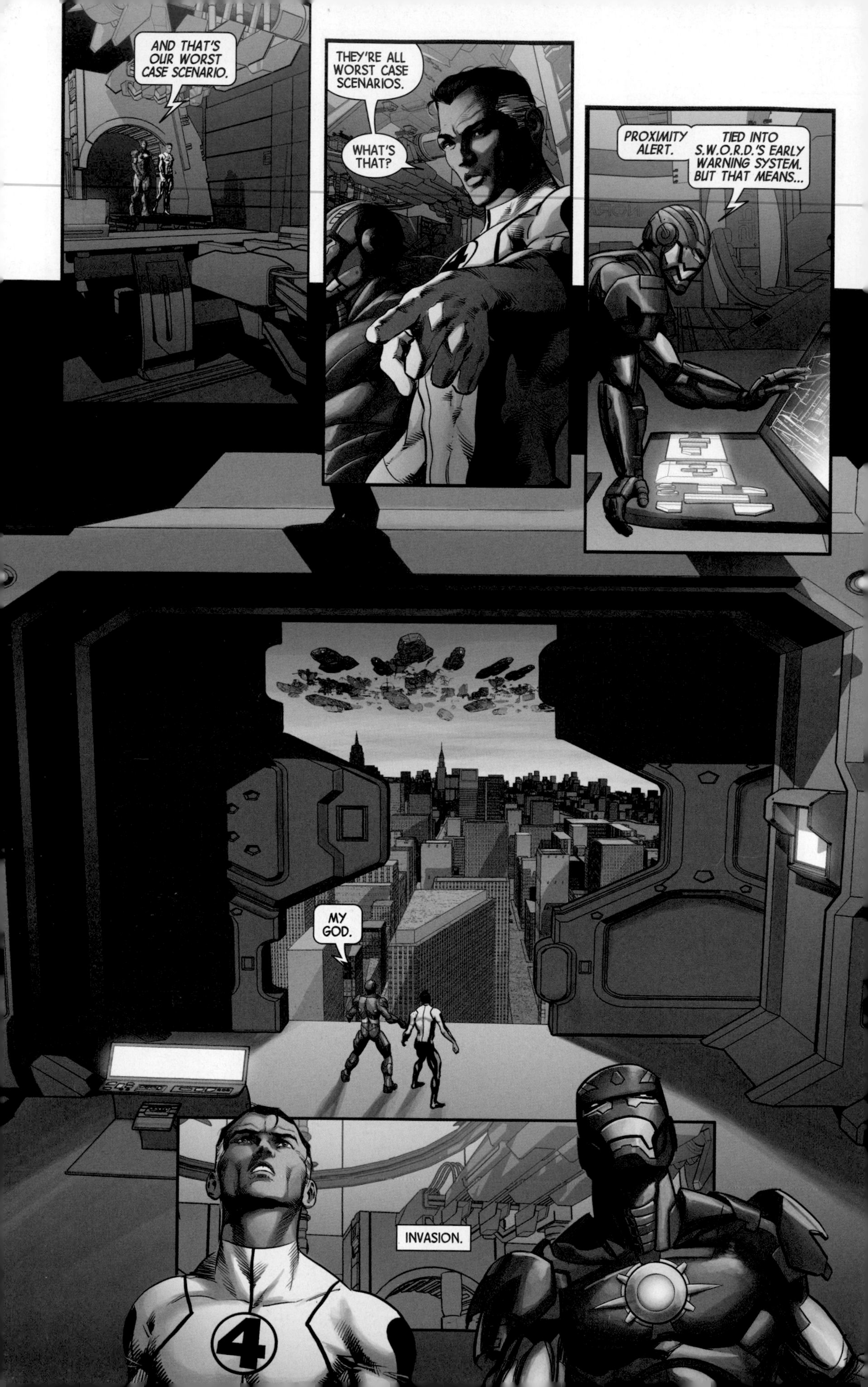
AND THAT'S OUR WORST CASE SCENARIO.
THEY'RE ALL WORST CASE SCENARIOS.
WHAT'S THAT?
PROXIMITY ALERT.
TIED INTO S.W.O.R.D.'S EARLY WARNING SYSTEM. BUT THAT MEANS...
MY GOD.
INVASION.

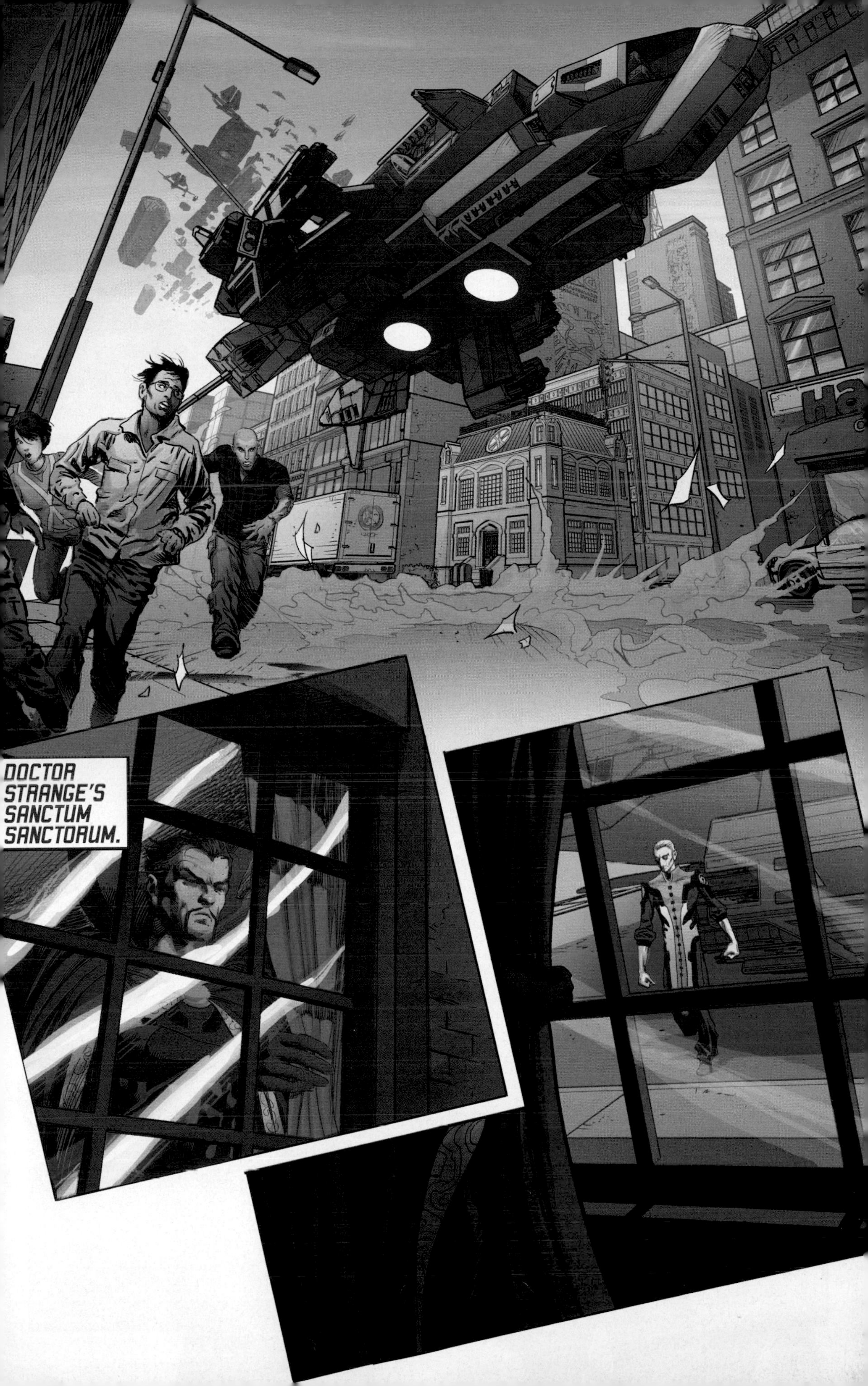
DOCTOR STRANGE'S SANCTUM SANCTORUM.

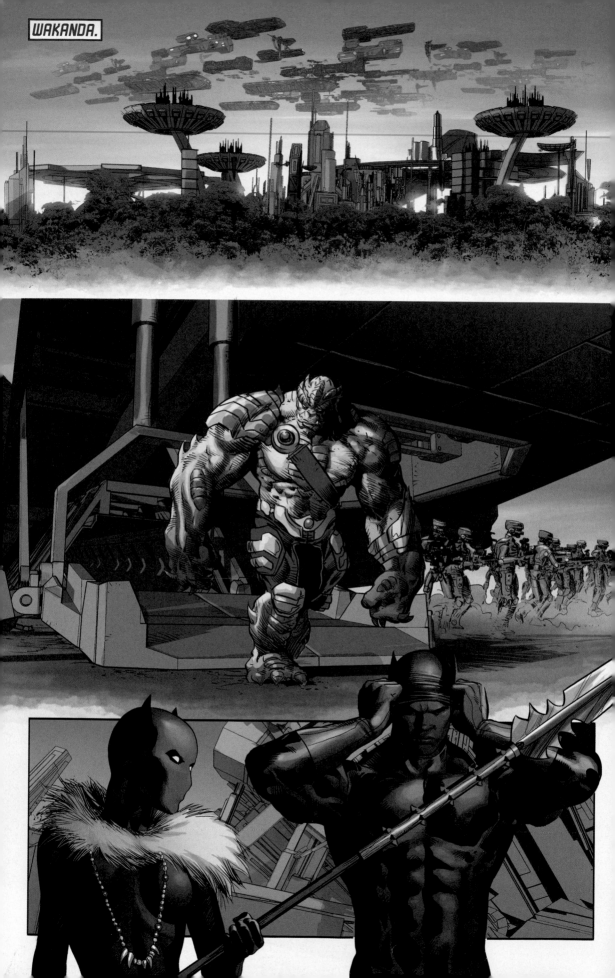

WAKANDA.

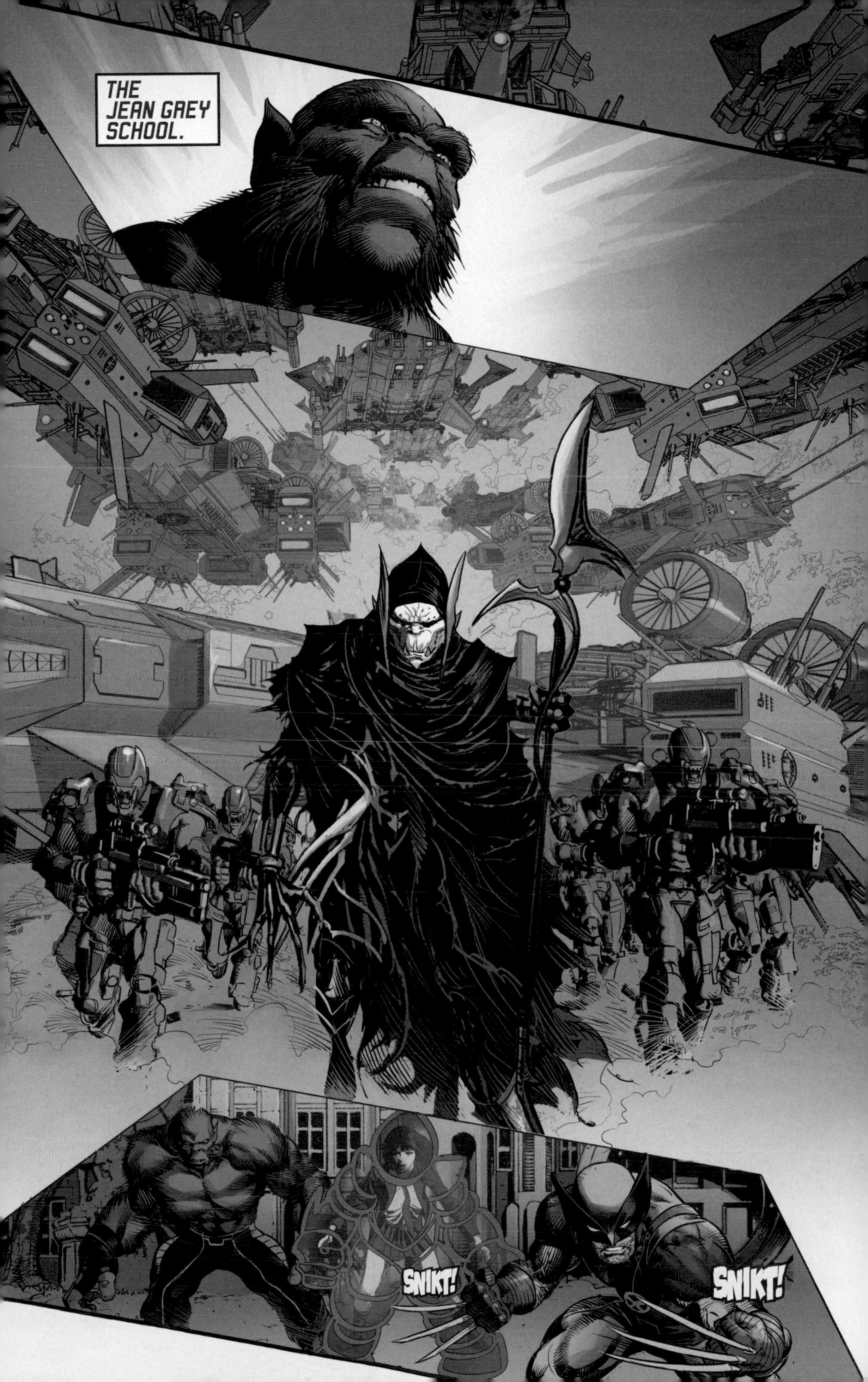
THE JEAN GREY SCHOOL.
SNIKT!
SNIKT!

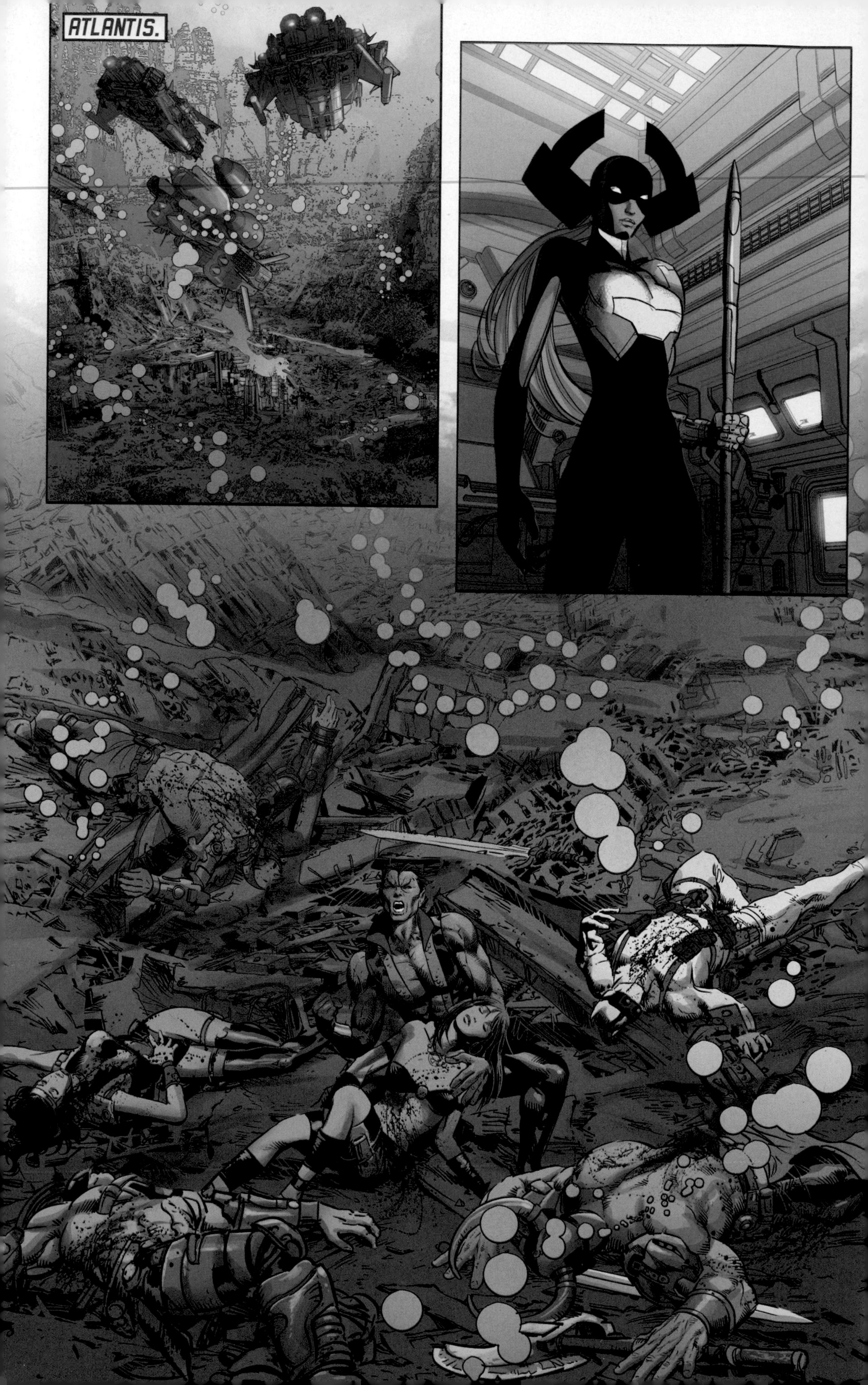
ATLANTIS.

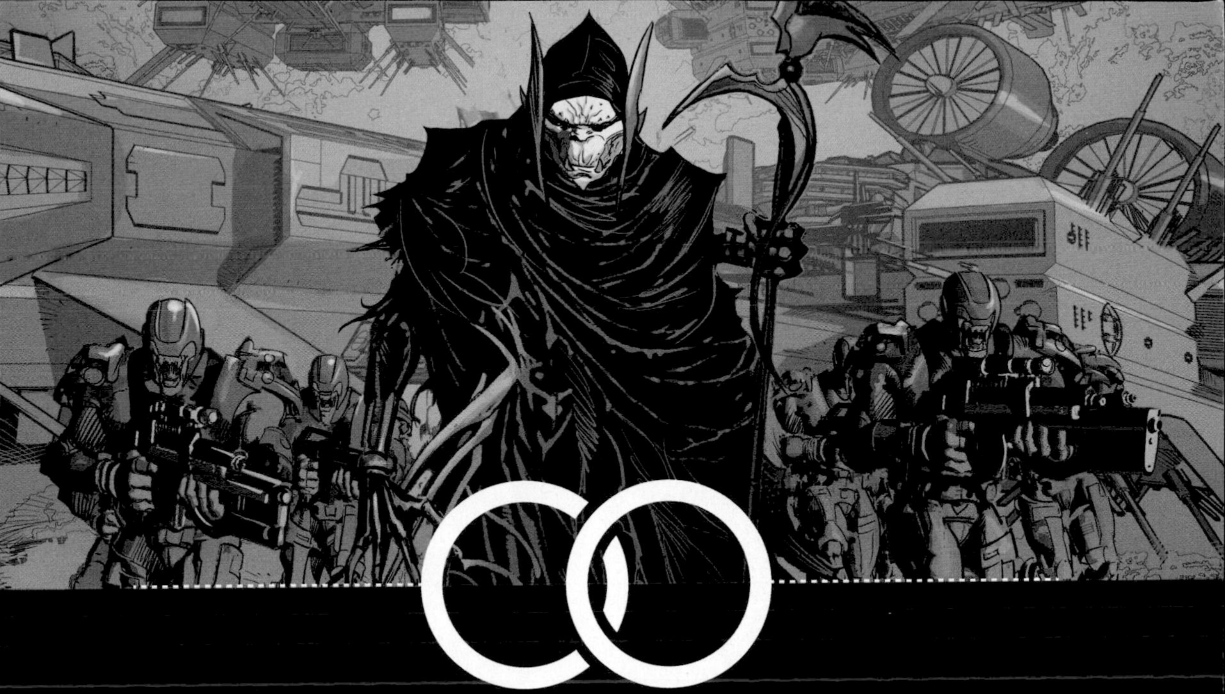

PREVIOUSLY IN INFINITY

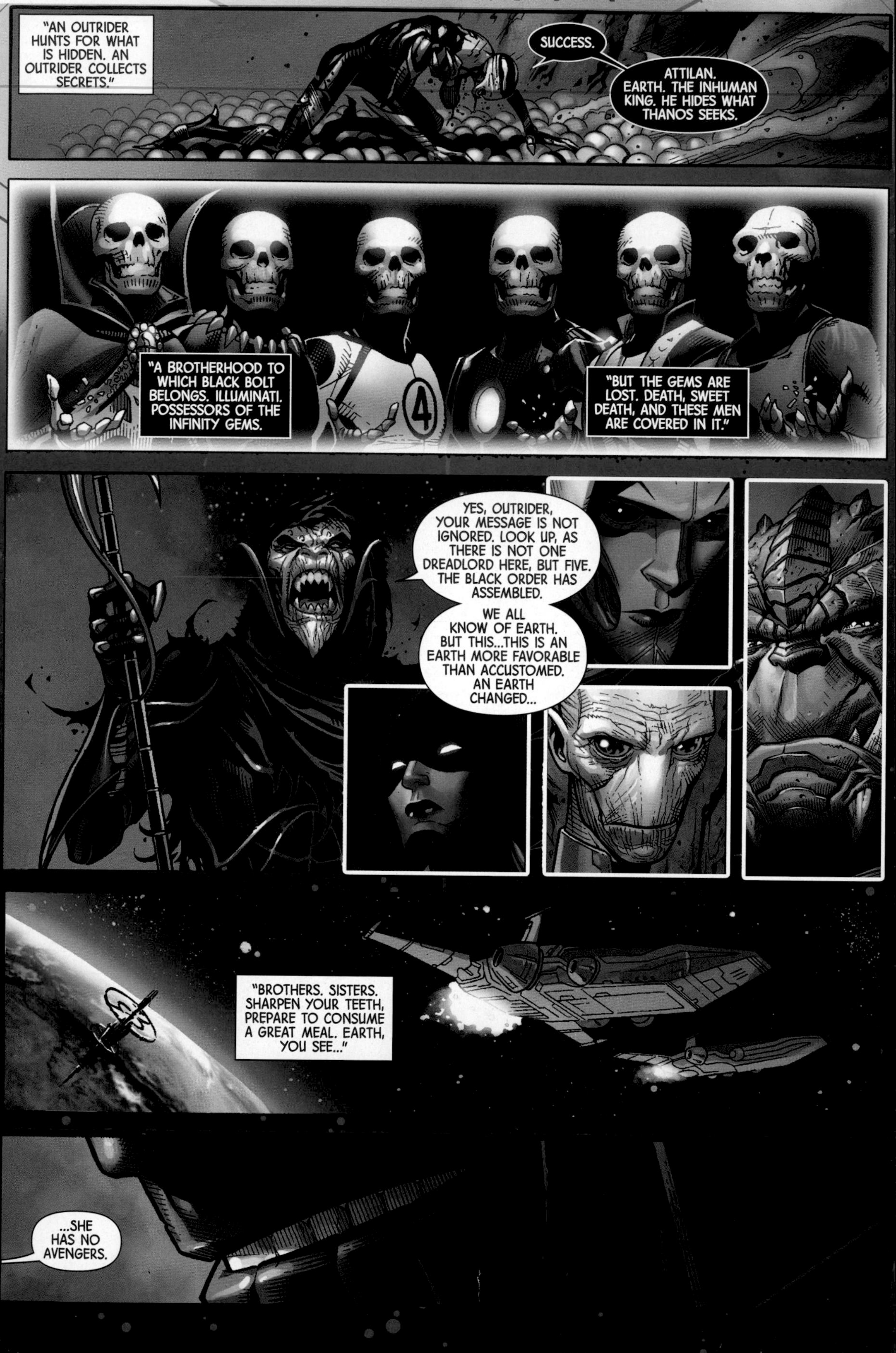
"AN OUTRIDER HUNTS FOR WHAT IS HIDDEN. AN OUTRIDER COLLECTS SECRETS."
SUCCESS.
ATTILAN. EARTH. THE INHUMAN KING. HE HIDES WHAT THANOS SEEKS.
"A BROTHERHOOD TO WHICH BLACK BOLT BELONGS. ILLUMINATI. POSSESSORS OF THE INFINITY GEMS.
"BUT THE GEMS ARE LOST. DEATH, SWEET DEATH, AND THESE MEN ARE COVERED IN IT."
YES, OUTRIDER, YOUR MESSAGE IS NOT IGNORED. LOOK UP, AS THERE IS NOT ONE DREADLORD HERE, BUT FIVE. THE BLACK ORDER HAS ASSEMBLED.
WE ALL KNOW OF EARTH. BUT THIS...THIS IS AN EARTH MORE FAVORABLE THAN ACCUSTOMED. AN EARTH CHANGED...
"BROTHERS. SISTERS. SHARPEN YOUR TEETH, PREPARE TO CONSUME A GREAT MEAL. EARTH, YOU SEE..."
...SHE HAS NO AVENGERS.

CAST

THE ILLUMINATI

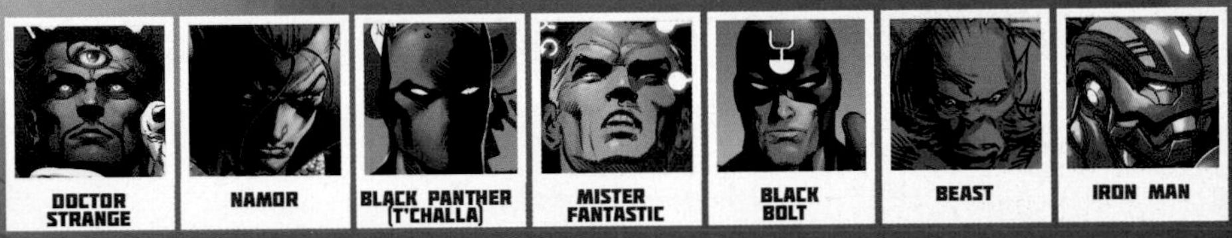
DOCTOR STRANGE
NAMOR
BLACK PANTHER (T'CHALLA)
MISTER FANTASTIC
BLACK BOLT
BEAST
IRON MAN

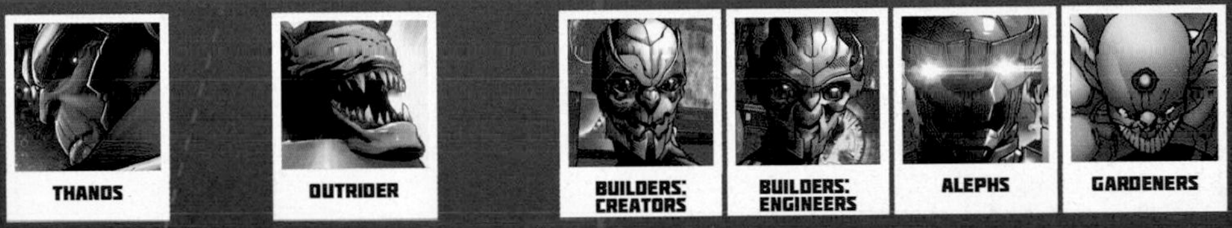
THANOS
OUTRIDER
BUILDERS: CREATORS
BUILDERS: ENGINEERS
ALEPHS
GARDENERS

THE BLACK ORDER

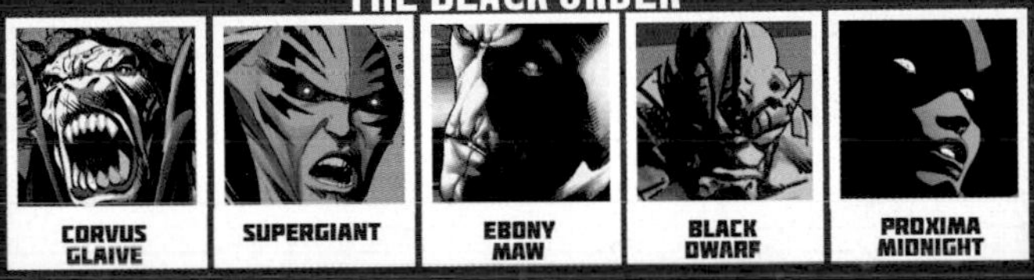
CORVUS GLAIVE
SUPERGIANT
EBONY MAW
BLACK DWARF
PROXIMA MIDNIGHT

X-MEN

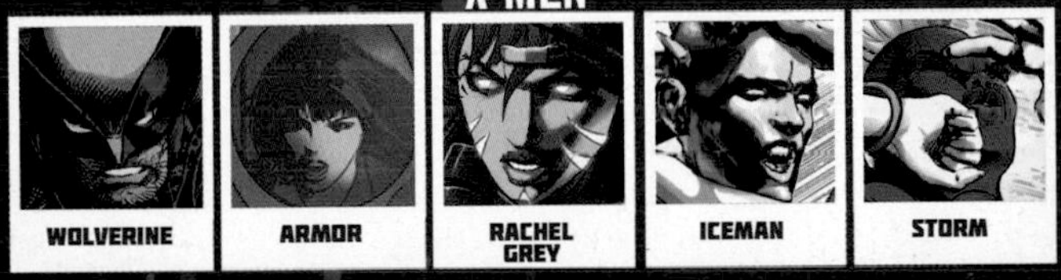
WOLVERINE
ARMOR
RACHEL GREY
ICEMAN
STORM

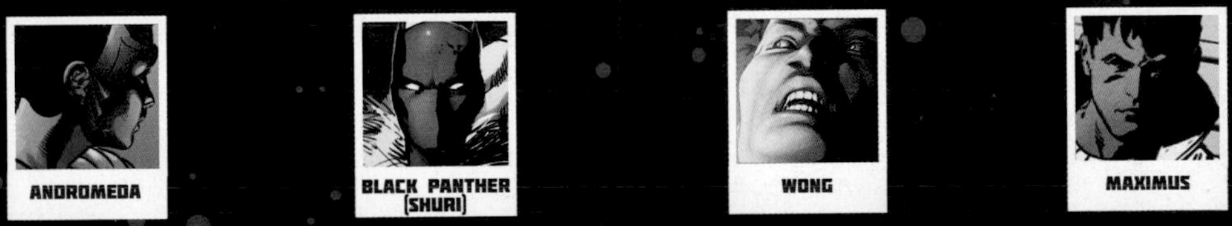
ANDROMEDA
BLACK PANTHER (SHURI)
WONG
MAXIMUS

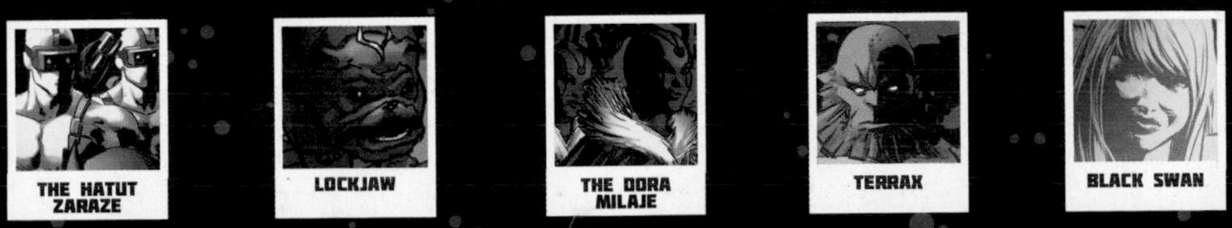
THE HATUT ZARAZE
LOCKJAW
THE DORA MILAJE
TERRAX
BLACK SWAN

THE STONES, SHATTERED

◆

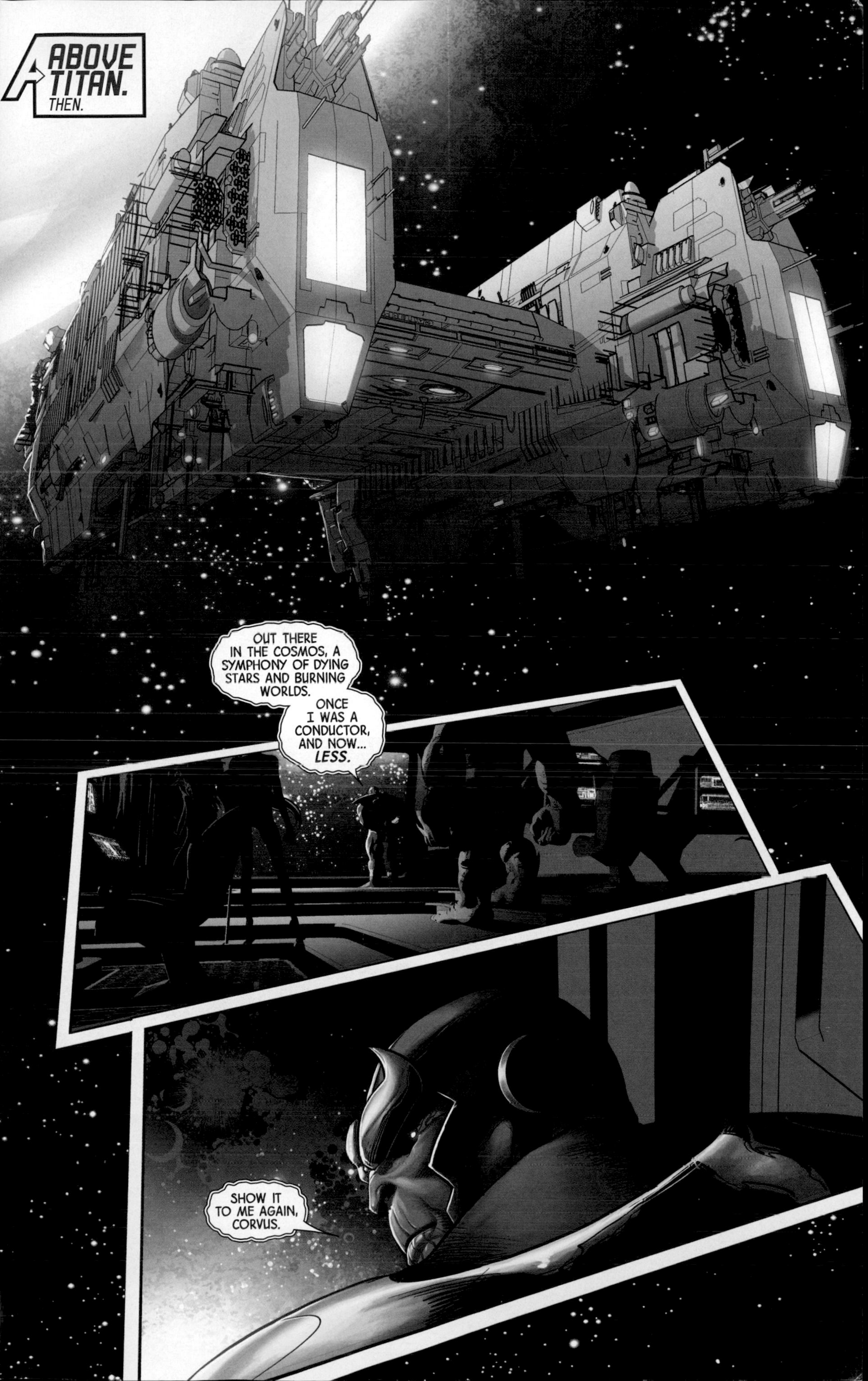
ABOVE TITAN. THEN.
OUT THERE IN THE COSMOS, A SYMPHONY OF DYING STARS AND BURNING WORLDS.
ONCE I WAS A CONDUCTOR, AND NOW... LESS.
SHOW IT TO ME AGAIN, CORVUS.

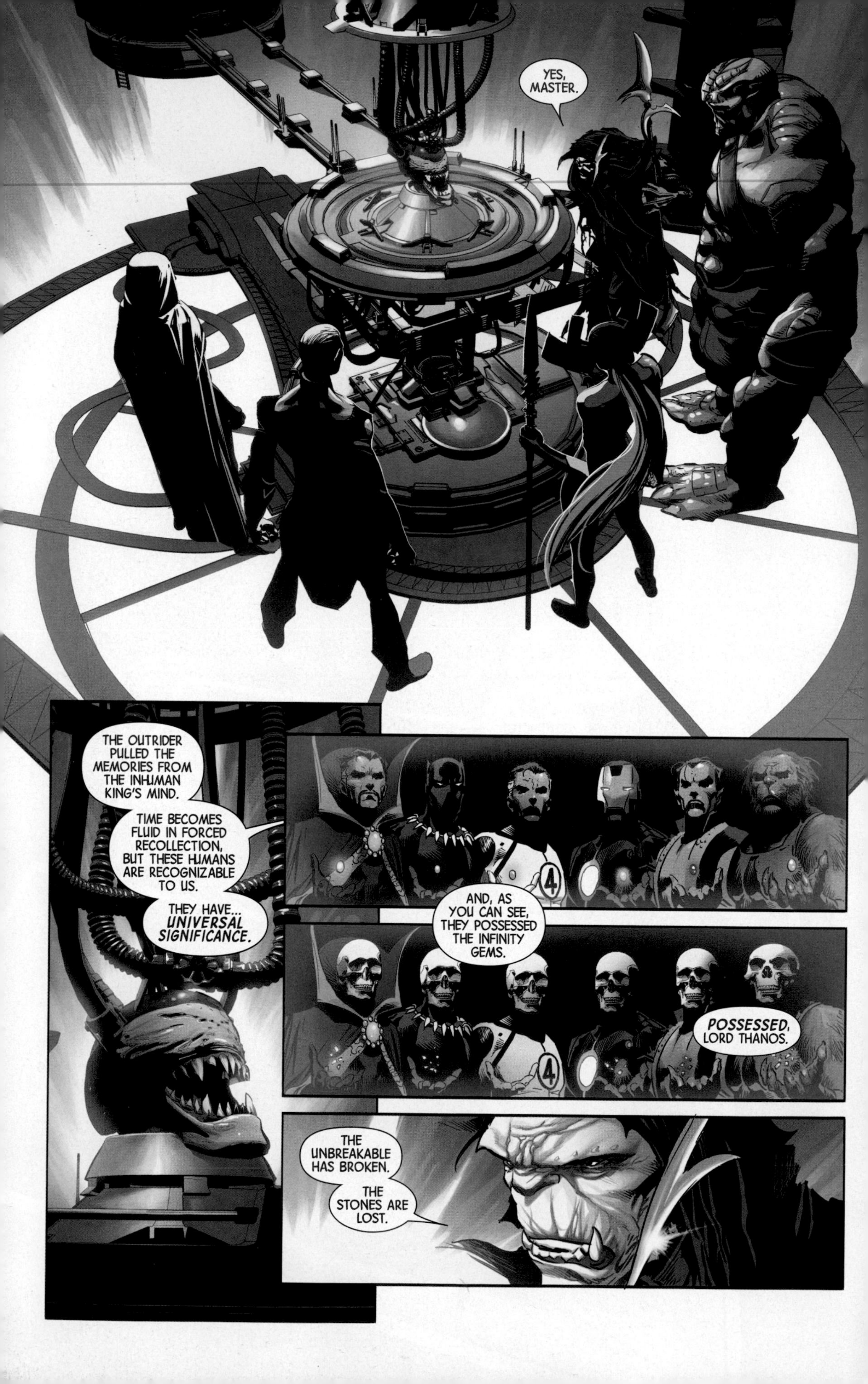
YES, MASTER.
THE OUTRIDER PULLED THE MEMORIES FROM THE INHUMAN KING'S MIND.
TIME BECOMES FLUID IN FORCED RECOLLECTION, BUT THESE HUMANS ARE RECOGNIZABLE TO US.
THEY HAVE... *UNIVERSAL SIGNIFICANCE.*
AND, AS YOU CAN SEE, THEY POSSESSED THE INFINITY GEMS.
POSSESSED, LORD THANOS.
THE UNBREAKABLE HAS BROKEN.
THE STONES ARE LOST.

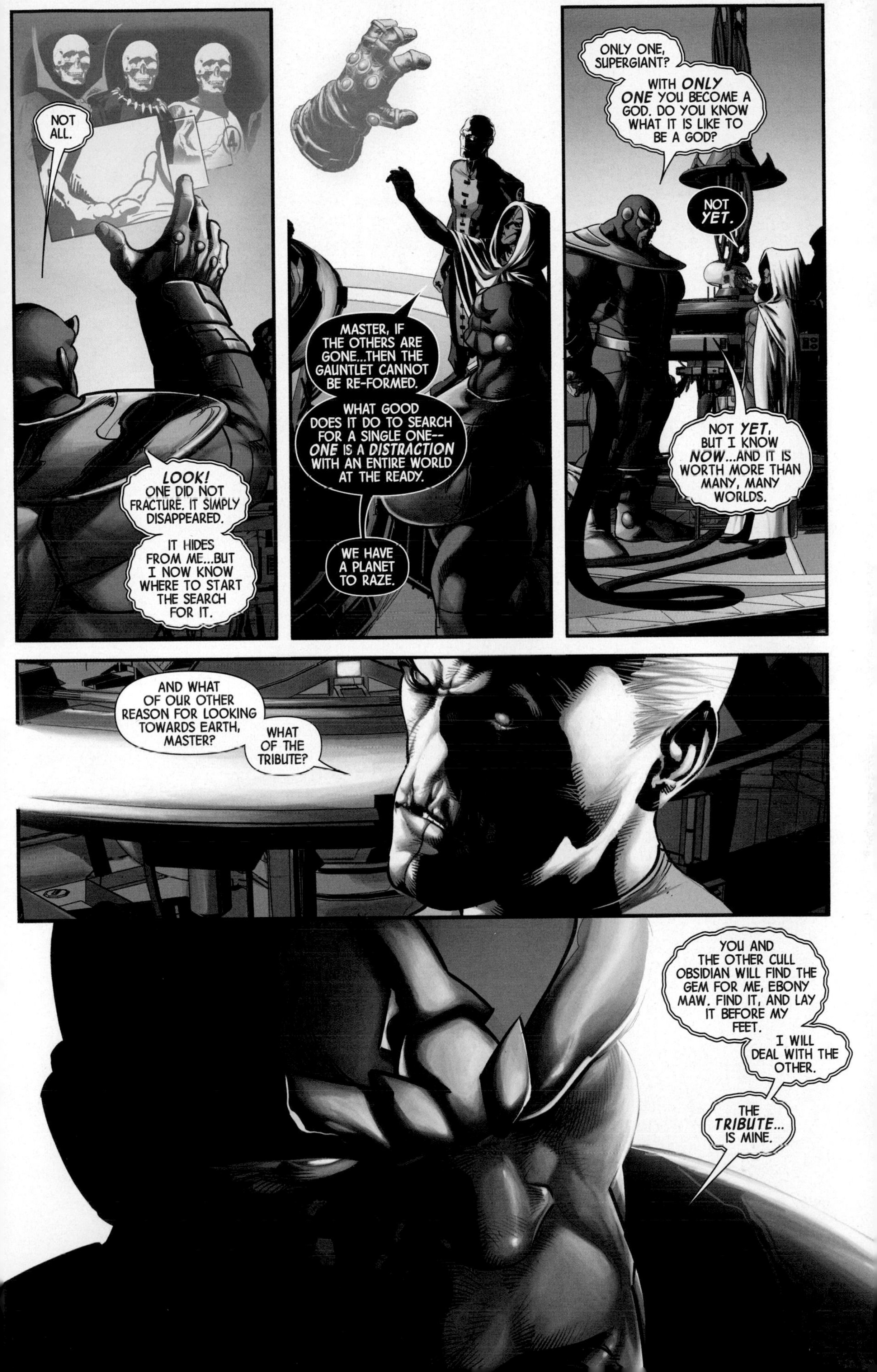
NOT ALL.
LOOK! ONE DID NOT FRACTURE. IT SIMPLY DISAPPEARED.
IT HIDES FROM ME...BUT I NOW KNOW WHERE TO START THE SEARCH FOR IT.
MASTER, IF THE OTHERS ARE GONE...THEN THE GAUNTLET CANNOT BE RE-FORMED.
WHAT GOOD DOES IT DO TO SEARCH FOR A SINGLE ONE-- ONE IS A DISTRACTION WITH AN ENTIRE WORLD AT THE READY.
WE HAVE A PLANET TO RAZE.
ONLY ONE, SUPERGIANT?
WITH ONLY ONE YOU BECOME A GOD. DO YOU KNOW WHAT IT IS LIKE TO BE A GOD?
NOT YET.
NOT YET, BUT I KNOW NOW...AND IT IS WORTH MORE THAN MANY, MANY WORLDS.
AND WHAT OF OUR OTHER REASON FOR LOOKING TOWARDS EARTH, MASTER?
WHAT OF THE TRIBUTE?
YOU AND THE OTHER CULL OBSIDIAN WILL FIND THE GEM FOR ME, EBONY MAW. FIND IT, AND LAY IT BEFORE MY FEET.
I WILL DEAL WITH THE OTHER.
THE TRIBUTE... IS MINE.

THE CULL OBSIDIAN

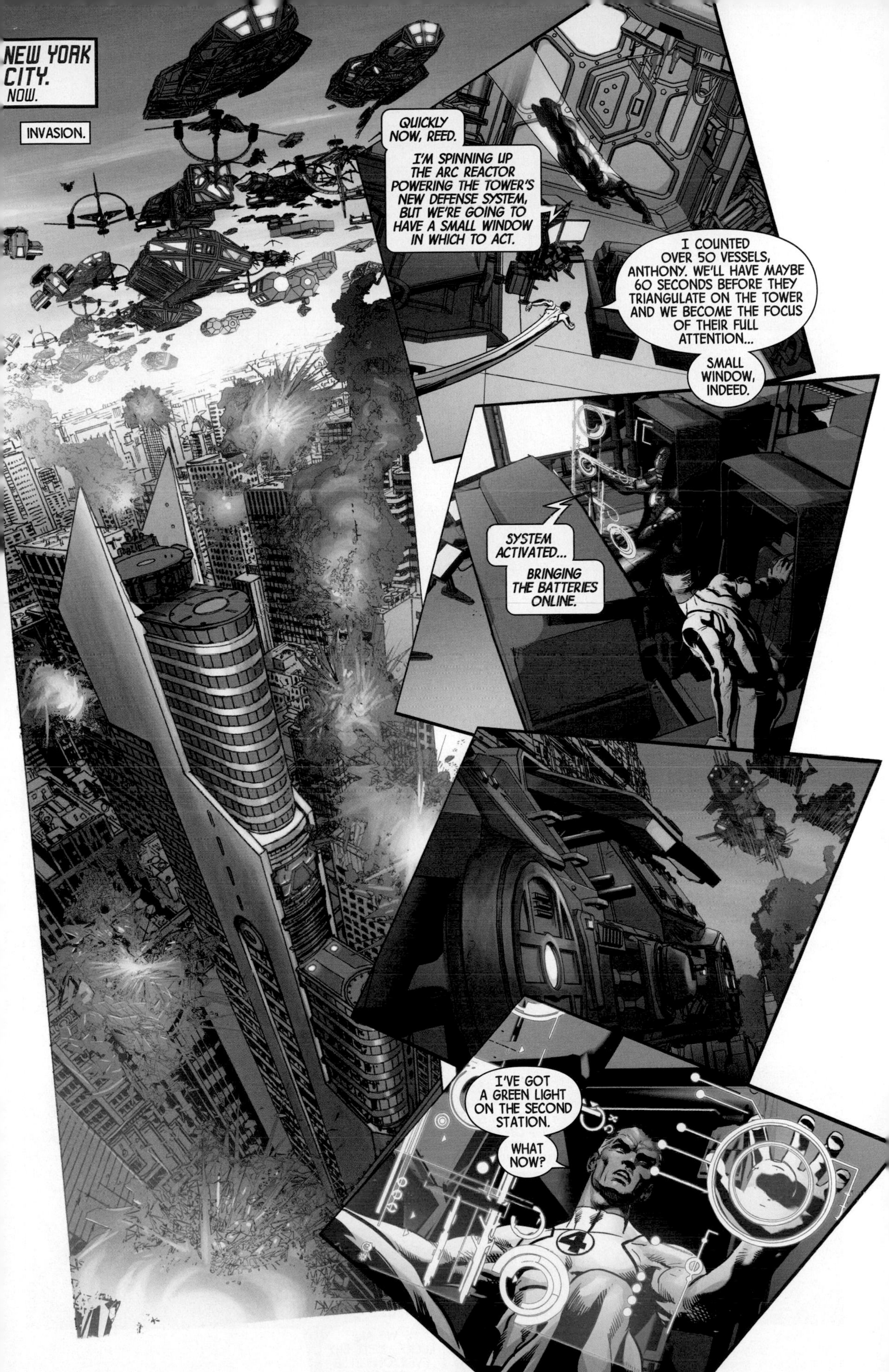
NEW YORK CITY. NOW.
INVASION.
QUICKLY NOW, REED.
I'M SPINNING UP THE ARC REACTOR POWERING THE TOWER'S NEW DEFENSE SYSTEM, BUT WE'RE GOING TO HAVE A SMALL WINDOW IN WHICH TO ACT.
I COUNTED OVER 50 VESSELS, ANTHONY. WE'LL HAVE MAYBE 60 SECONDS BEFORE THEY TRIANGULATE ON THE TOWER AND WE BECOME THE FOCUS OF THEIR FULL ATTENTION...
SMALL WINDOW, INDEED.
SYSTEM ACTIVATED...
BRINGING THE BATTERIES ONLINE.
I'VE GOT A GREEN LIGHT ON THE SECOND STATION.
WHAT NOW?

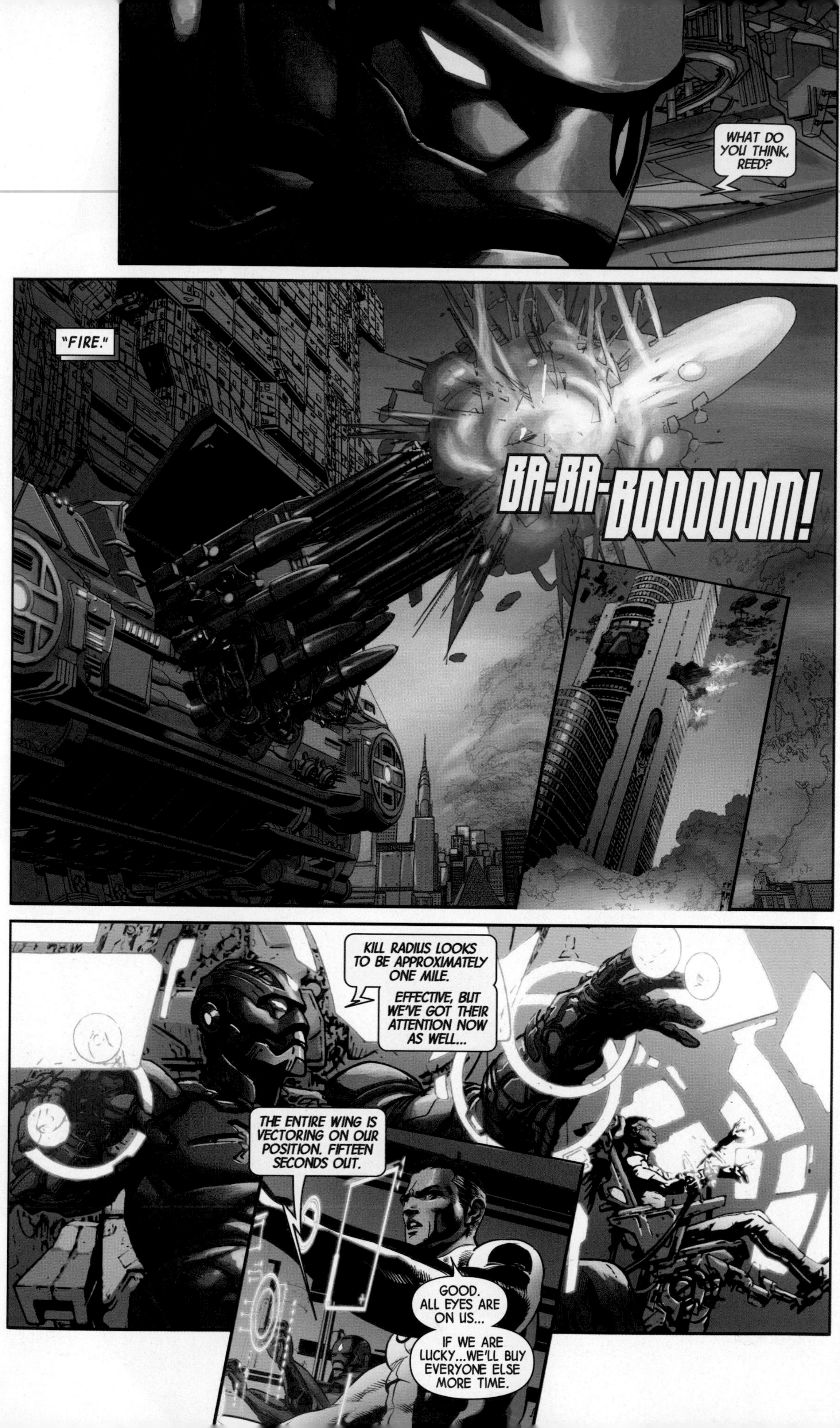
WHAT DO YOU THINK, REED?
"FIRE."
BA-BA-BOOOOOM!
KILL RADIUS LOOKS TO BE APPROXIMATELY ONE MILE.
EFFECTIVE, BUT WE'VE GOT THEIR ATTENTION NOW AS WELL...
THE ENTIRE WING IS VECTORING ON OUR POSITION. FIFTEEN SECONDS OUT.
GOOD. ALL EYES ARE ON US...
IF WE ARE LUCKY...WE'LL BUY EVERYONE ELSE MORE TIME.

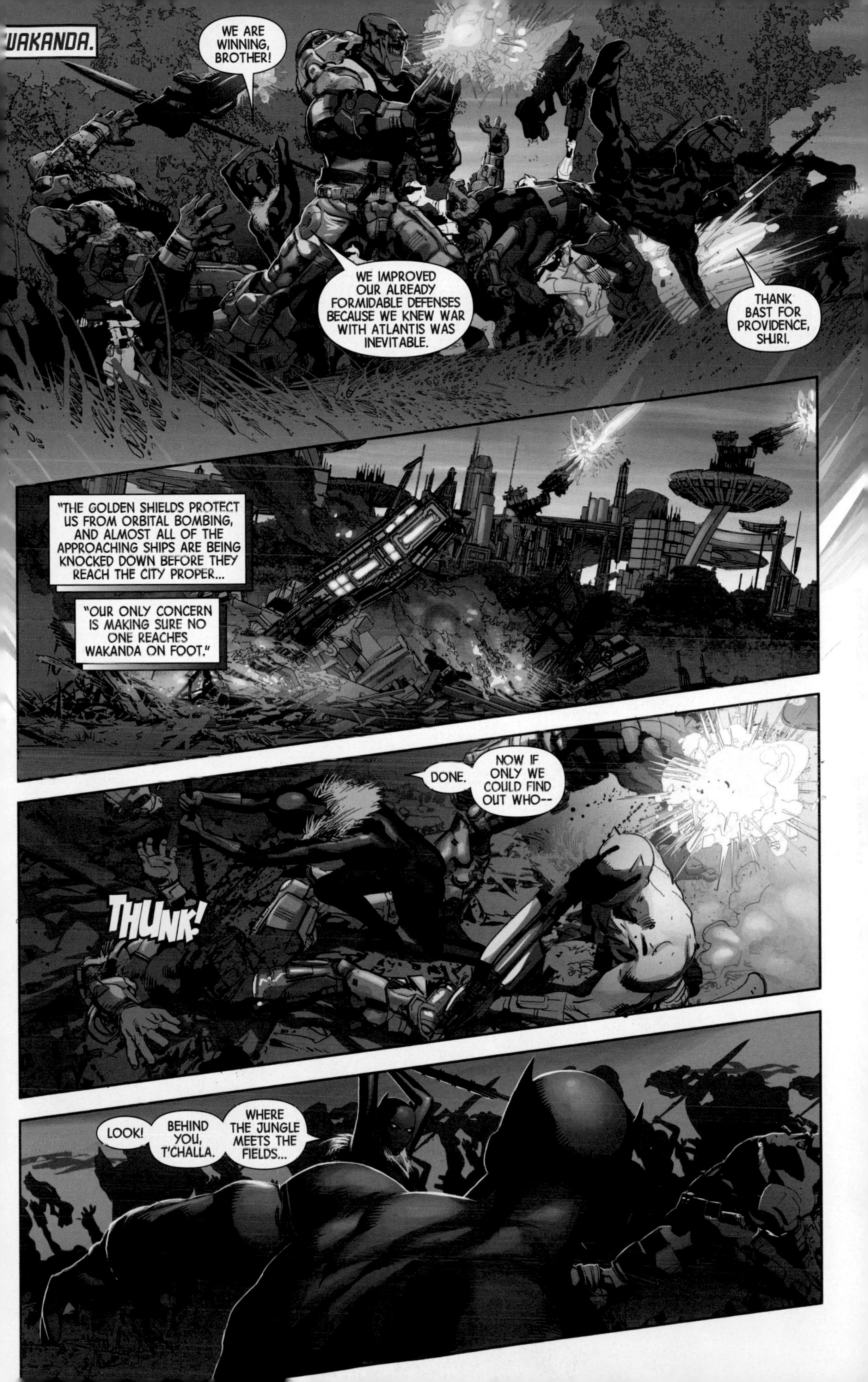
WAKANDA.
WE ARE WINNING, BROTHER!
WE IMPROVED OUR ALREADY FORMIDABLE DEFENSES BECAUSE WE KNEW WAR WITH ATLANTIS WAS INEVITABLE.
THANK BAST FOR PROVIDENCE, SHURI.
"THE GOLDEN SHIELDS PROTECT US FROM ORBITAL BOMBING, AND ALMOST ALL OF THE APPROACHING SHIPS ARE BEING KNOCKED DOWN BEFORE THEY REACH THE CITY PROPER...
"OUR ONLY CONCERN IS MAKING SURE NO ONE REACHES WAKANDA ON FOOT."
DONE.
NOW IF ONLY WE COULD FIND OUT WHO--
THUNK!
LOOK!
BEHIND YOU, T'CHALLA.
WHERE THE JUNGLE MEETS THE FIELDS...

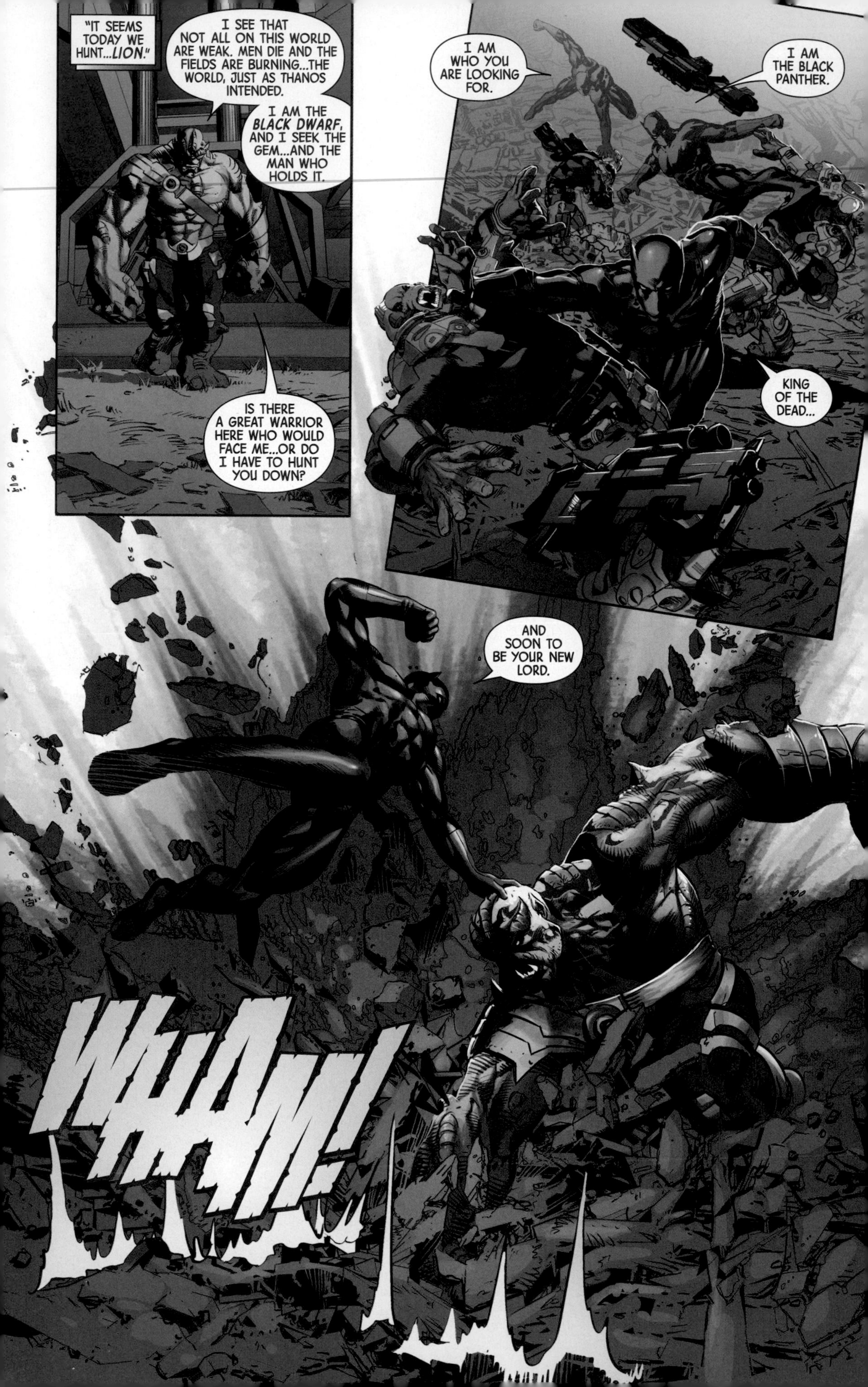
"IT SEEMS TODAY WE HUNT...LION."
I SEE THAT NOT ALL ON THIS WORLD ARE WEAK. MEN DIE AND THE FIELDS ARE BURNING...THE WORLD, JUST AS THANOS INTENDED.
I AM THE BLACK DWARF, AND I SEEK THE GEM...AND THE MAN WHO HOLDS IT.
IS THERE A GREAT WARRIOR HERE WHO WOULD FACE ME...OR DO I HAVE TO HUNT YOU DOWN?
I AM WHO YOU ARE LOOKING FOR.
I AM THE BLACK PANTHER.
KING OF THE DEAD...
AND SOON TO BE YOUR NEW LORD.
WHAM!

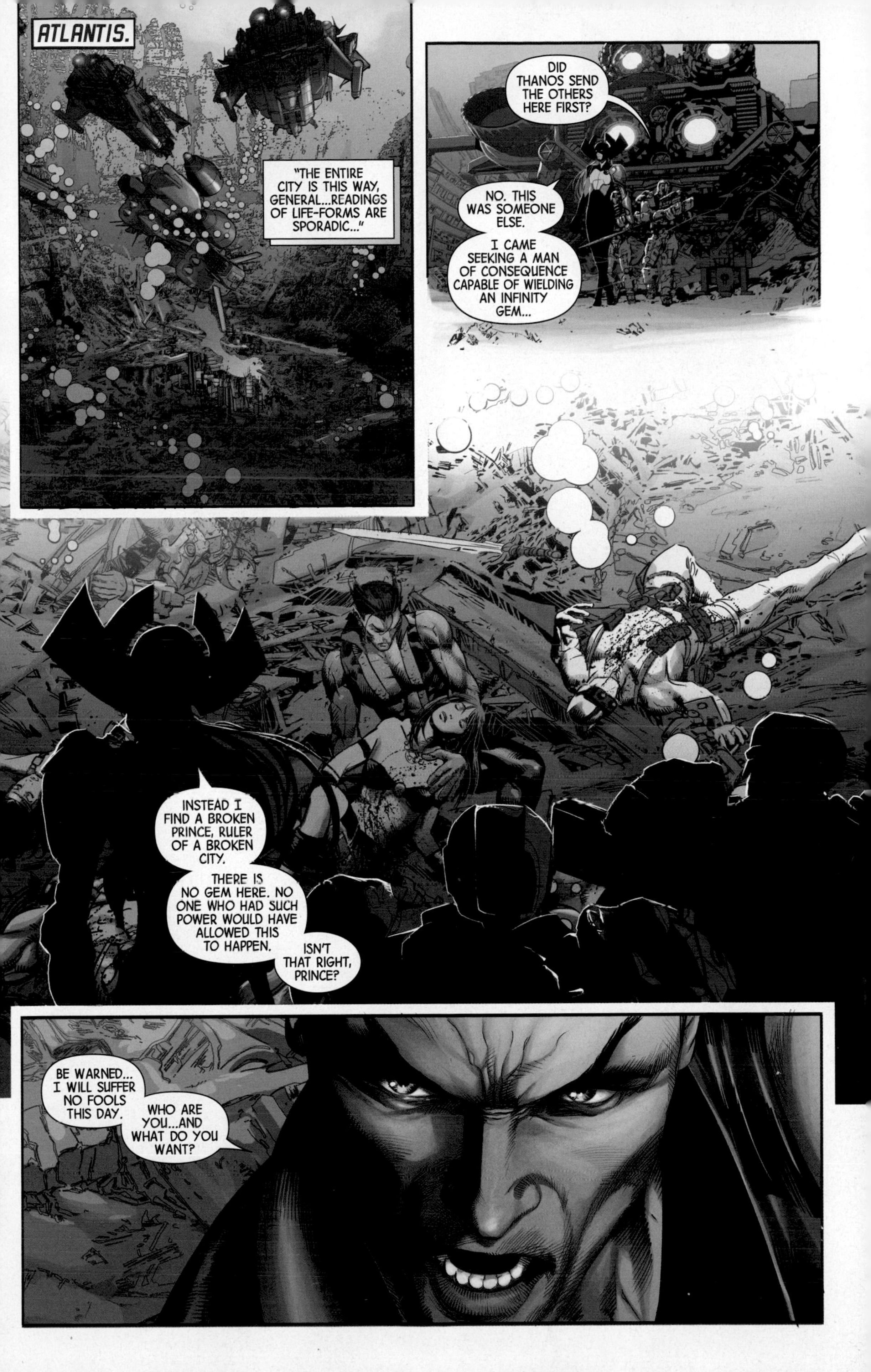
ATLANTIS.
"THE ENTIRE CITY IS THIS WAY, GENERAL...READINGS OF LIFE-FORMS ARE SPORADIC..."
DID THANOS SEND THE OTHERS HERE FIRST?
NO. THIS WAS SOMEONE ELSE.
I CAME SEEKING A MAN OF CONSEQUENCE CAPABLE OF WIELDING AN INFINITY GEM...
INSTEAD I FIND A BROKEN PRINCE, RULER OF A BROKEN CITY.
THERE IS NO GEM HERE. NO ONE WHO HAD SUCH POWER WOULD HAVE ALLOWED THIS TO HAPPEN.
ISN'T THAT RIGHT, PRINCE?
BE WARNED... I WILL SUFFER NO FOOLS THIS DAY.
WHO ARE YOU...AND WHAT DO YOU WANT?

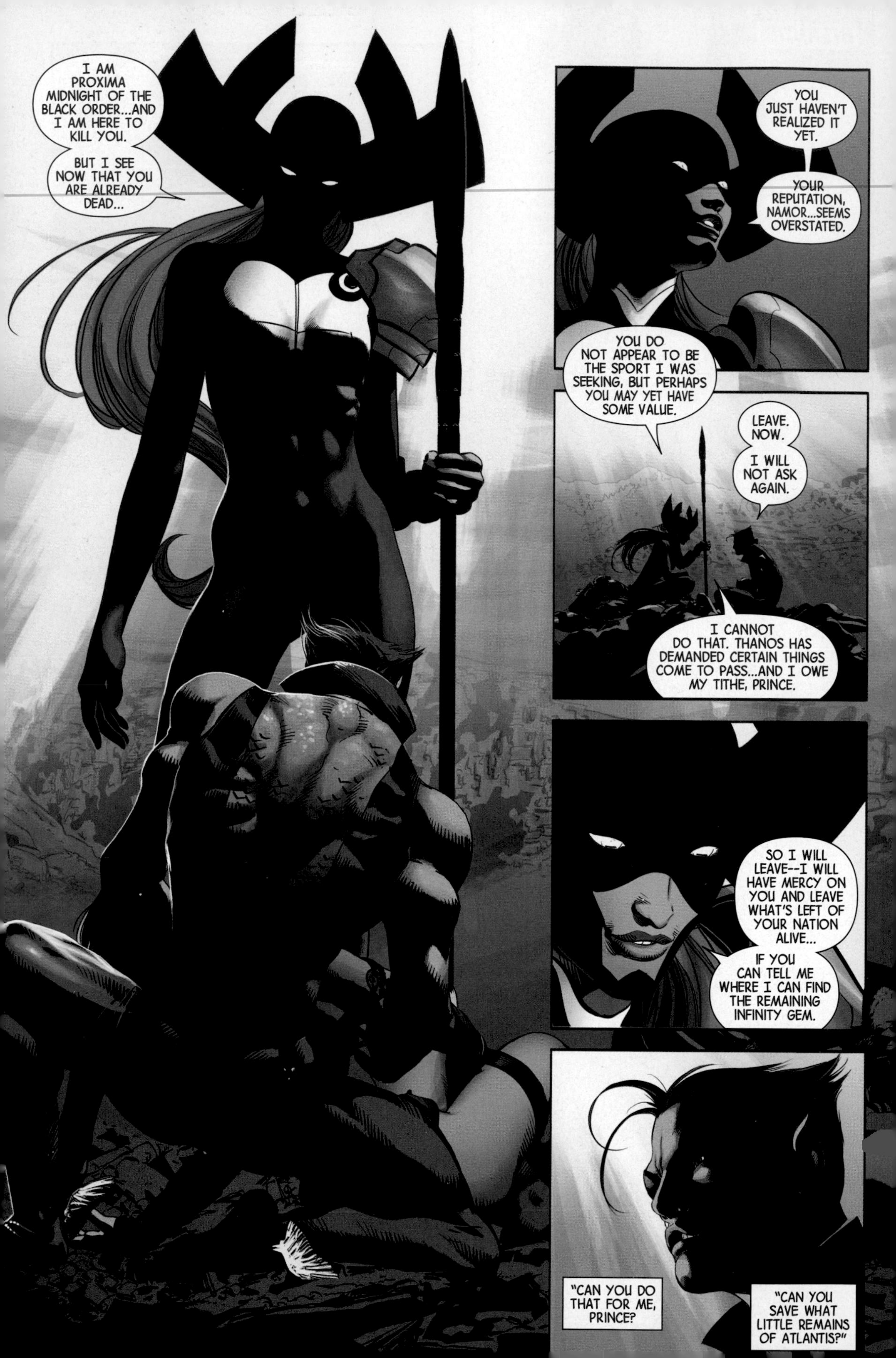
I AM PROXIMA MIDNIGHT OF THE BLACK ORDER...AND I AM HERE TO KILL YOU.
BUT I SEE NOW THAT YOU ARE ALREADY DEAD...
YOU JUST HAVEN'T REALIZED IT YET.
YOUR REPUTATION, NAMOR...SEEMS OVERSTATED.
YOU DO NOT APPEAR TO BE THE SPORT I WAS SEEKING, BUT PERHAPS YOU MAY YET HAVE SOME VALUE.
LEAVE. NOW.
I WILL NOT ASK AGAIN.
I CANNOT DO THAT. THANOS HAS DEMANDED CERTAIN THINGS COME TO PASS...AND I OWE MY TITHE, PRINCE.
SO I WILL LEAVE--I WILL HAVE MERCY ON YOU AND LEAVE WHAT'S LEFT OF YOUR NATION ALIVE...
IF YOU CAN TELL ME WHERE I CAN FIND THE REMAINING INFINITY GEM.
"CAN YOU DO THAT FOR ME, PRINCE?
"CAN YOU SAVE WHAT LITTLE REMAINS OF ATLANTIS?"

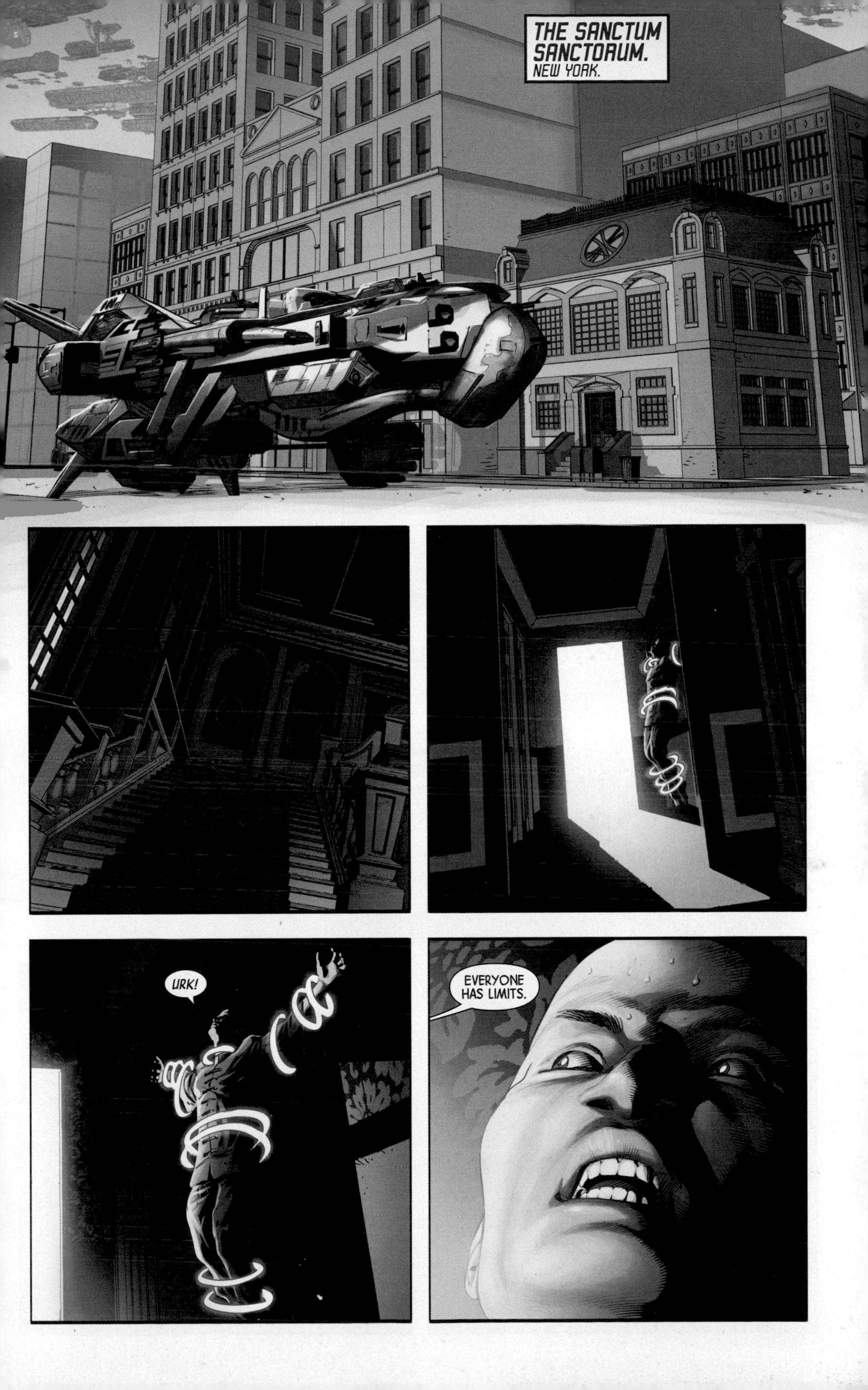
THE SANCTUM SANCTORUM.
NEW YORK.
URK!
EVERYONE HAS LIMITS.

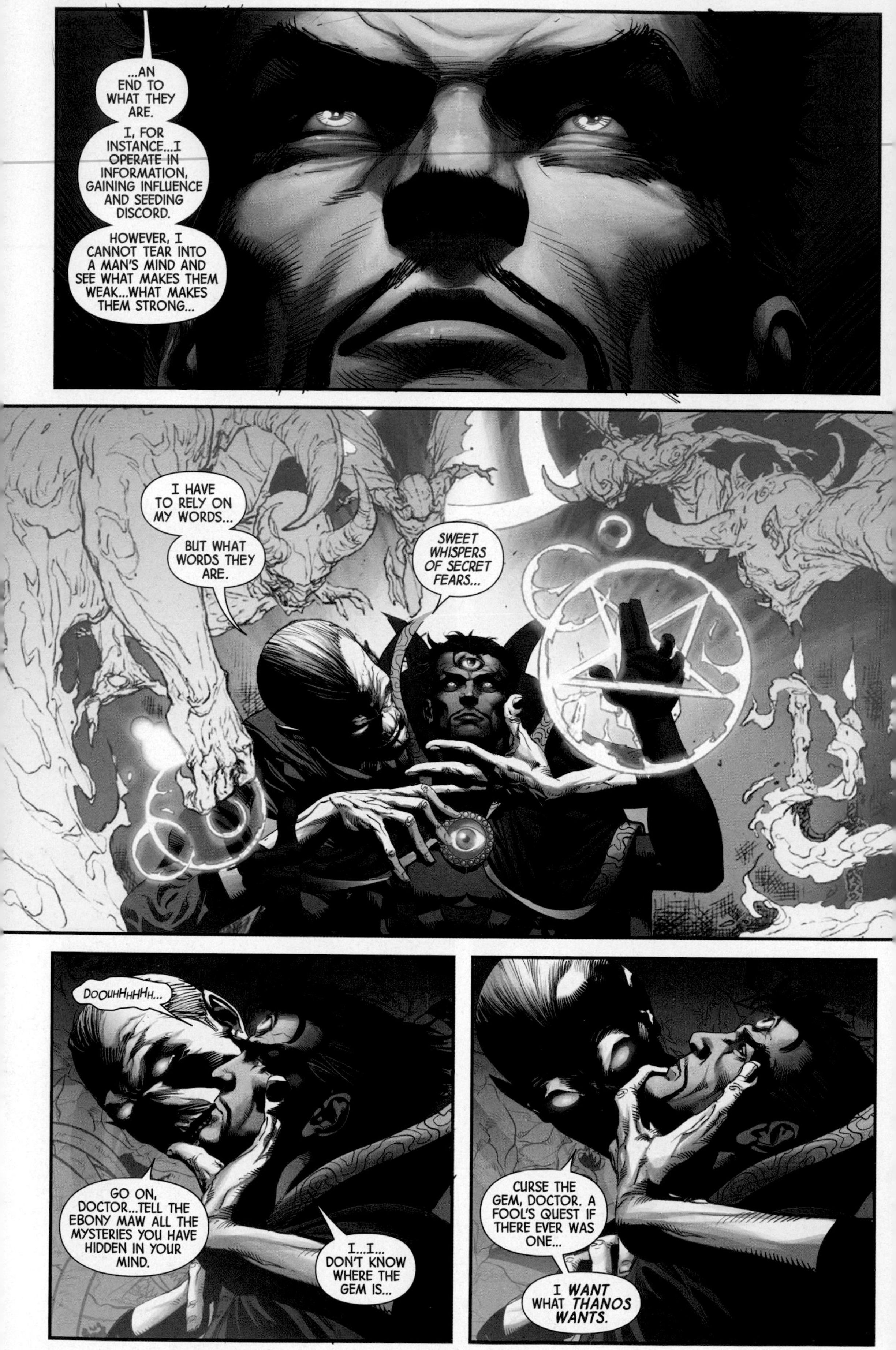
...AN END TO WHAT THEY ARE.
I, FOR INSTANCE...I OPERATE IN INFORMATION, GAINING INFLUENCE AND SEEDING DISCORD.
HOWEVER, I CANNOT TEAR INTO A MAN'S MIND AND SEE WHAT MAKES THEM WEAK...WHAT MAKES THEM STRONG...
I HAVE TO RELY ON MY WORDS...
BUT WHAT WORDS THEY ARE.
SWEET WHISPERS OF SECRET FEARS...
DOOUHHHHHH...
GO ON, DOCTOR...TELL THE EBONY MAW ALL THE MYSTERIES YOU HAVE HIDDEN IN YOUR MIND.
I...I... DON'T KNOW WHERE THE GEM IS...
CURSE THE GEM, DOCTOR. A FOOL'S QUEST IF THERE EVER WAS ONE...
I WANT WHAT THANOS WANTS.

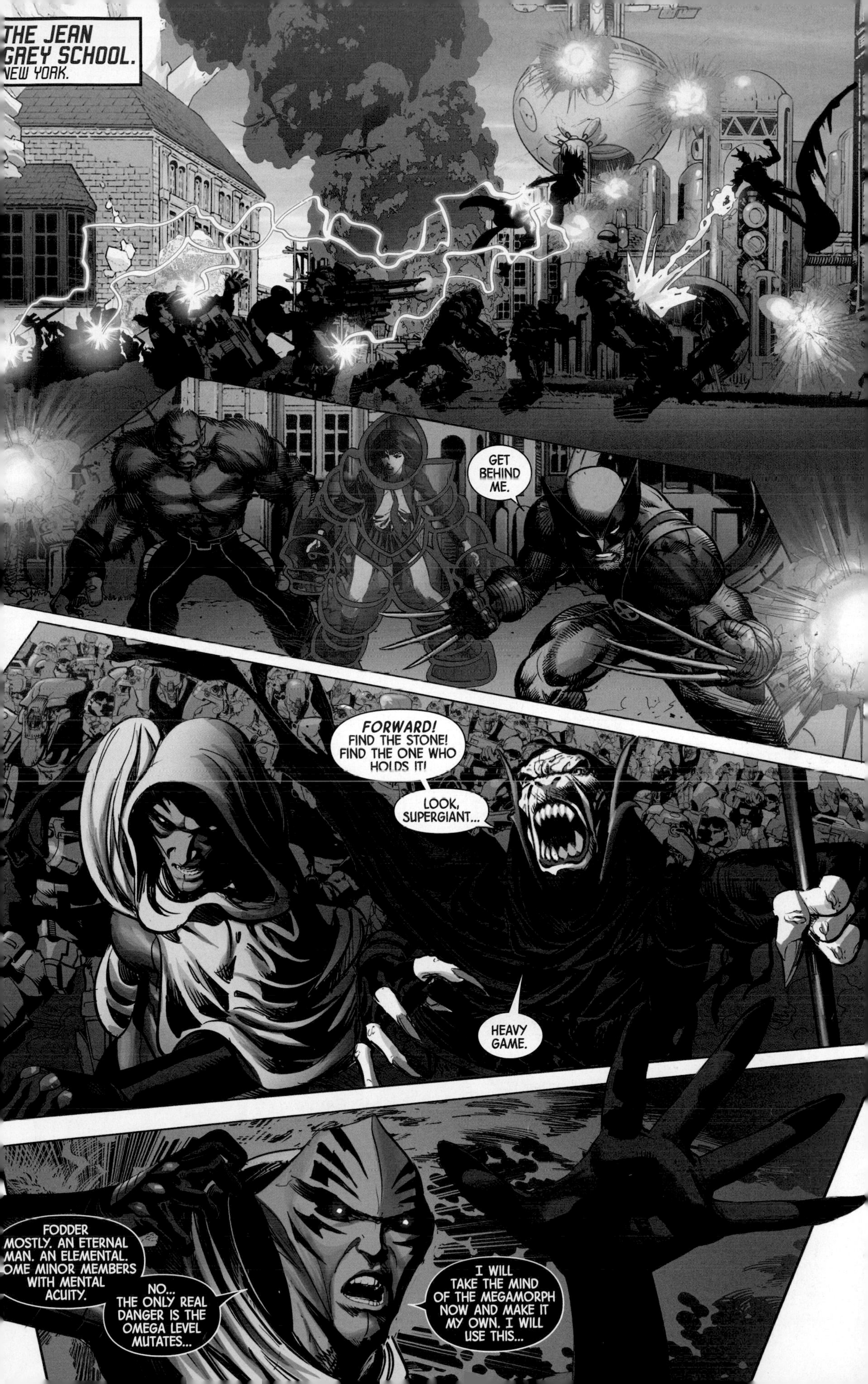
THE JEAN GREY SCHOOL. NEW YORK.
GET BEHIND ME.
FORWARD! FIND THE STONE! FIND THE ONE WHO HOLDS IT!
LOOK, SUPERGIANT...
HEAVY GAME.
FODDER MOSTLY. AN ETERNAL MAN. AN ELEMENTAL. SOME MINOR MEMBERS WITH MENTAL ACUITY.
NO... THE ONLY REAL DANGER IS THE OMEGA LEVEL MUTATES...
I WILL TAKE THE MIND OF THE MEGAMORPH NOW AND MAKE IT MY OWN. I WILL USE THIS...

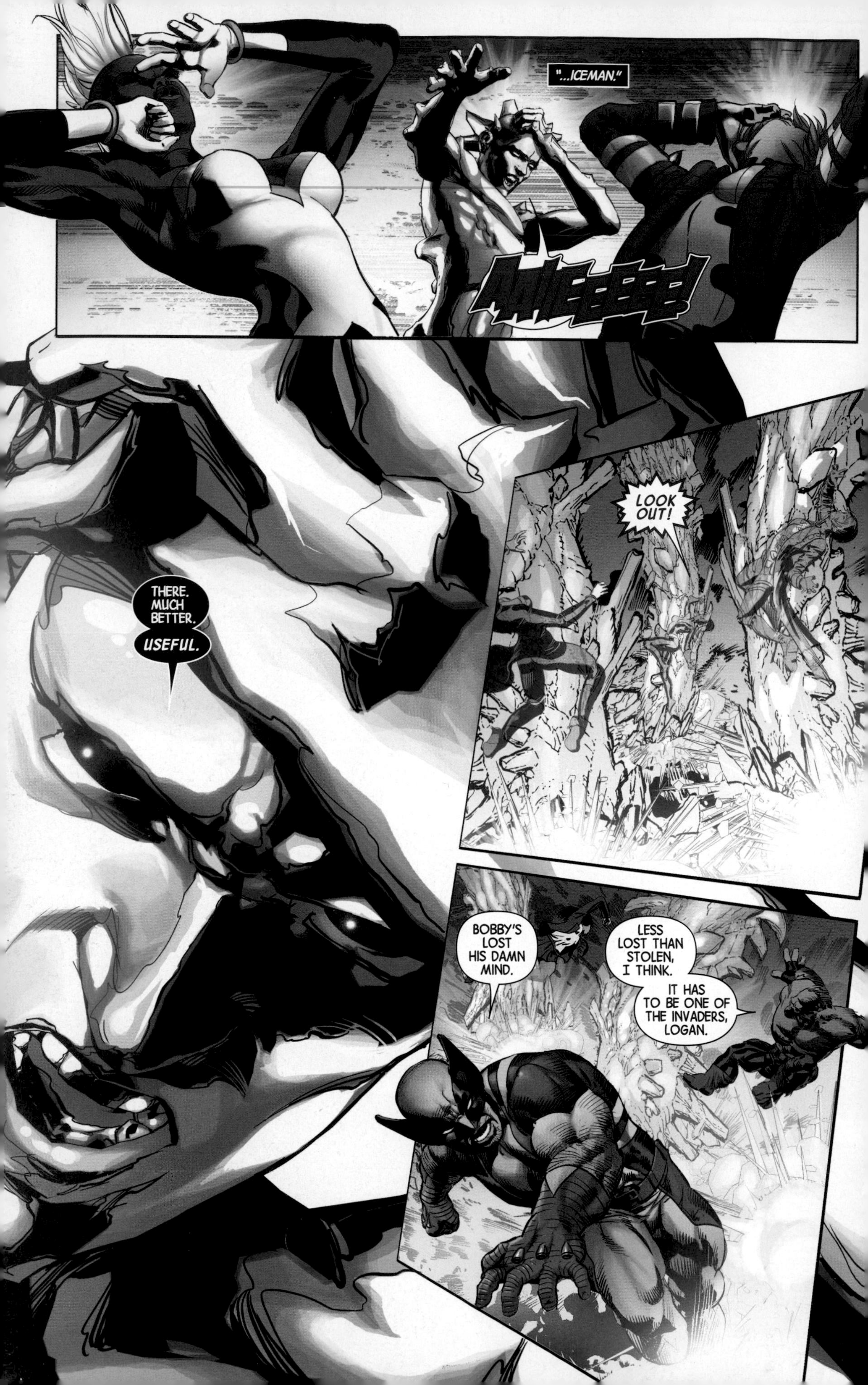

"...ICEMAN."
AIIEEEEE!
THERE. MUCH BETTER.
USEFUL.
LOOK OUT!
BOBBY'S LOST HIS DAMN MIND.
LESS LOST THAN STOLEN, I THINK.
IT HAS TO BE ONE OF THE INVADERS, LOGAN.

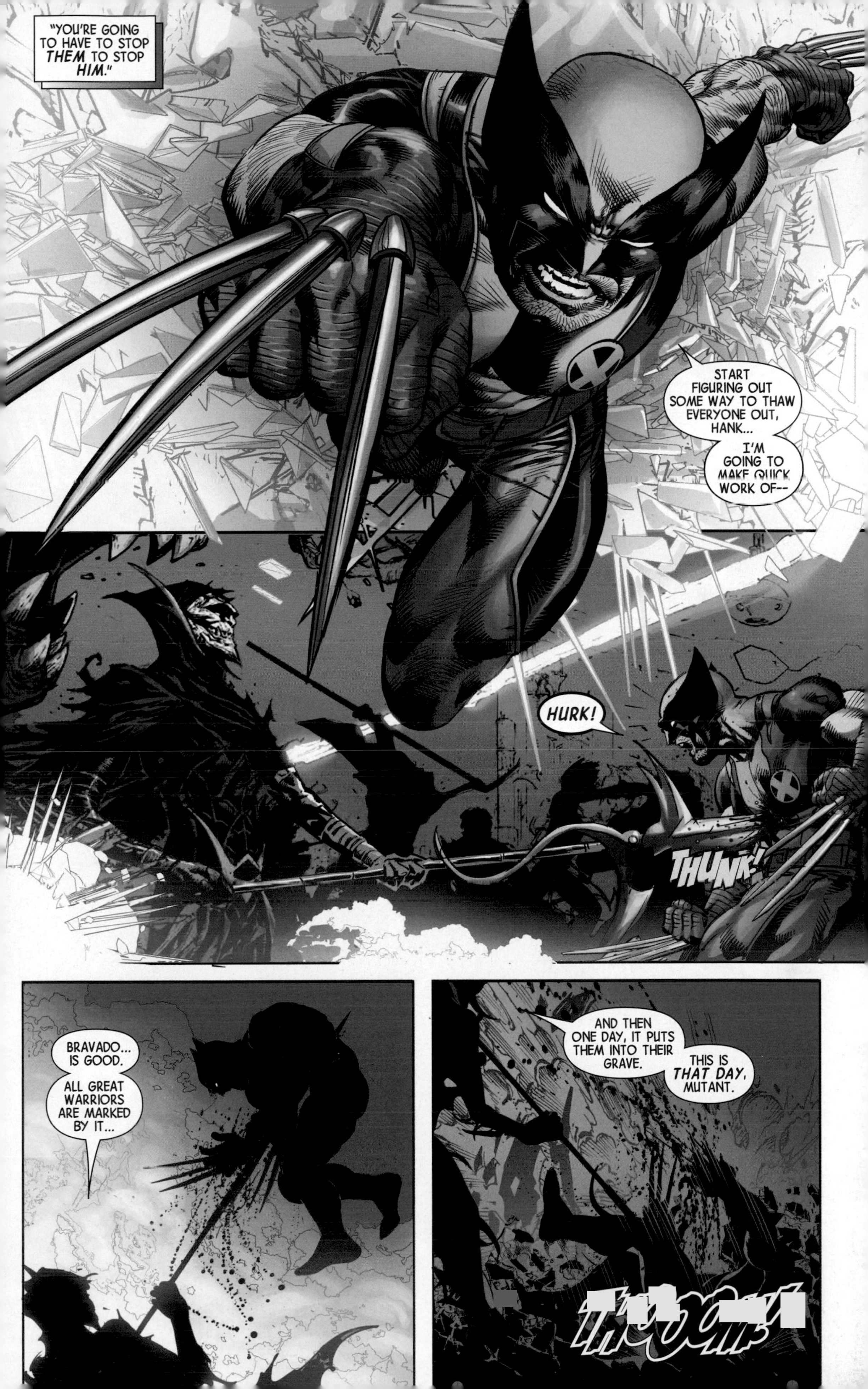
"YOU'RE GOING TO HAVE TO STOP *THEM* TO STOP *HIM*."
START FIGURING OUT SOME WAY TO THAW EVERYONE OUT, HANK...
I'M GOING TO MAKE QUICK WORK OF--
HURK!
THUNK!
BRAVADO... IS GOOD.
ALL GREAT WARRIORS ARE MARKED BY IT...
AND THEN ONE DAY, IT PUTS THEM INTO THEIR GRAVE.
THIS IS *THAT DAY*, MUTANT.

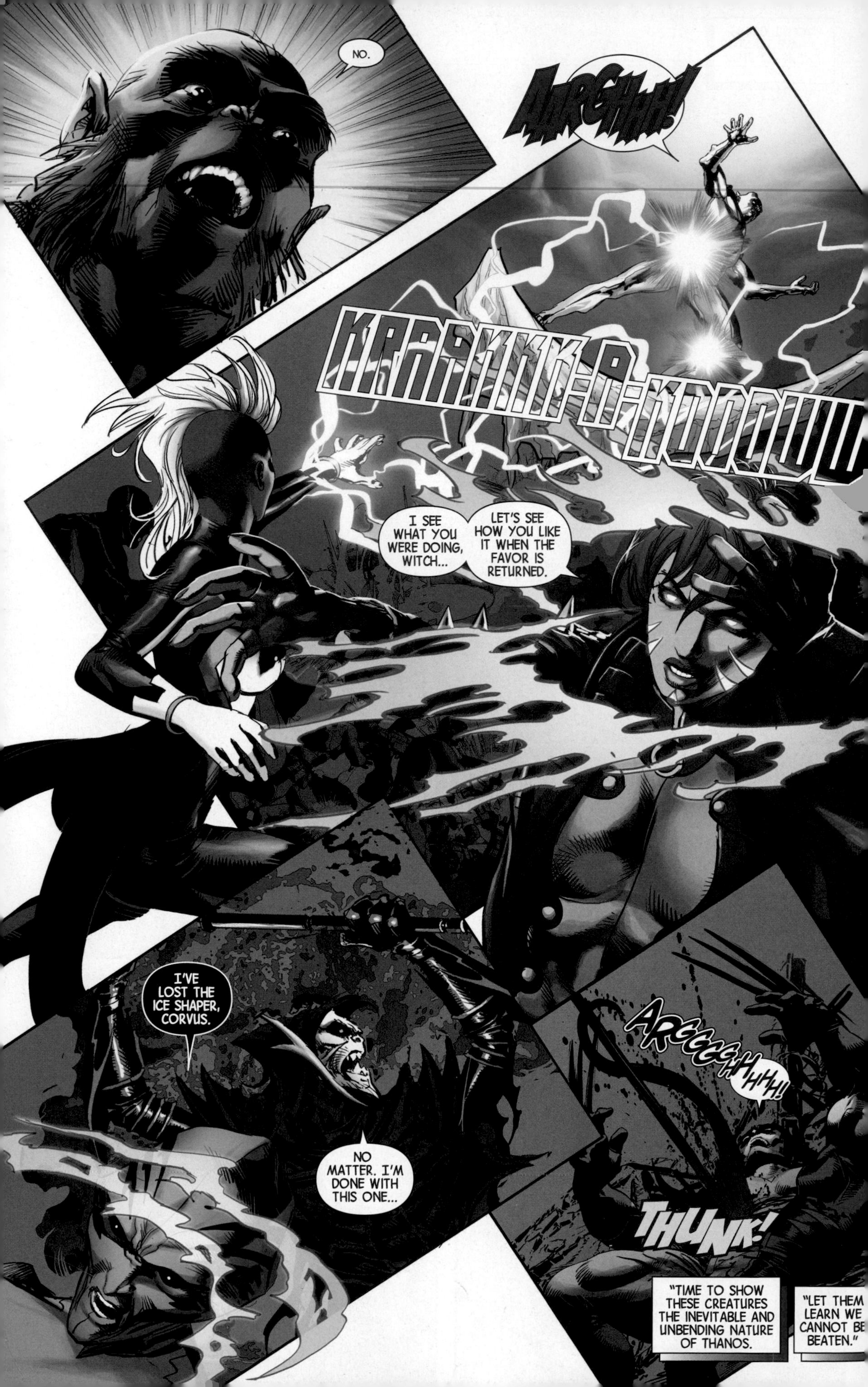

NO.
AARGHHH!
KRAAKKK-A-DOOOOOM
I SEE WHAT YOU WERE DOING, WITCH...
LET'S SEE HOW YOU LIKE IT WHEN THE FAVOR IS RETURNED.
I'VE LOST THE ICE SHAPER, CORVUS.
NO MATTER. I'M DONE WITH THIS ONE...
ARGGGHHHH!
THUNK!
"TIME TO SHOW THESE CREATURES THE INEVITABLE AND UNBENDING NATURE OF THANOS.
"LET THEM LEARN WE CANNOT BE BEATEN."

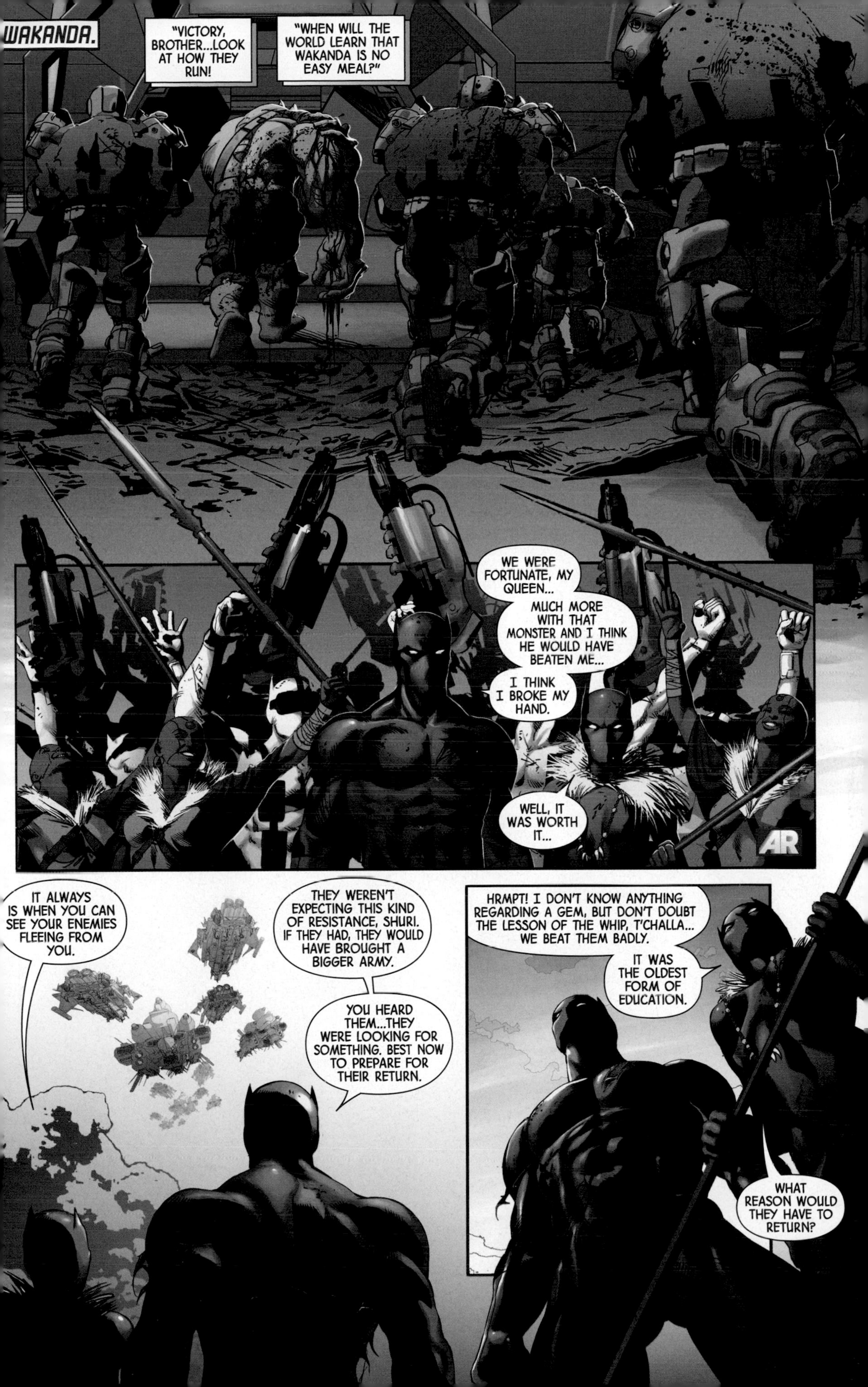
WAKANDA.
"VICTORY, BROTHER...LOOK AT HOW THEY RUN!
"WHEN WILL THE WORLD LEARN THAT WAKANDA IS NO EASY MEAL?"
WE WERE FORTUNATE, MY QUEEN...
MUCH MORE WITH THAT MONSTER AND I THINK HE WOULD HAVE BEATEN ME...
I THINK I BROKE MY HAND.
WELL, IT WAS WORTH IT...
AR
IT ALWAYS IS WHEN YOU CAN SEE YOUR ENEMIES FLEEING FROM YOU.
THEY WEREN'T EXPECTING THIS KIND OF RESISTANCE, SHURI. IF THEY HAD, THEY WOULD HAVE BROUGHT A BIGGER ARMY.
YOU HEARD THEM...THEY WERE LOOKING FOR SOMETHING. BEST NOW TO PREPARE FOR THEIR RETURN.
HRMPT! I DON'T KNOW ANYTHING REGARDING A GEM, BUT DON'T DOUBT THE LESSON OF THE WHIP, T'CHALLA... WE BEAT THEM BADLY.
IT WAS THE OLDEST FORM OF EDUCATION.
WHAT REASON WOULD THEY HAVE TO RETURN?

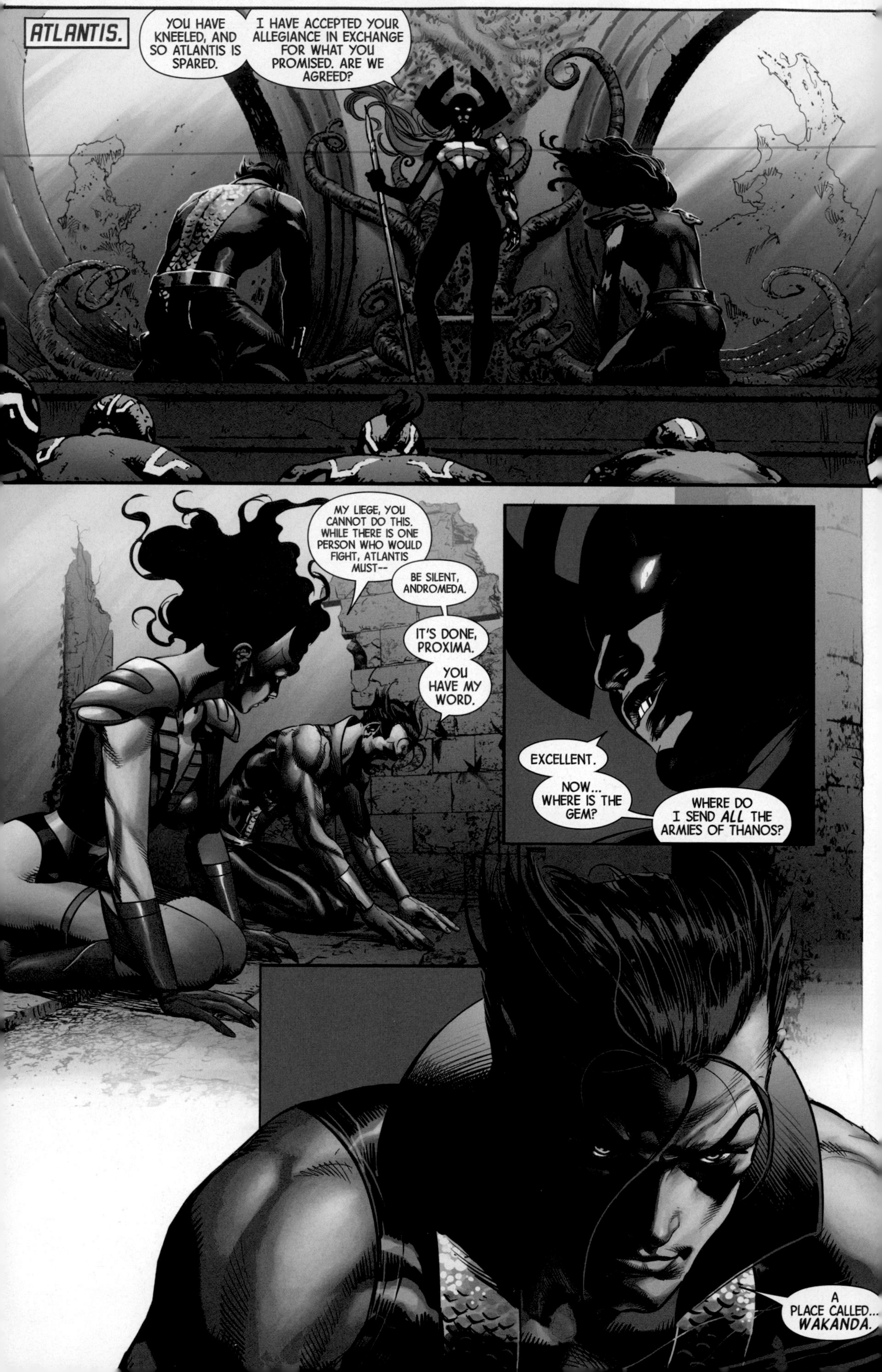
ATLANTIS.
YOU HAVE KNEELED, AND SO ATLANTIS IS SPARED.
I HAVE ACCEPTED YOUR ALLEGIANCE IN EXCHANGE FOR WHAT YOU PROMISED. ARE WE AGREED?
MY LIEGE, YOU CANNOT DO THIS. WHILE THERE IS ONE PERSON WHO WOULD FIGHT, ATLANTIS MUST--
BE SILENT, ANDROMEDA.
IT'S DONE, PROXIMA.
YOU HAVE MY WORD.
EXCELLENT.
NOW... WHERE IS THE GEM?
WHERE DO I SEND ALL THE ARMIES OF THANOS?
A PLACE CALLED... WAKANDA.

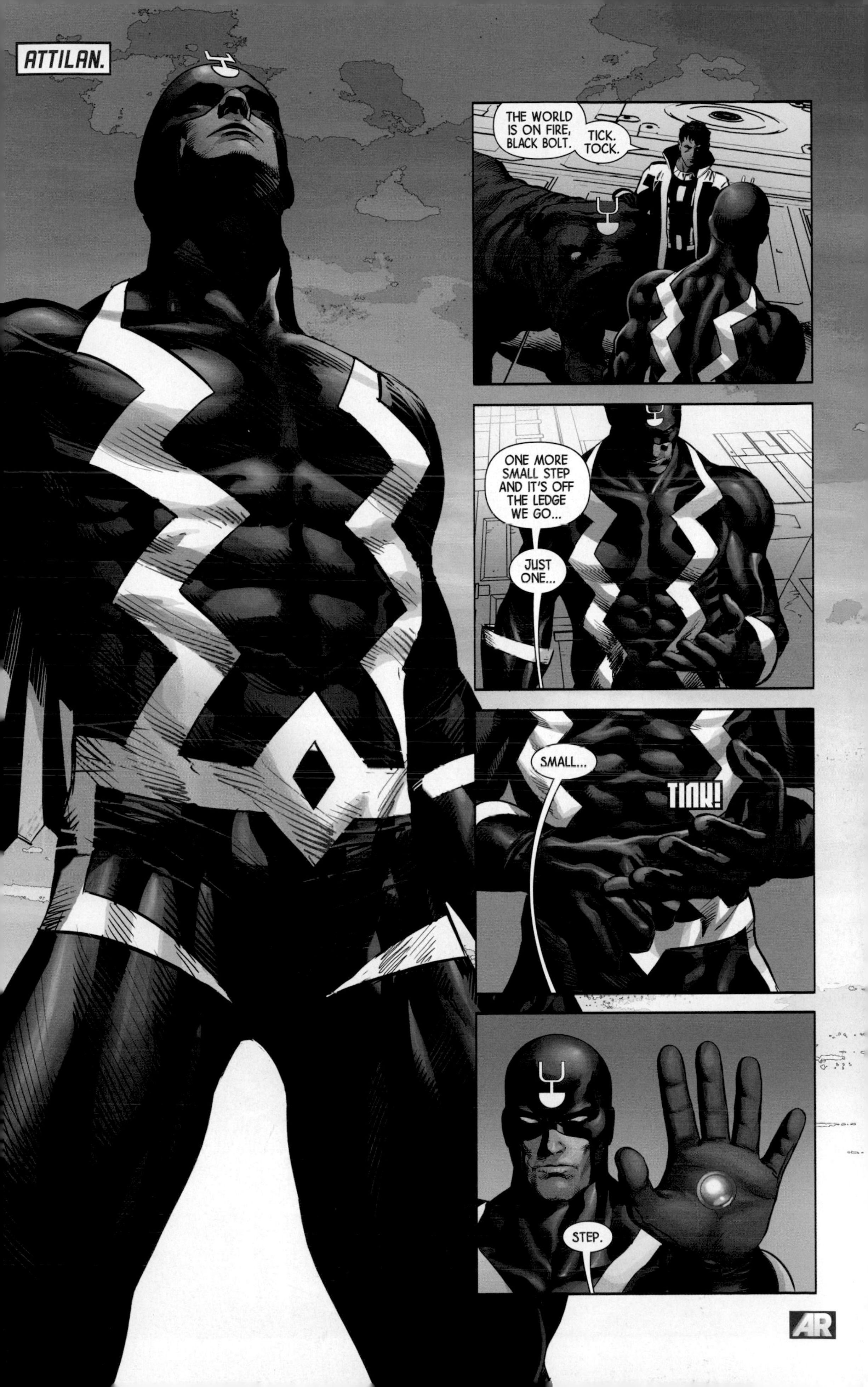
ATTILAN.
THE WORLD IS ON FIRE, BLACK BOLT.
TICK. TOCK.
ONE MORE SMALL STEP AND IT'S OFF THE LEDGE WE GO...
JUST ONE...
SMALL...
TINK!
STEP.

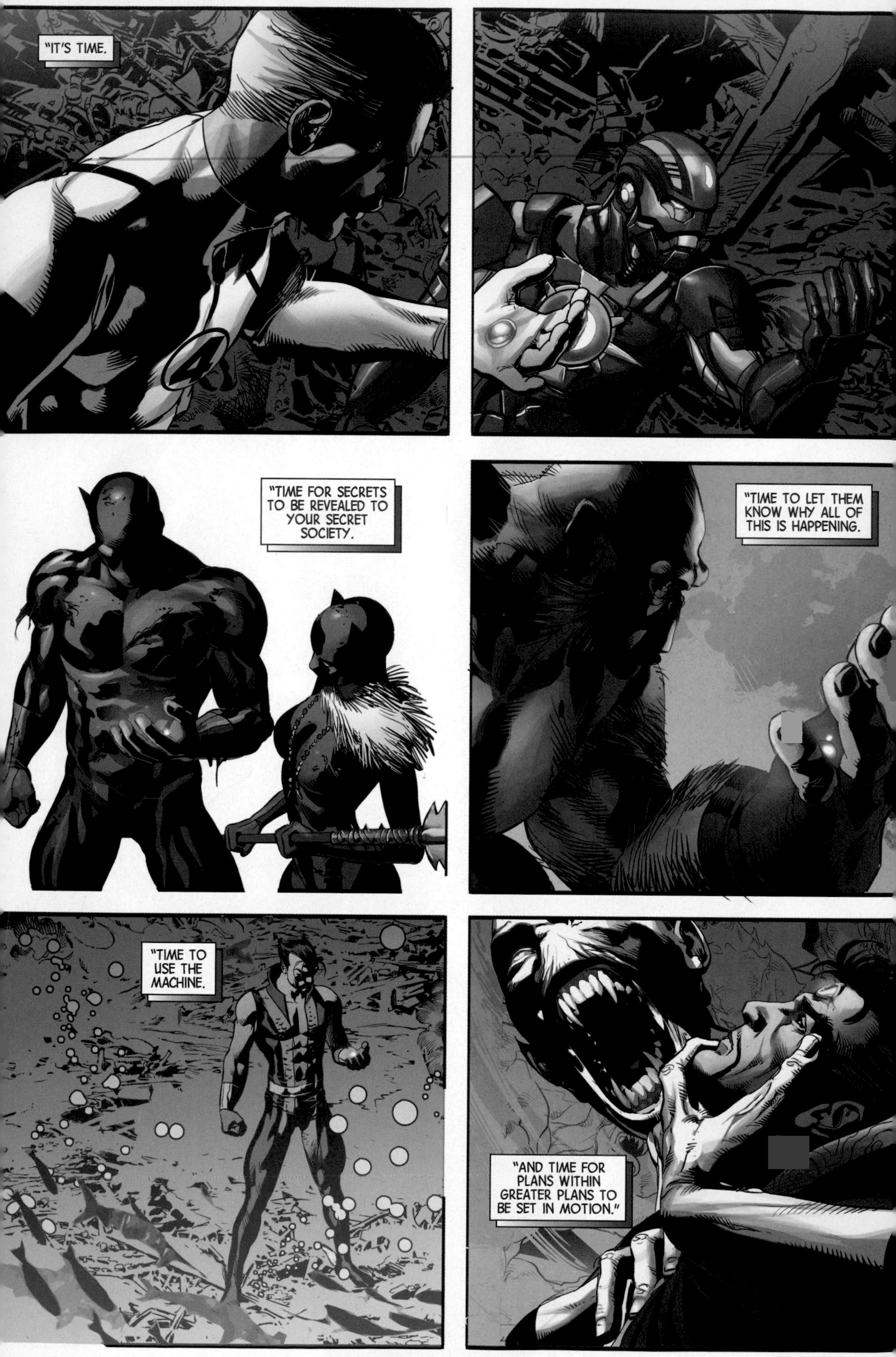
"IT'S TIME.
"TIME FOR SECRETS TO BE REVEALED TO YOUR SECRET SOCIETY.
"TIME TO LET THEM KNOW WHY ALL OF THIS IS HAPPENING.
"TIME TO USE THE MACHINE.
"AND TIME FOR PLANS WITHIN GREATER PLANS TO BE SET IN MOTION."

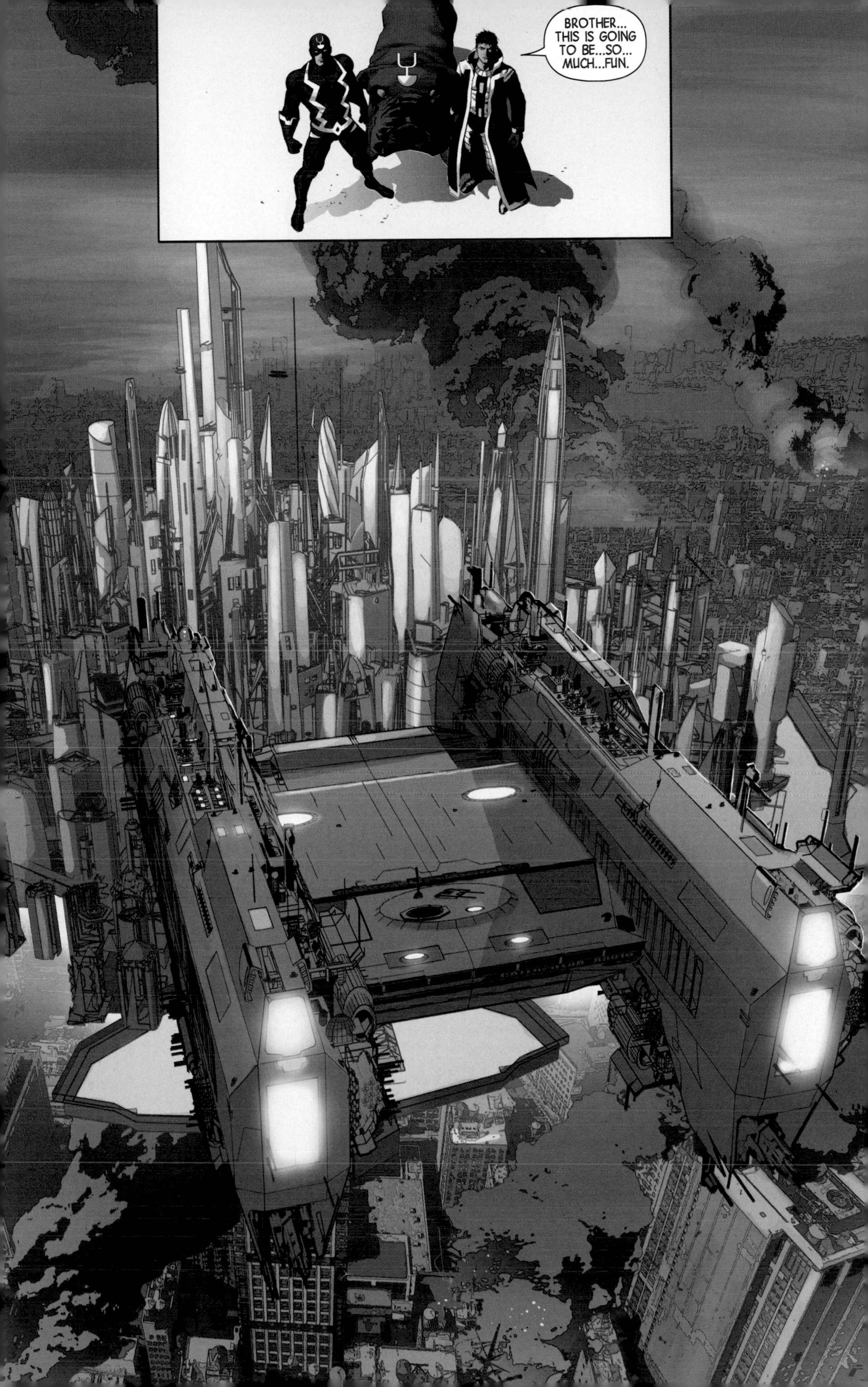
BROTHER... THIS IS GOING TO BE...SO... MUCH...FUN.

CULL OBSIDIAN
(THE BLACK ORDER)

◆

CORVUS GLAIVE: The first of the five. Thanos' most favored. Corvus is cruel, arrogant and the most loyal of the Black Order. A warrior who betrayed his people and sold his soul to Thanos to pursue a different kind of glory.

POWERS: Strength, speed…As long as his otherworldly blade remains whole, he cannot die.

PROXIMA MIDNIGHT: The cruelest of Thanos' generals. A predator in every sense of the word, Proxima Midnight is the greatest warrior in Thanos' army.

POWERS: Savage hand-to-hand fighter. Her spear, when thrown, transforms into three tracers of black light that never miss. These beams are lethal to most creatures.

BLACK DWARF: When compared to the others of the Black Order, Black Dwarf seems almost normal. Feigning joy and contentment, in reality this celestial nihilist is simply more at peace with the oblivion Thanos seeks than the others of the Black Order.

POWERS: Super-strength. Super-dense, unbreakable skin.

SUPERGIANT: History unknown. An mentally unstable omnipath and telepathic parasite, Supergiant seeks out intellect and devours it. What she knows, Thanos knows.

POWERS: Mental parasite. Controls, steals or devours the minds of her victims.

THE EBONY MAW: A thin razor of a man. Not a fighter, a thinker. A black tongue that spreads mischief and evil wherever he goes. He seems to be the weakest of the Black Order, but in truth, he is the most dangerous of them all.

POWERS: Believed to be none, but that, like most things about him could be a lie.

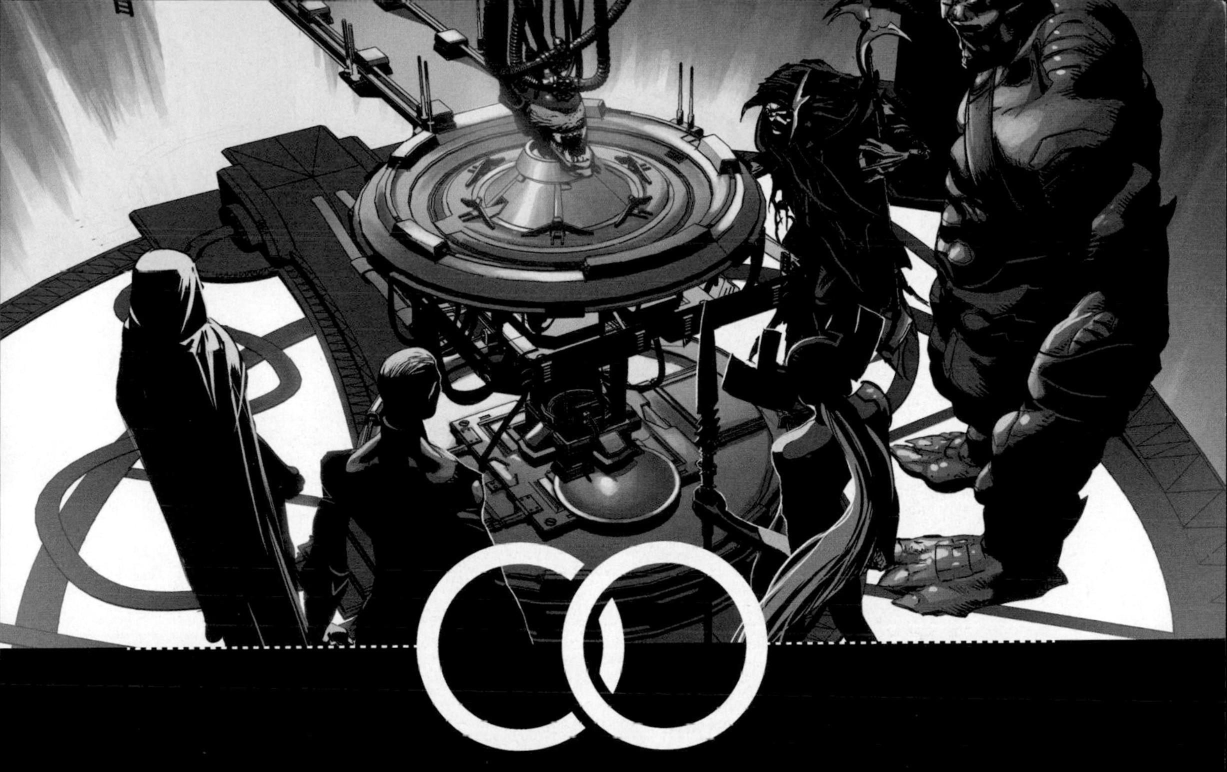

"THE THANOS SEED"

PREVIOUSLY IN INFINITY

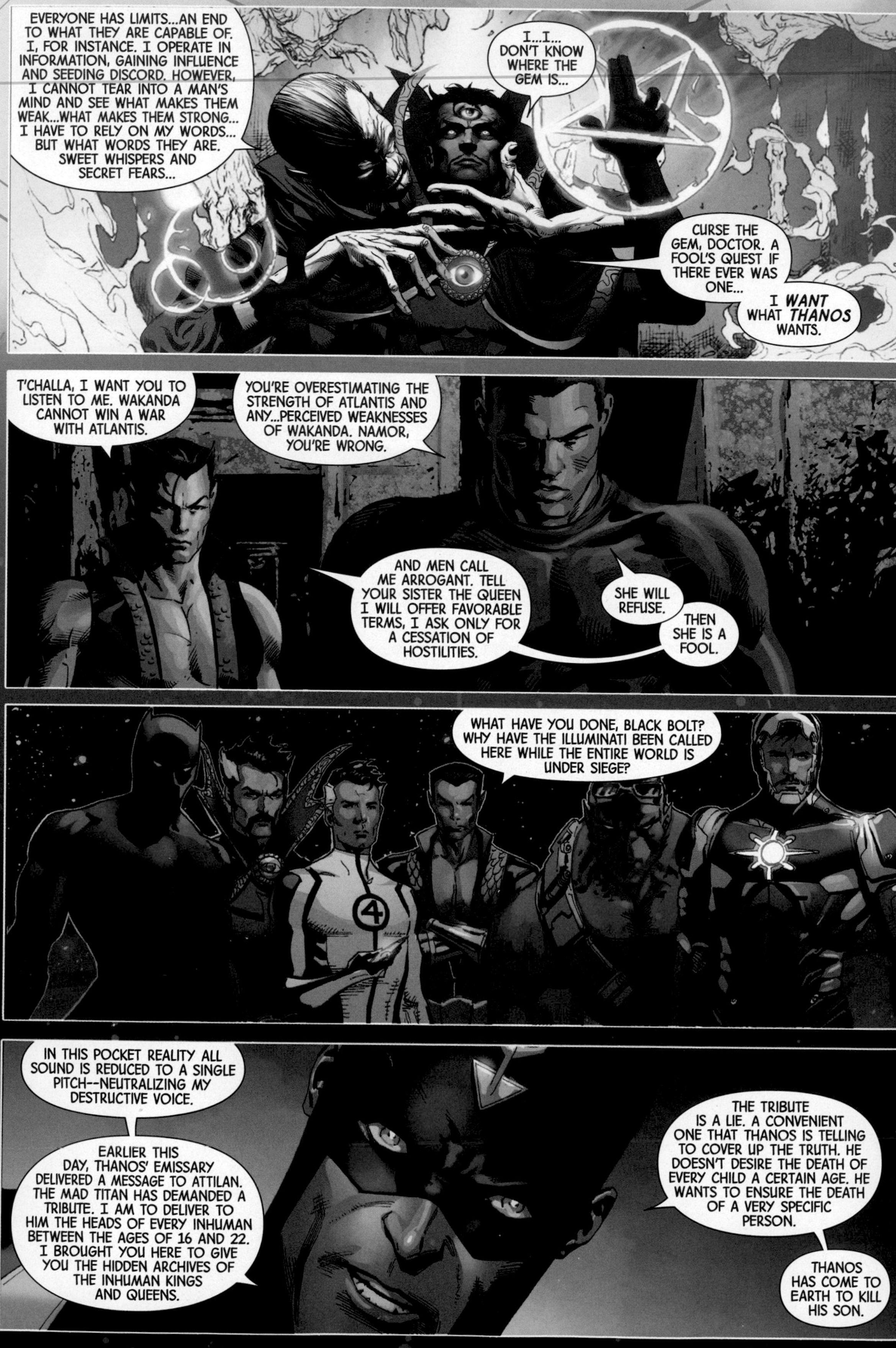

EVERYONE HAS LIMITS...AN END TO WHAT THEY ARE CAPABLE OF. I, FOR INSTANCE. I OPERATE IN INFORMATION, GAINING INFLUENCE AND SEEDING DISCORD. HOWEVER, I CANNOT TEAR INTO A MAN'S MIND AND SEE WHAT MAKES THEM WEAK...WHAT MAKES THEM STRONG... I HAVE TO RELY ON MY WORDS... BUT WHAT WORDS THEY ARE. SWEET WHISPERS AND SECRET FEARS...
I...I... DON'T KNOW WHERE THE GEM IS...
CURSE THE GEM, DOCTOR. A FOOL'S QUEST IF THERE EVER WAS ONE...
I *WANT* WHAT *THANOS* WANTS.
T'CHALLA, I WANT YOU TO LISTEN TO ME. WAKANDA CANNOT WIN A WAR WITH ATLANTIS.
YOU'RE OVERESTIMATING THE STRENGTH OF ATLANTIS AND ANY...PERCEIVED WEAKNESSES OF WAKANDA. NAMOR, YOU'RE WRONG.
AND MEN CALL ME ARROGANT. TELL YOUR SISTER THE QUEEN I WILL OFFER FAVORABLE TERMS, I ASK ONLY FOR A CESSATION OF HOSTILITIES.
SHE WILL REFUSE.
THEN SHE IS A FOOL.
WHAT HAVE YOU DONE, BLACK BOLT? WHY HAVE THE ILLUMINATI BEEN CALLED HERE WHILE THE ENTIRE WORLD IS UNDER SIEGE?
IN THIS POCKET REALITY ALL SOUND IS REDUCED TO A SINGLE PITCH--NEUTRALIZING MY DESTRUCTIVE VOICE.
EARLIER THIS DAY, THANOS' EMISSARY DELIVERED A MESSAGE TO ATTILAN. THE MAD TITAN HAS DEMANDED A TRIBUTE. I AM TO DELIVER TO HIM THE HEADS OF EVERY INHUMAN BETWEEN THE AGES OF 16 AND 22. I BROUGHT YOU HERE TO GIVE YOU THE HIDDEN ARCHIVES OF THE INHUMAN KINGS AND QUEENS.
THE TRIBUTE IS A LIE. A CONVENIENT ONE THAT THANOS IS TELLING TO COVER UP THE TRUTH. HE DOESN'T DESIRE THE DEATH OF EVERY CHILD A CERTAIN AGE. HE WANTS TO ENSURE THE DEATH OF A VERY SPECIFIC PERSON.
THANOS HAS COME TO EARTH TO KILL HIS SON.

THE THANOS SEED

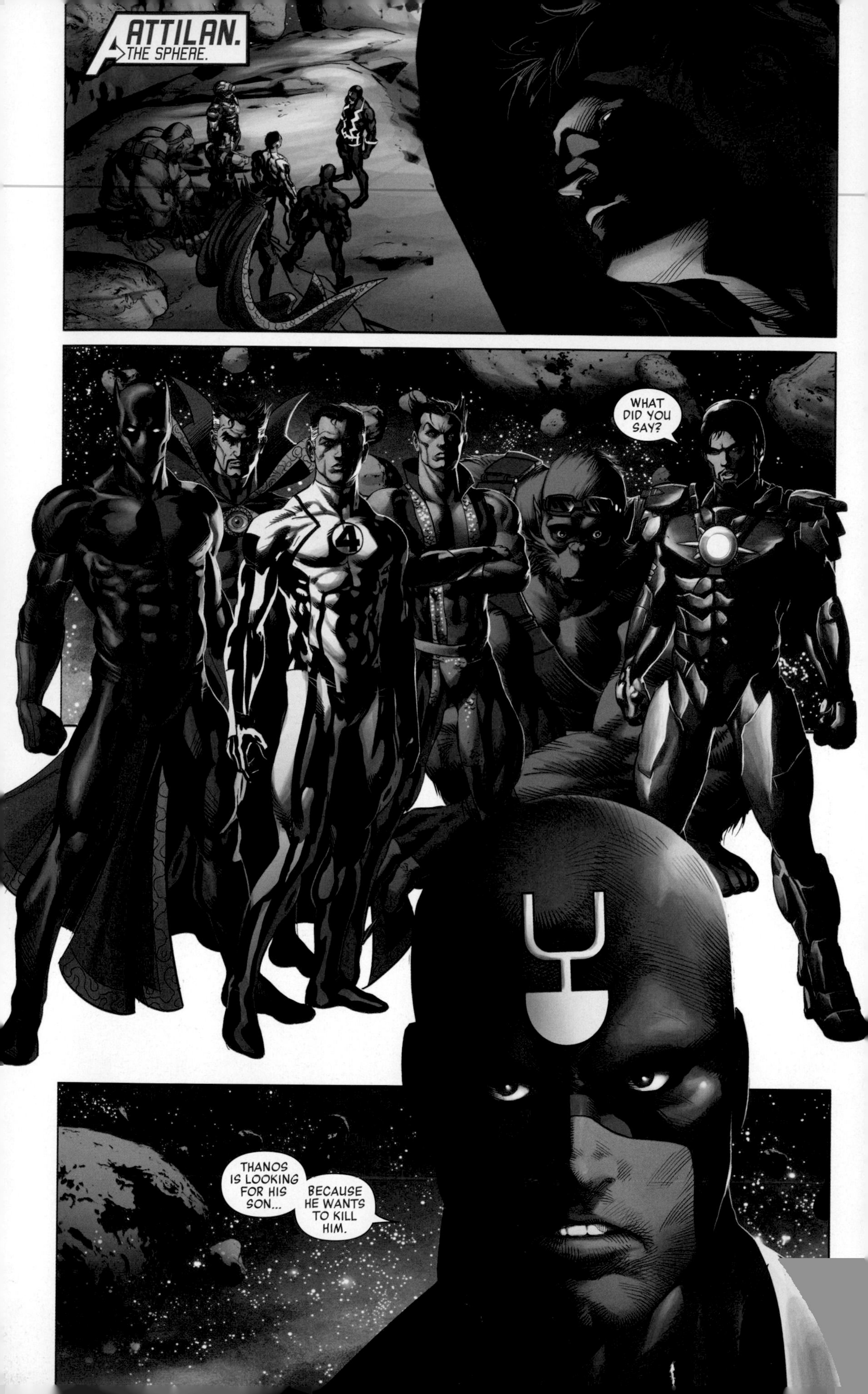
ATTILAN.
THE SPHERE.
WHAT DID YOU SAY?
THANOS IS LOOKING FOR HIS SON...
BECAUSE HE WANTS TO KILL HIM.

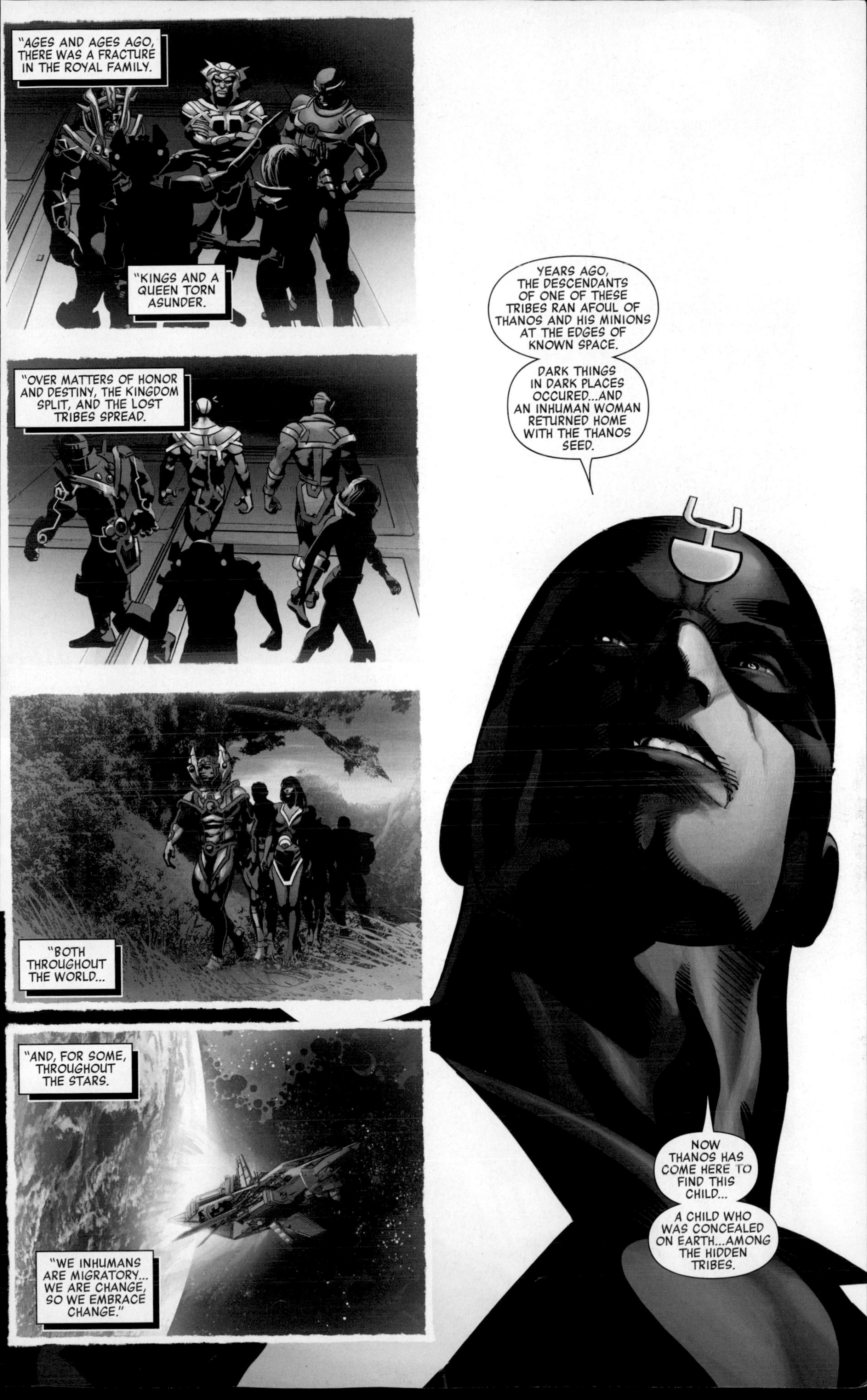
"AGES AND AGES AGO, THERE WAS A FRACTURE IN THE ROYAL FAMILY.
"KINGS AND A QUEEN TORN ASUNDER.
"OVER MATTERS OF HONOR AND DESTINY, THE KINGDOM SPLIT, AND THE LOST TRIBES SPREAD.
"BOTH THROUGHOUT THE WORLD...
"AND, FOR SOME, THROUGHOUT THE STARS.
"WE INHUMANS ARE MIGRATORY... WE ARE CHANGE, SO WE EMBRACE CHANGE."
YEARS AGO, THE DESCENDANTS OF ONE OF THESE TRIBES RAN AFOUL OF THANOS AND HIS MINIONS AT THE EDGES OF KNOWN SPACE.
DARK THINGS IN DARK PLACES OCCURED...AND AN INHUMAN WOMAN RETURNED HOME WITH THE THANOS SEED.
NOW THANOS HAS COME HERE TO FIND THIS CHILD...
A CHILD WHO WAS CONCEALED ON EARTH...AMONG THE HIDDEN TRIBES.

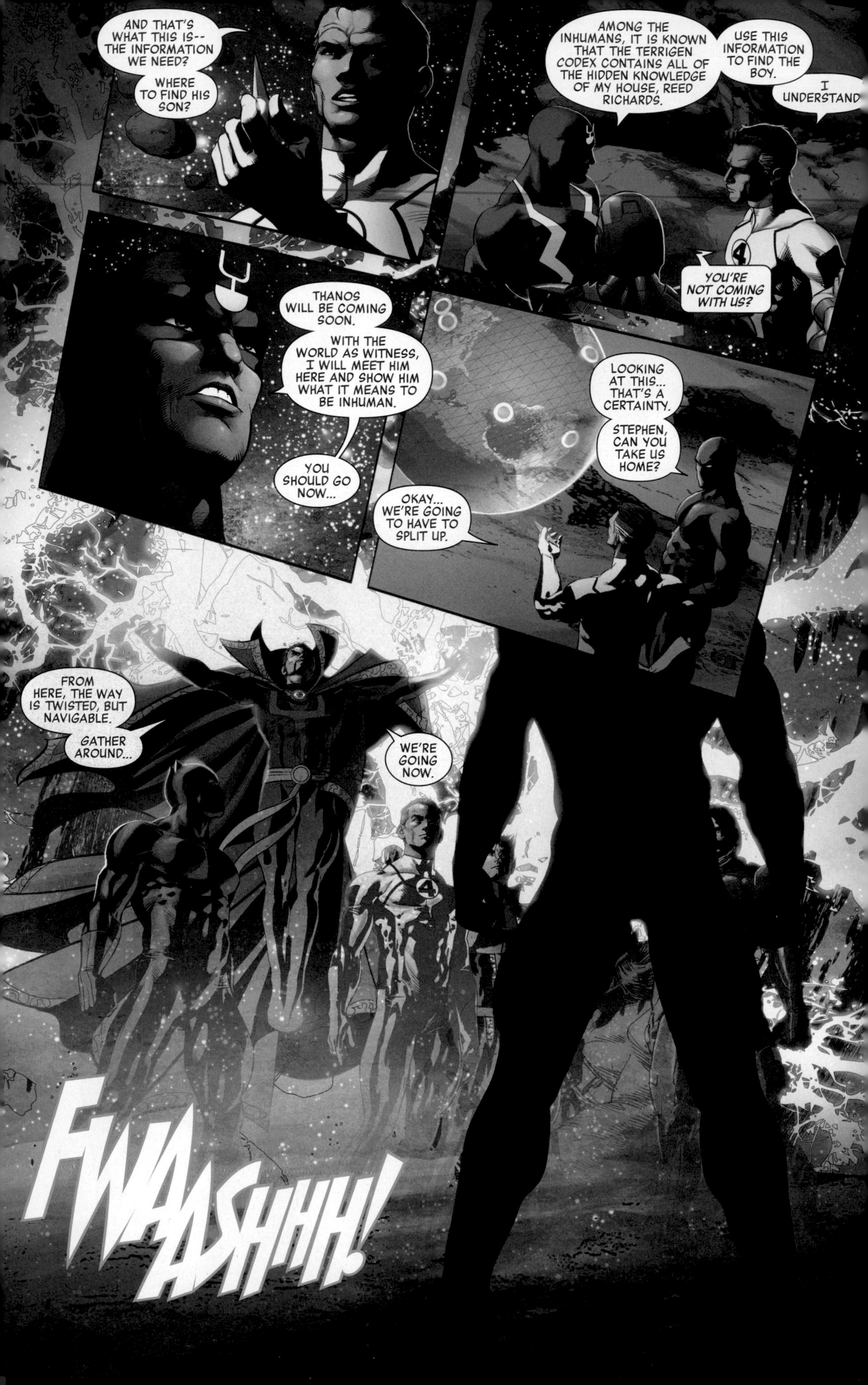
AND THAT'S WHAT THIS IS-- THE INFORMATION WE NEED?
WHERE TO FIND HIS SON?
AMONG THE INHUMANS, IT IS KNOWN THAT THE TERRIGEN CODEX CONTAINS ALL OF THE HIDDEN KNOWLEDGE OF MY HOUSE, REED RICHARDS.
USE THIS INFORMATION TO FIND THE BOY.
I UNDERSTAND
YOU'RE NOT COMING WITH US?
THANOS WILL BE COMING SOON.
WITH THE WORLD AS WITNESS, I WILL MEET HIM HERE AND SHOW HIM WHAT IT MEANS TO BE INHUMAN.
YOU SHOULD GO NOW...
LOOKING AT THIS... THAT'S A CERTAINTY.
STEPHEN, CAN YOU TAKE US HOME?
OKAY... WE'RE GOING TO HAVE TO SPLIT UP.
FROM HERE, THE WAY IS TWISTED, BUT NAVIGABLE.
GATHER AROUND...
WE'RE GOING NOW.
FWAASHHH!

FLASH, AND OFF THEY GO. IT WAS FOOLISH, BROTHER.

FOOLISH AND UNLIKE YOU...

DON'T YOU TRUST ME, MAXIMUS?

NOT IF YOU REALLY GAVE THE HUMANS THE CODEX.

SO MANY SECRETS.

WHY WOULD YOU DO SOMETHING LIKE THAT?

WHY WOULD YO--

OH... I LIKE THIS PLAN.

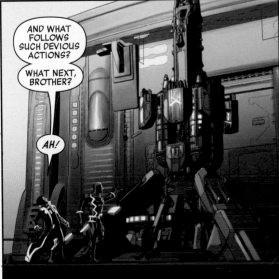

AND WHAT FOLLOWS SUCH DEVIOUS ACTIONS?

WHAT NEXT, BROTHER?

AH!

VERY GOOD. I'LL MAKE READY THE MACHINE!

FAVOR AND DISFAVOR

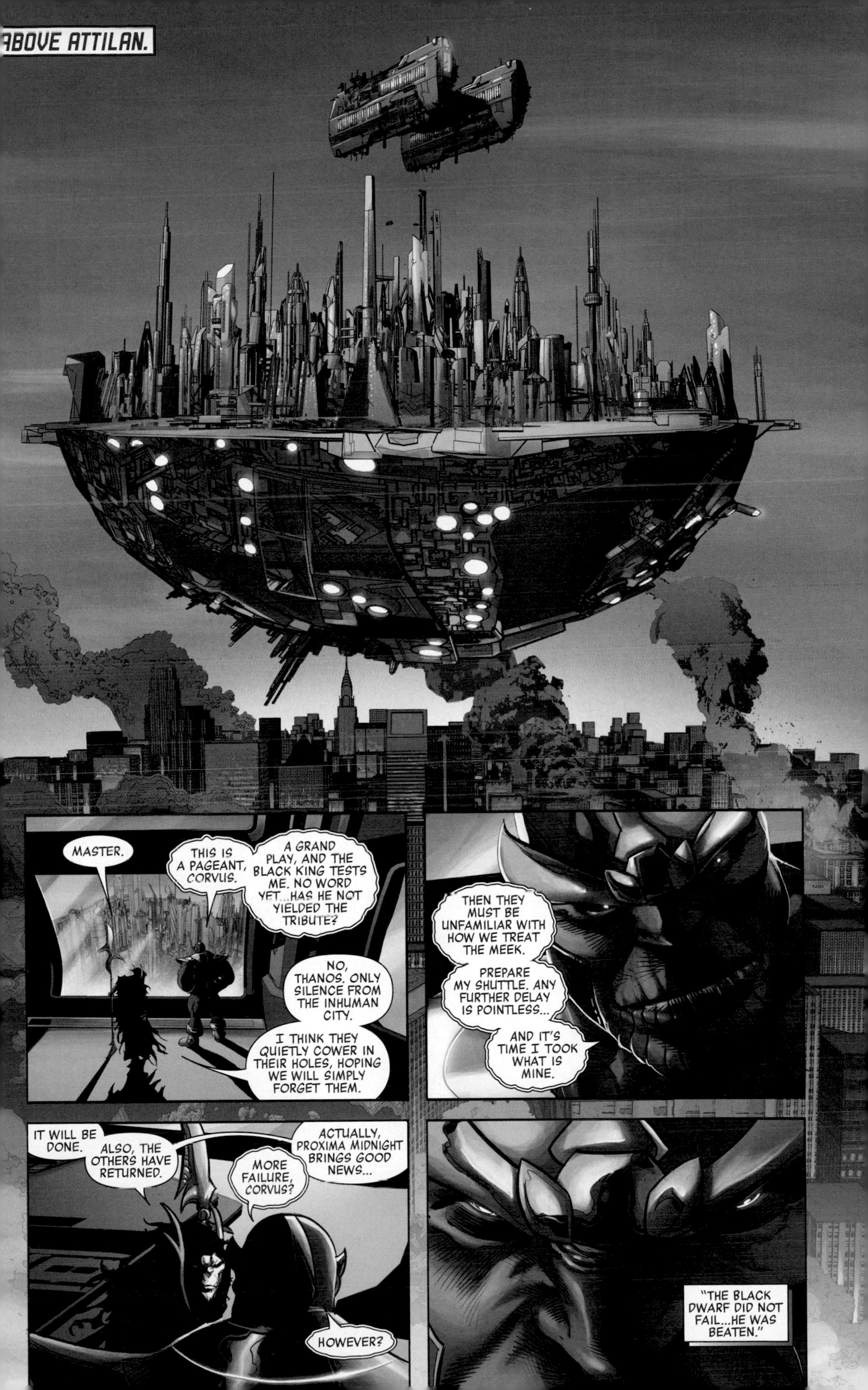
ABOVE ATTILAN.
MASTER.
THIS IS A PAGEANT, CORVUS.
A GRAND PLAY, AND THE BLACK KING TESTS ME. NO WORD YET...HAS HE NOT YIELDED THE TRIBUTE?
NO, THANOS. ONLY SILENCE FROM THE INHUMAN CITY.
I THINK THEY QUIETLY COWER IN THEIR HOLES, HOPING WE WILL SIMPLY FORGET THEM.
THEN THEY MUST BE UNFAMILIAR WITH HOW WE TREAT THE MEEK.
PREPARE MY SHUTTLE. ANY FURTHER DELAY IS POINTLESS...
AND IT'S TIME I TOOK WHAT IS MINE.
IT WILL BE DONE.
ALSO, THE OTHERS HAVE RETURNED.
MORE FAILURE, CORVUS?
ACTUALLY, PROXIMA MIDNIGHT BRINGS GOOD NEWS...
HOWEVER?
"THE BLACK DWARF DID NOT FAIL...HE WAS BEATEN."

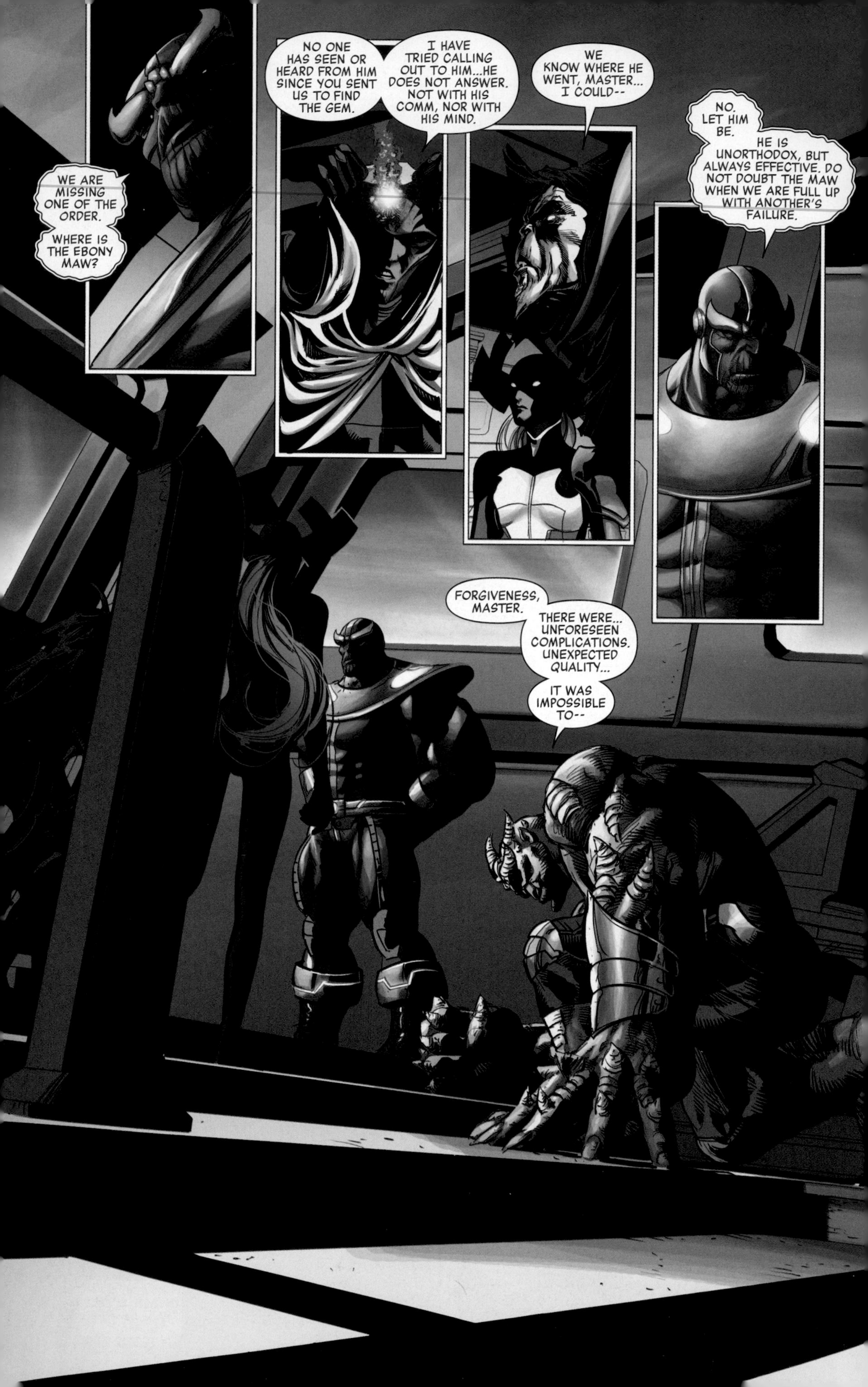
WE ARE MISSING ONE OF THE ORDER.
WHERE IS THE EBONY MAW?
NO ONE HAS SEEN OR HEARD FROM HIM SINCE YOU SENT US TO FIND THE GEM.
I HAVE TRIED CALLING OUT TO HIM...HE DOES NOT ANSWER. NOT WITH HIS COMM, NOR WITH HIS MIND.
WE KNOW WHERE HE WENT, MASTER... I COULD--
NO. LET HIM BE.
HE IS UNORTHODOX, BUT ALWAYS EFFECTIVE. DO NOT DOUBT THE MAW WHEN WE ARE FULL UP WITH ANOTHER'S FAILURE.
FORGIVENESS, MASTER.
THERE WERE... UNFORESEEN COMPLICATIONS. UNEXPECTED QUALITY...
IT WAS IMPOSSIBLE TO--

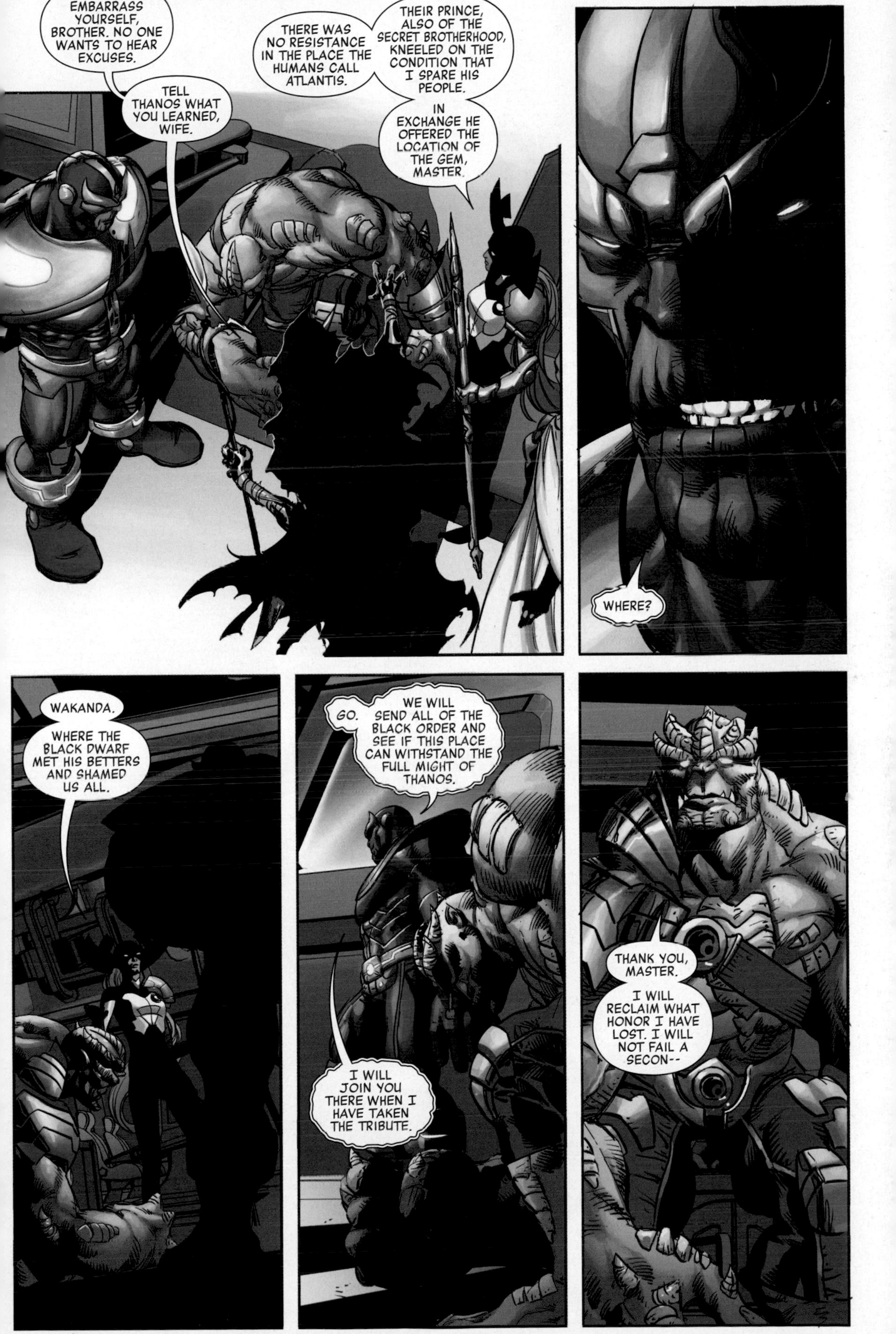
YOU EMBARRASS YOURSELF, BROTHER. NO ONE WANTS TO HEAR EXCUSES.
TELL THANOS WHAT YOU LEARNED, WIFE.
THERE WAS NO RESISTANCE IN THE PLACE THE HUMANS CALL ATLANTIS.
THEIR PRINCE, ALSO OF THE SECRET BROTHERHOOD, KNEELED ON THE CONDITION THAT I SPARE HIS PEOPLE.
IN EXCHANGE HE OFFERED THE LOCATION OF THE GEM, MASTER.
WHERE?
WAKANDA.
WHERE THE BLACK DWARF MET HIS BETTERS AND SHAMED US ALL.
GO.
WE WILL SEND ALL OF THE BLACK ORDER AND SEE IF THIS PLACE CAN WITHSTAND THE FULL MIGHT OF THANOS.
I WILL JOIN YOU THERE WHEN I HAVE TAKEN THE TRIBUTE.
THANK YOU, MASTER.
I WILL RECLAIM WHAT HONOR I HAVE LOST. I WILL NOT FAIL A SECON--

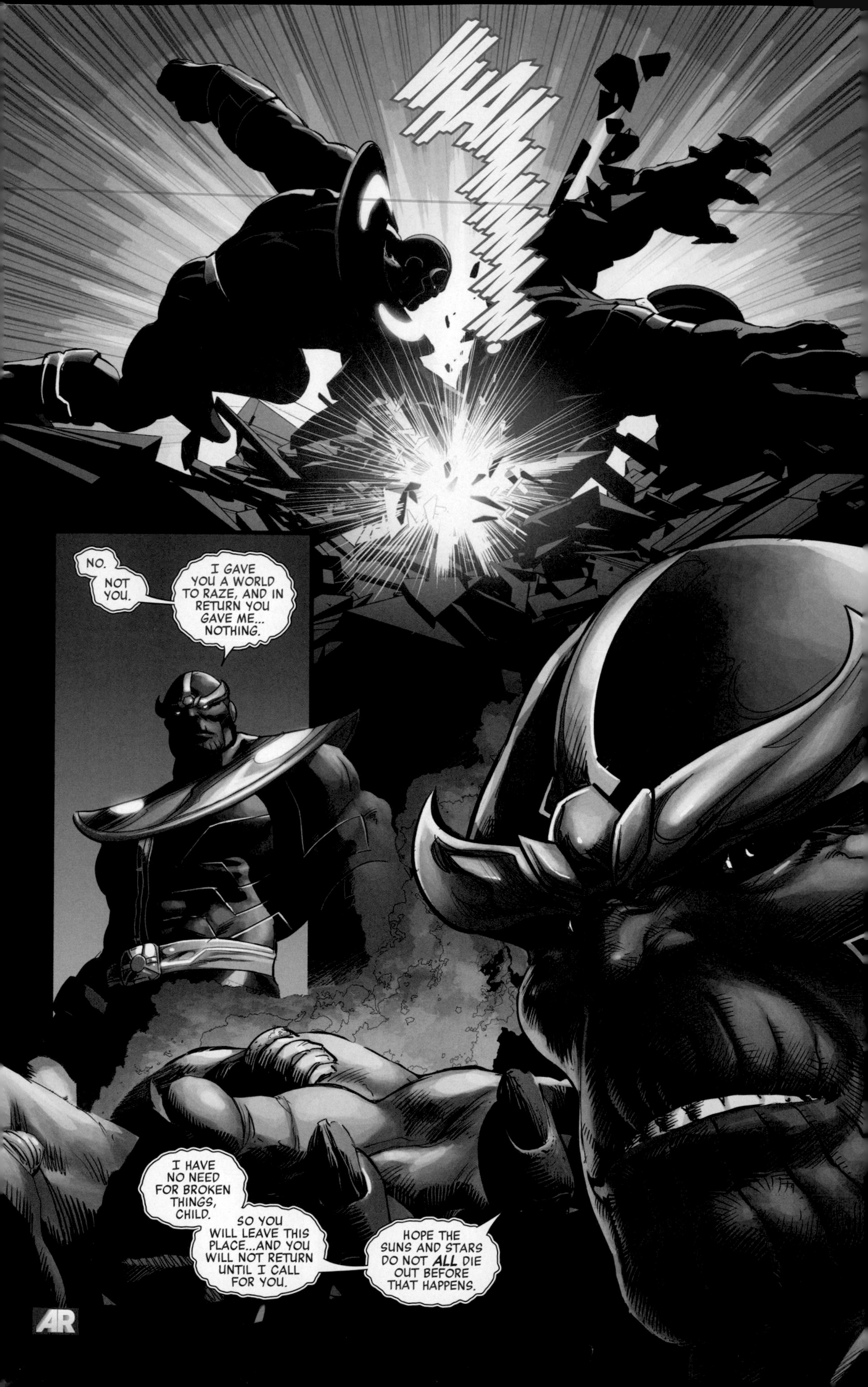
NO. NOT YOU.
I GAVE YOU A WORLD TO RAZE, AND IN RETURN YOU GAVE ME... NOTHING.
I HAVE NO NEED FOR BROKEN THINGS, CHILD.
SO YOU WILL LEAVE THIS PLACE...AND YOU WILL NOT RETURN UNTIL I CALL FOR YOU.
HOPE THE SUNS AND STARS DO NOT ALL DIE OUT BEFORE THAT HAPPENS.

THE HUNT

◆

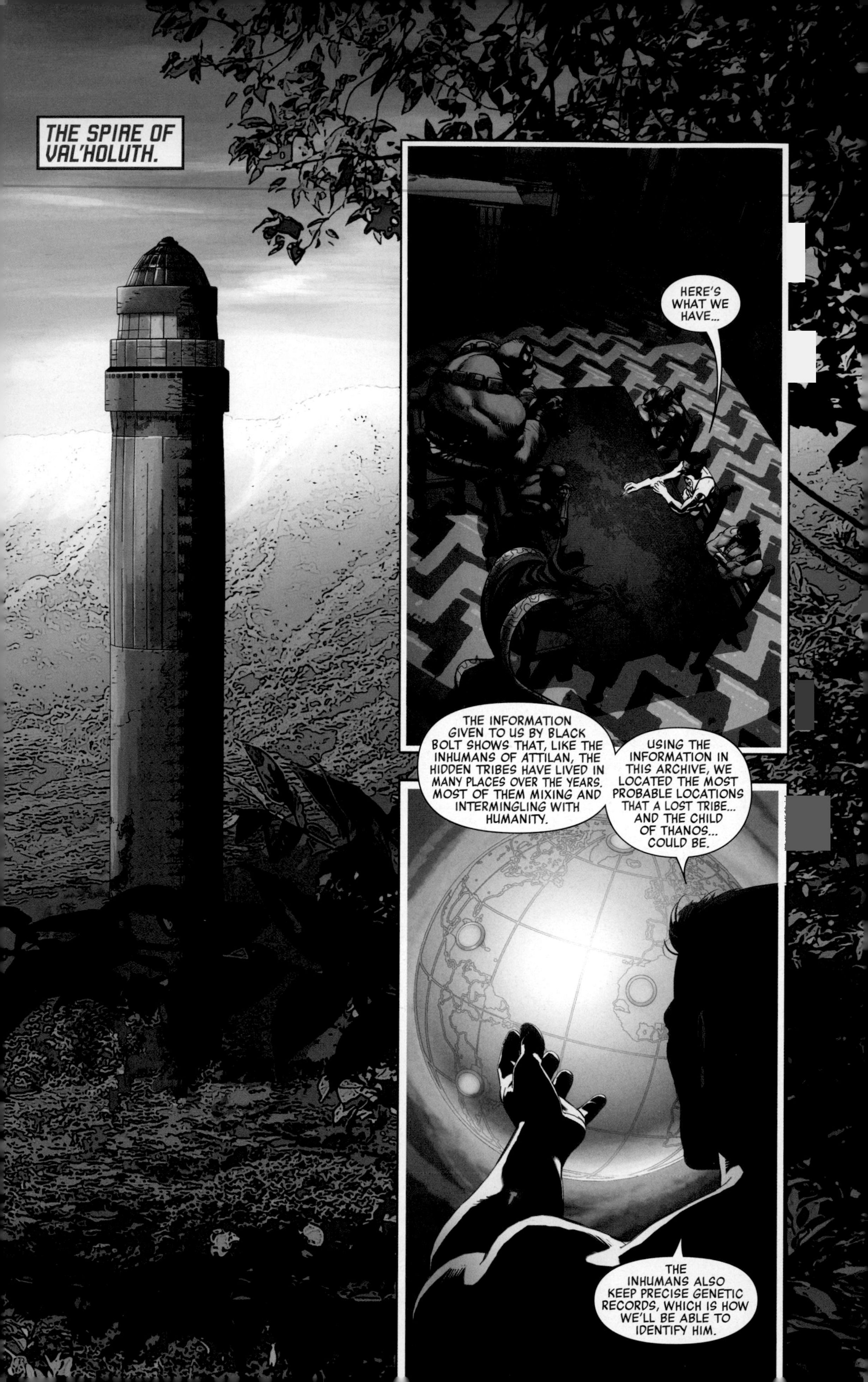
THE SPIRE OF VAL'HOLUTH.
HERE'S WHAT WE HAVE...
THE INFORMATION GIVEN TO US BY BLACK BOLT SHOWS THAT, LIKE THE INHUMANS OF ATTILAN, THE HIDDEN TRIBES HAVE LIVED IN MANY PLACES OVER THE YEARS. MOST OF THEM MIXING AND INTERMINGLING WITH HUMANITY.
USING THE INFORMATION IN THIS ARCHIVE, WE LOCATED THE MOST PROBABLE LOCATIONS THAT A LOST TRIBE... AND THE CHILD OF THANOS... COULD BE.
THE INHUMANS ALSO KEEP PRECISE GENETIC RECORDS, WHICH IS HOW WE'LL BE ABLE TO IDENTIFY HIM.

I'M COUNTING SIX LOCATIONS... THE SIX OF US...

CONVENIENCE OR PROVIDENCE?

NEITHER. STILL...I'D LIKE US TO DOUBLE UP. TWO TO A SITE WILL TAKE TWICE AS LONG, BUT WE'RE TALKING ABOUT, WELL, THE SON OF THANOS HERE.

ANYONE HAVE ANY IDEA WHAT THE SPAWN OF A SPACE TYRANT LOOKS LIKE?

I SUGGEST WE PROCEED CAUTIOUSLY.

PROCEED WITH CAUTION?

CAUTION WOULD DICTATE THAT WE WORK APART FROM EACH OTHER FOR THE FORESEEABLE FUTURE.

WHAT'S GOING ON HERE?

REED MEANS BEYOND THE NORMAL, TEDIOUS ACRIMONY, OF COURSE.

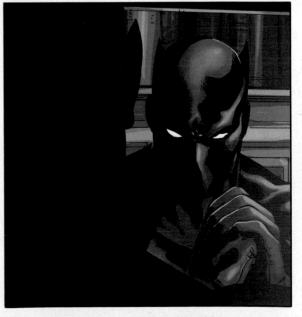

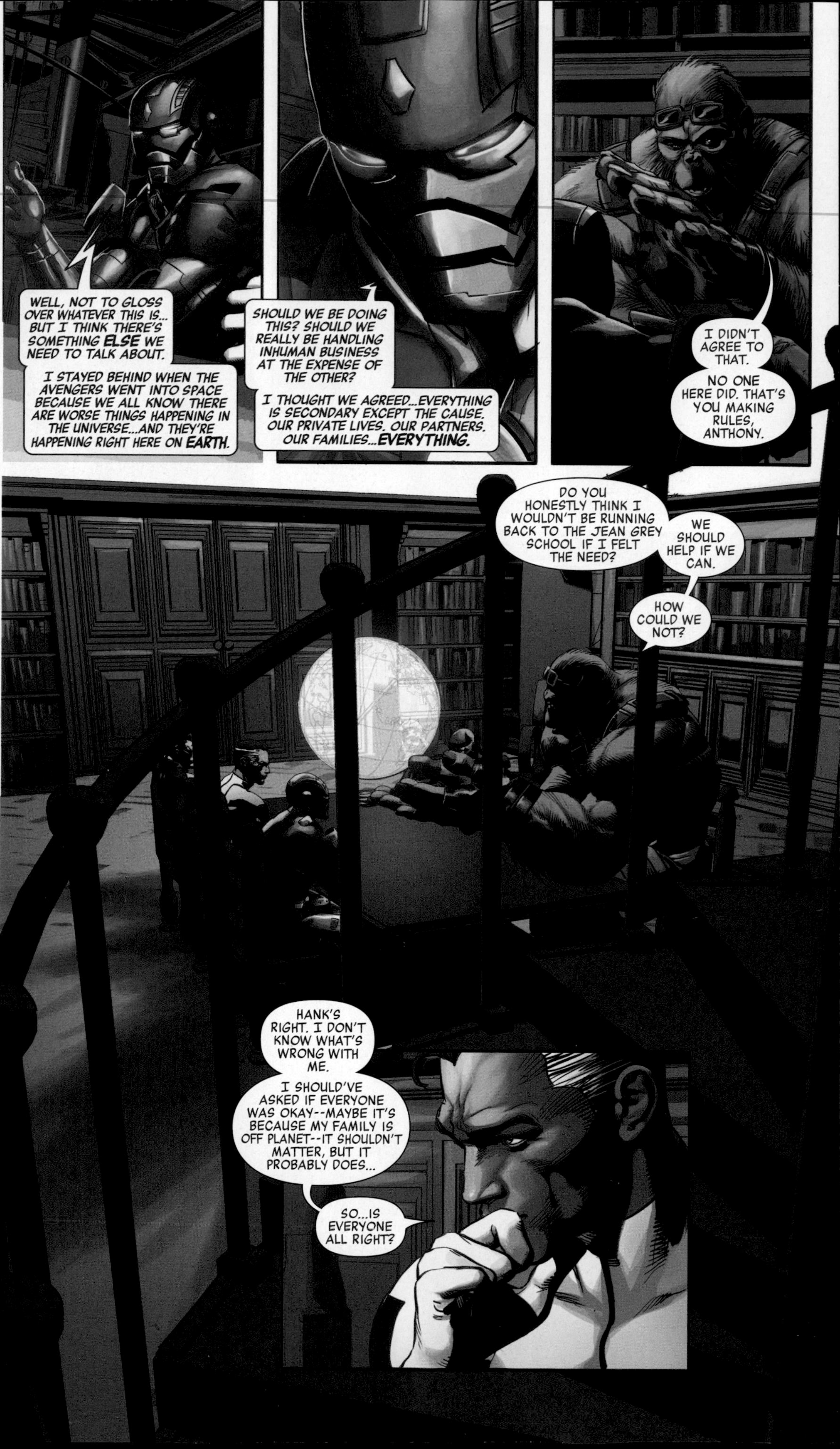
WELL, NOT TO GLOSS OVER WHATEVER THIS IS... BUT I THINK THERE'S SOMETHING ELSE WE NEED TO TALK ABOUT.
I STAYED BEHIND WHEN THE AVENGERS WENT INTO SPACE BECAUSE WE ALL KNOW THERE ARE WORSE THINGS HAPPENING IN THE UNIVERSE...AND THEY'RE HAPPENING RIGHT HERE ON EARTH.
SHOULD WE BE DOING THIS? SHOULD WE REALLY BE HANDLING INHUMAN BUSINESS AT THE EXPENSE OF THE OTHER?
I THOUGHT WE AGREED...EVERYTHING IS SECONDARY EXCEPT THE CAUSE. OUR PRIVATE LIVES. OUR PARTNERS. OUR FAMILIES...EVERYTHING.
I DIDN'T AGREE TO THAT.
NO ONE HERE DID. THAT'S YOU MAKING RULES, ANTHONY.
DO YOU HONESTLY THINK I WOULDN'T BE RUNNING BACK TO THE JEAN GREY SCHOOL IF I FELT THE NEED?
WE SHOULD HELP IF WE CAN.
HOW COULD WE NOT?
HANK'S RIGHT. I DON'T KNOW WHAT'S WRONG WITH ME.
I SHOULD'VE ASKED IF EVERYONE WAS OKAY--MAYBE IT'S BECAUSE MY FAMILY IS OFF PLANET--IT SHOULDN'T MATTER, BUT IT PROBABLY DOES...
SO...IS EVERYONE ALL RIGHT?

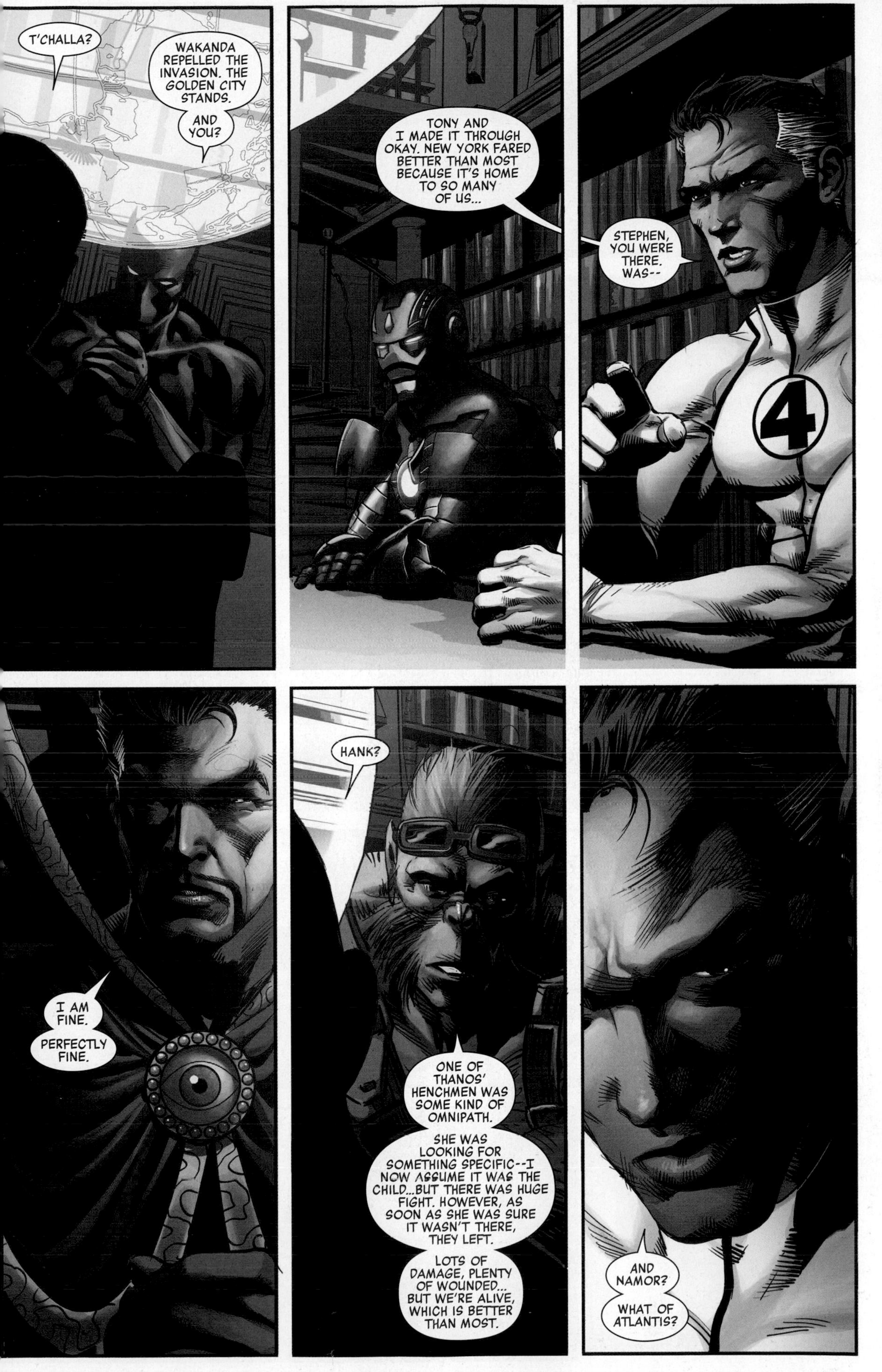
T'CHALLA?
WAKANDA REPELLED THE INVASION. THE GOLDEN CITY STANDS.
AND YOU?
TONY AND I MADE IT THROUGH OKAY. NEW YORK FARED BETTER THAN MOST BECAUSE IT'S HOME TO SO MANY OF US...
STEPHEN, YOU WERE THERE. WAS--
I AM FINE.
PERFECTLY FINE.
HANK?
ONE OF THANOS' HENCHMEN WAS SOME KIND OF OMNIPATH.
SHE WAS LOOKING FOR SOMETHING SPECIFIC--I NOW ASSUME IT WAS THE CHILD...BUT THERE WAS HUGE FIGHT. HOWEVER, AS SOON AS SHE WAS SURE IT WASN'T THERE, THEY LEFT.
LOTS OF DAMAGE, PLENTY OF WOUNDED... BUT WE'RE ALIVE, WHICH IS BETTER THAN MOST.
AND NAMOR?
WHAT OF ATLANTIS?

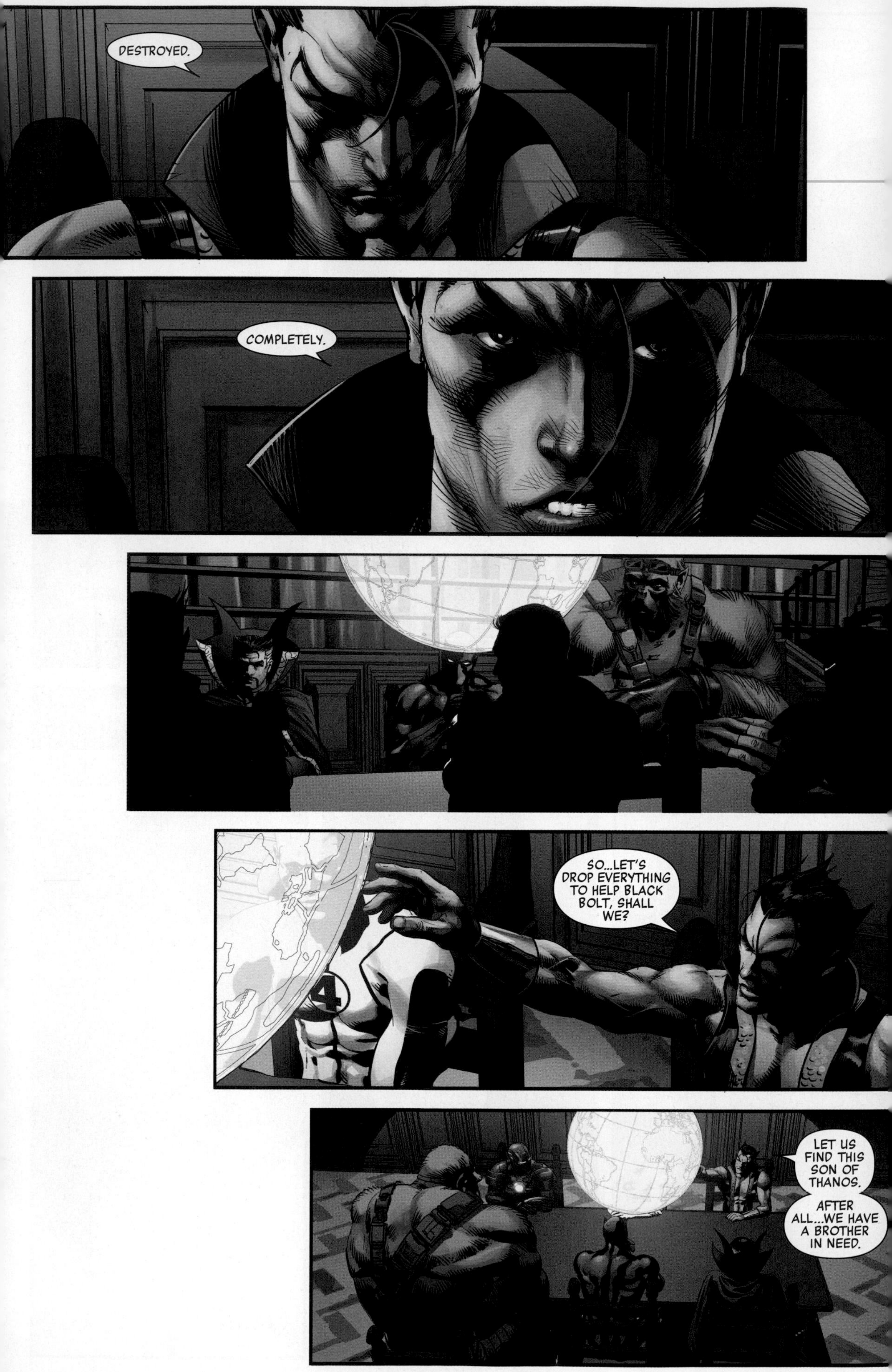
DESTROYED.
COMPLETELY.
SO...LET'S DROP EVERYTHING TO HELP BLACK BOLT, SHALL WE?
LET US FIND THIS SON OF THANOS.
AFTER ALL...WE HAVE A BROTHER IN NEED.

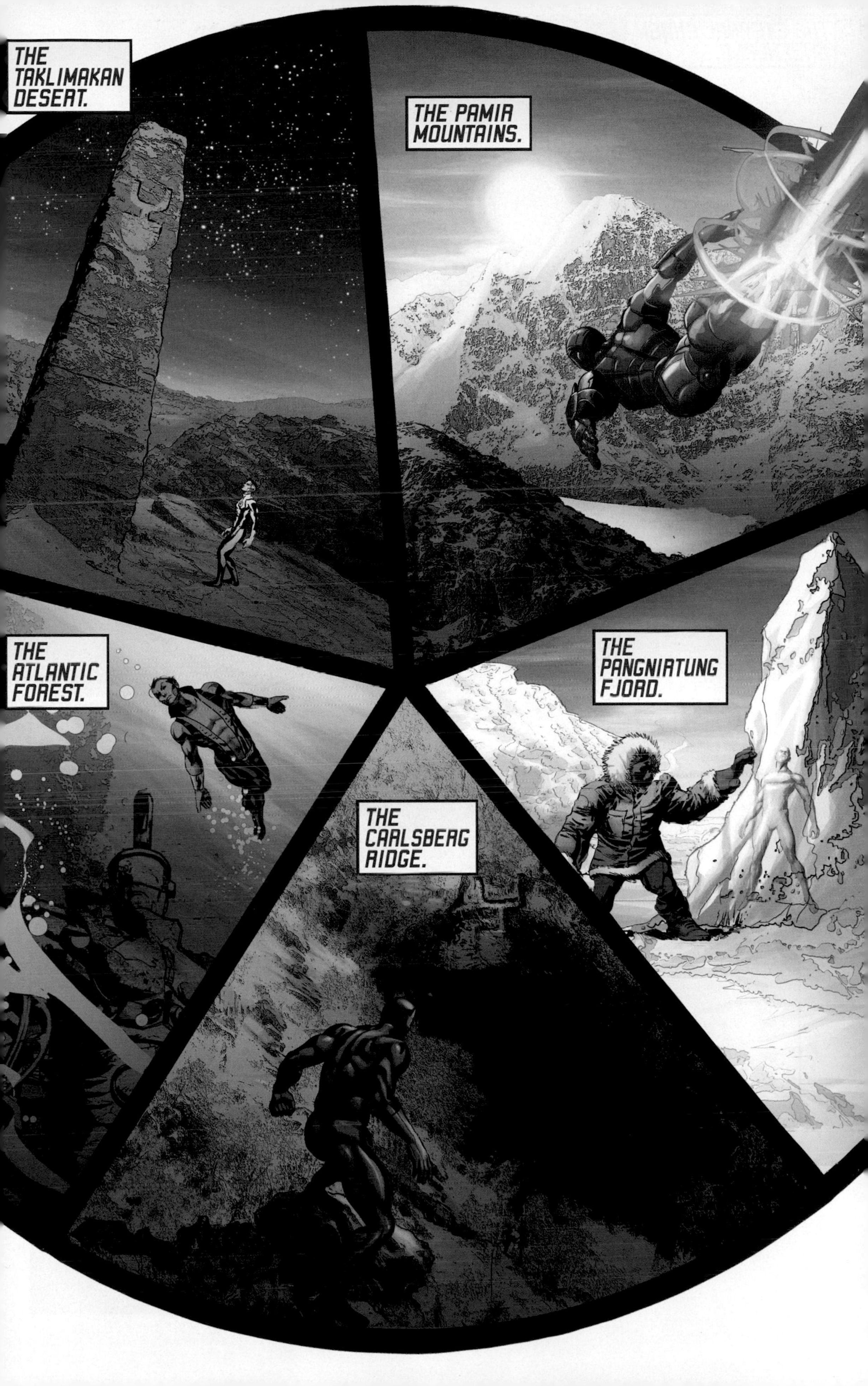
THE TAKLIMAKAN DESERT.
THE PAMIR MOUNTAINS.
THE ATLANTIC FOREST.
THE PANGNIRTUNG FJORD.
THE CARLSBERG RIDGE.

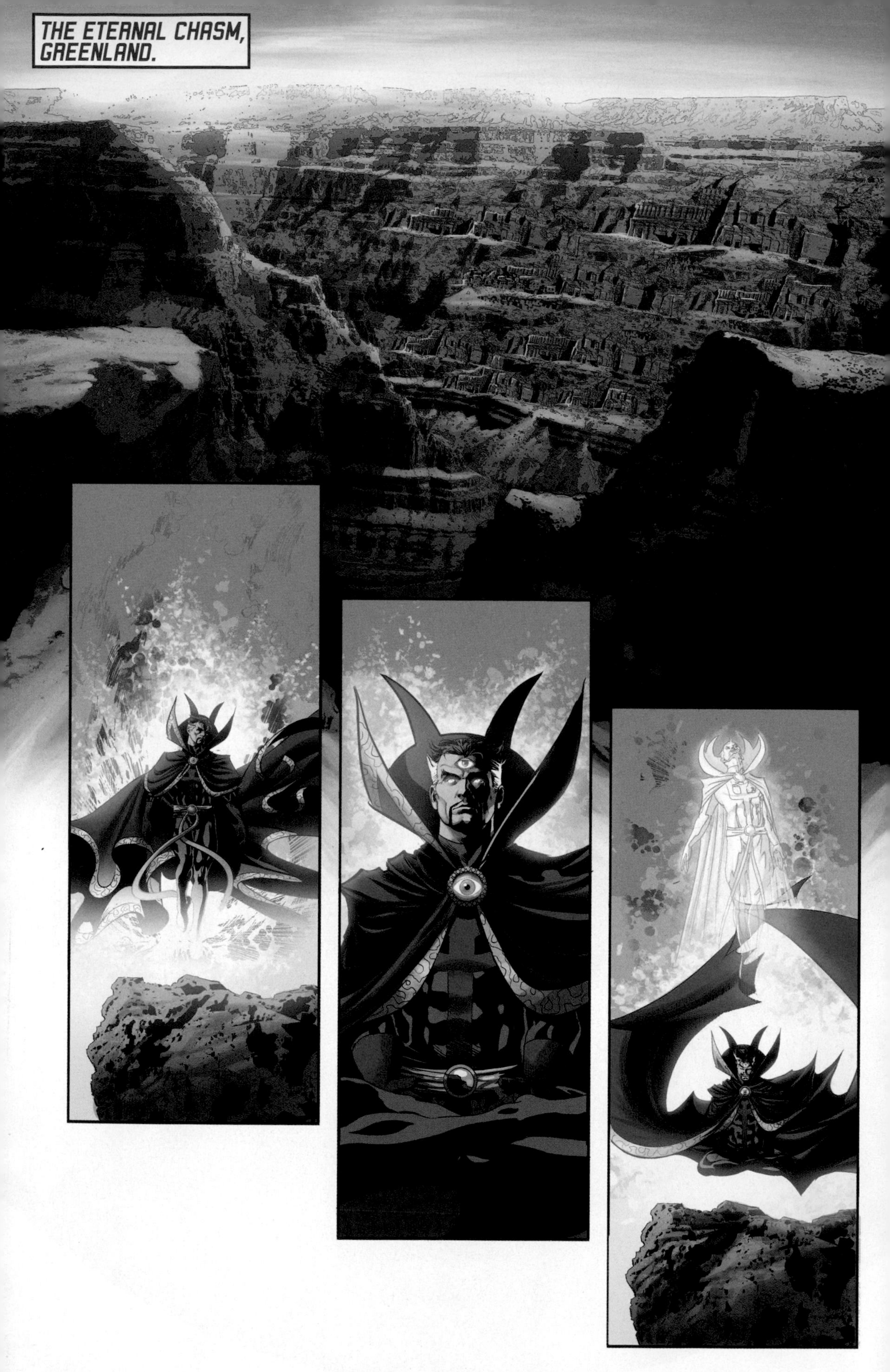
THE ETERNAL CHASM, GREENLAND.

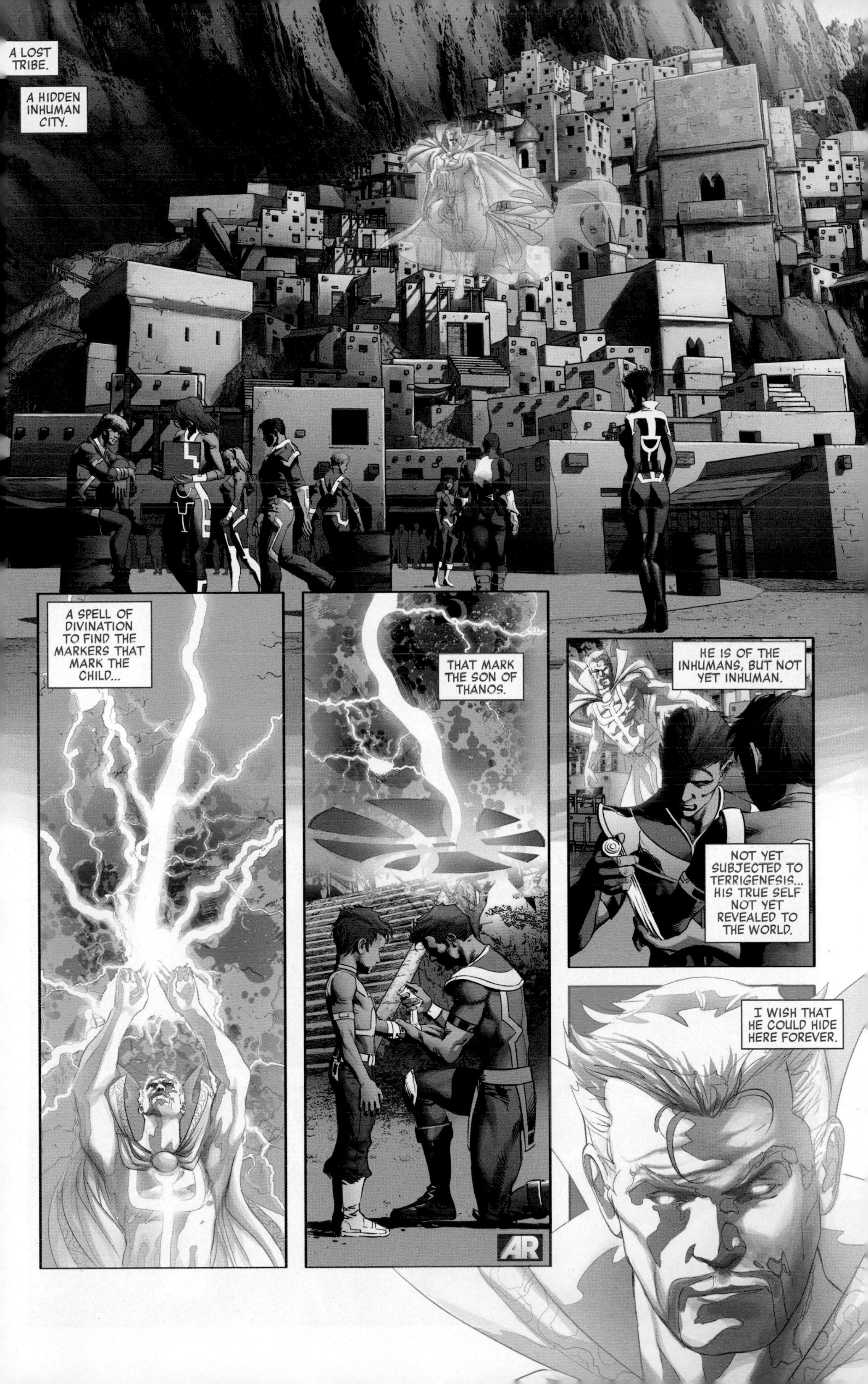
A LOST TRIBE.
A HIDDEN INHUMAN CITY.
A SPELL OF DIVINATION TO FIND THE MARKERS THAT MARK THE CHILD...
THAT MARK THE SON OF THANOS.
HE IS OF THE INHUMANS, BUT NOT YET INHUMAN.
NOT YET SUBJECTED TO TERRIGENESIS... HIS TRUE SELF NOT YET REVEALED TO THE WORLD.
I WISH THAT HE COULD HIDE HERE FOREVER.

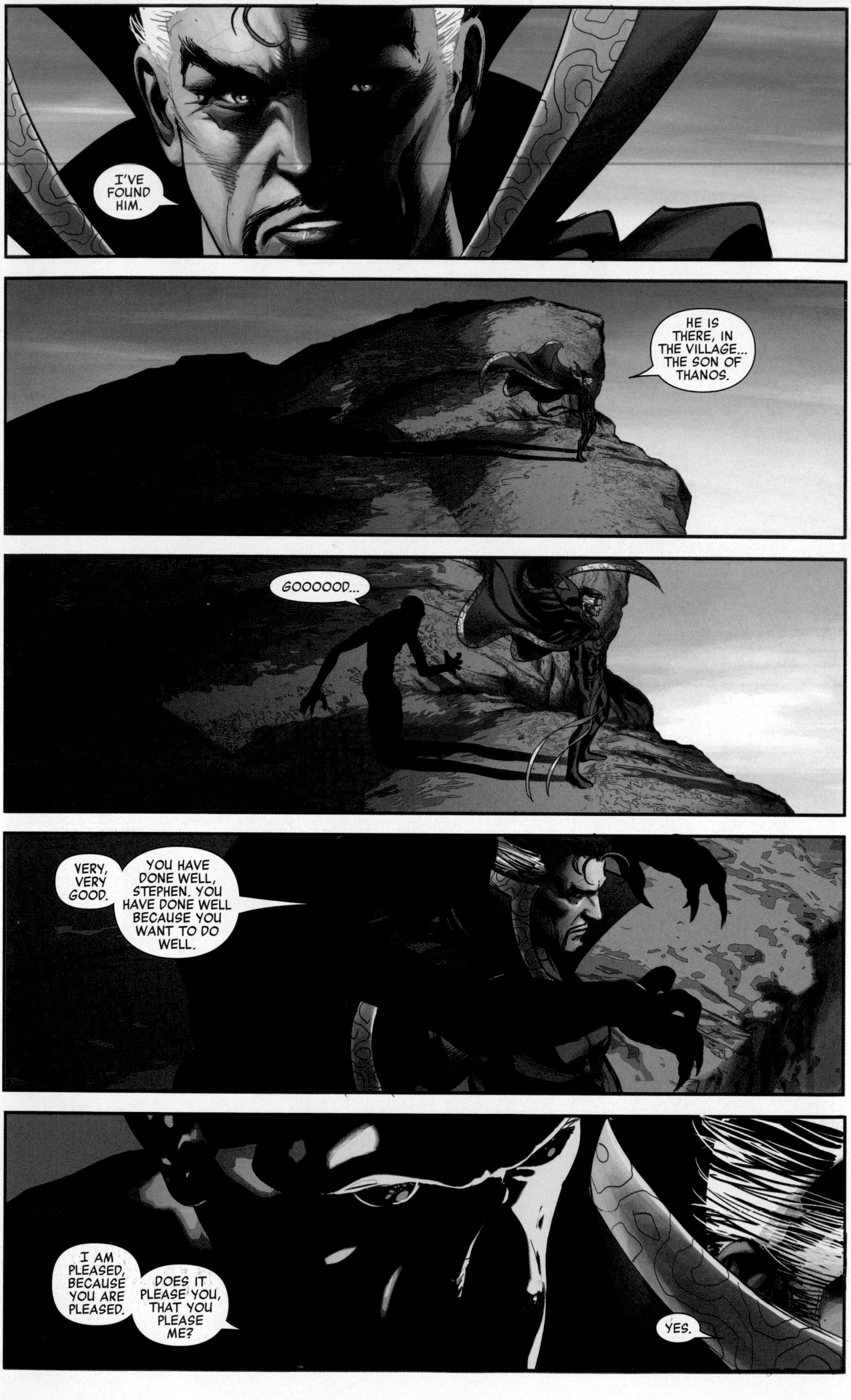
I'VE FOUND HIM.
HE IS THERE, IN THE VILLAGE... THE SON OF THANOS.
GOOOOOD...
VERY, VERY GOOD.
YOU HAVE DONE WELL, STEPHEN. YOU HAVE DONE WELL BECAUSE YOU WANT TO DO WELL.
I AM PLEASED, BECAUSE YOU ARE PLEASED.
DOES IT PLEASE YOU, THAT YOU PLEASE ME?
YES.

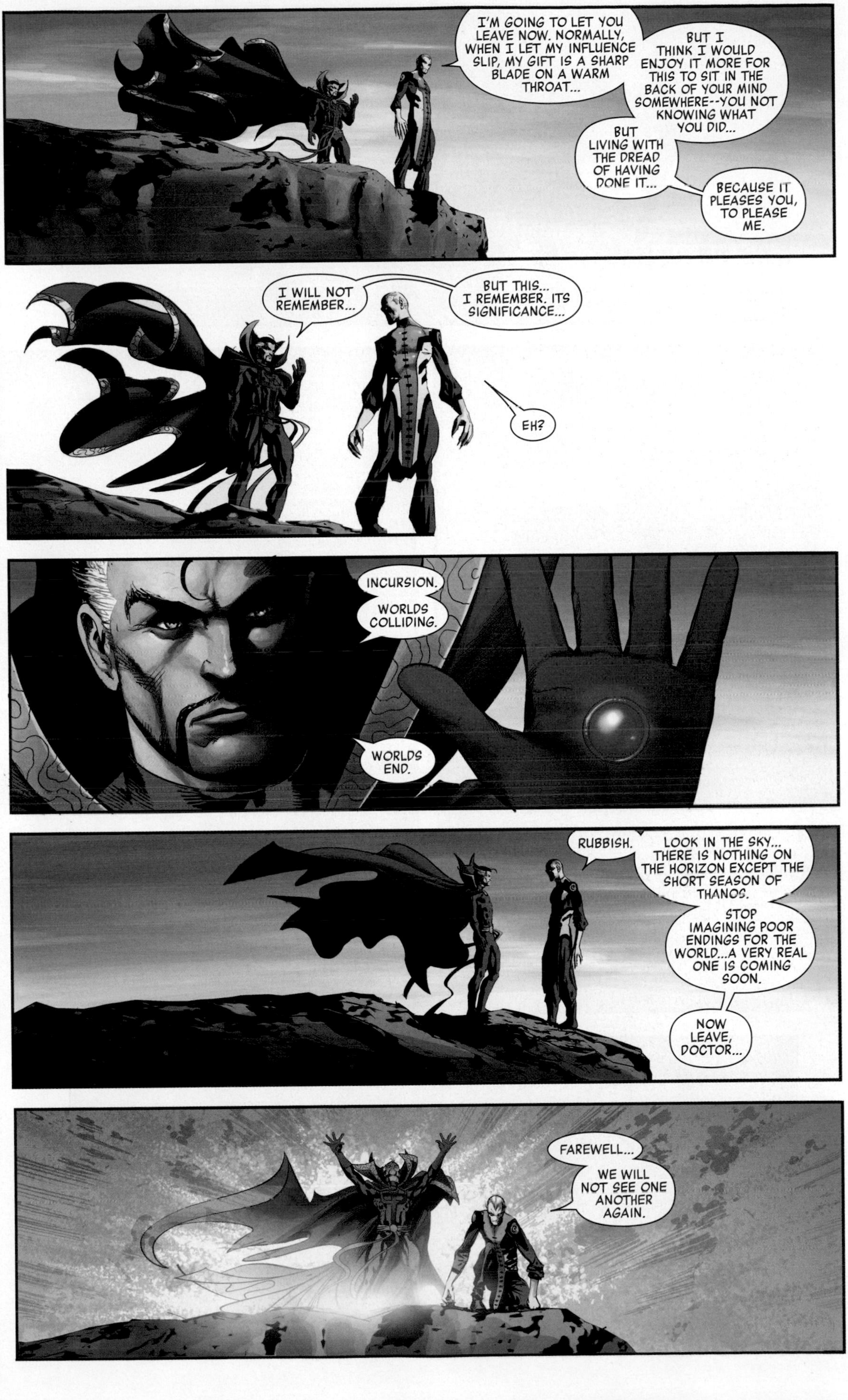

I'M GOING TO LET YOU LEAVE NOW. NORMALLY, WHEN I LET MY INFLUENCE SLIP, MY GIFT IS A SHARP BLADE ON A WARM THROAT...
BUT I THINK I WOULD ENJOY IT MORE FOR THIS TO SIT IN THE BACK OF YOUR MIND SOMEWHERE--YOU NOT KNOWING WHAT YOU DID...
BUT LIVING WITH THE DREAD OF HAVING DONE IT...
BECAUSE IT PLEASES YOU, TO PLEASE ME.
I WILL NOT REMEMBER...
BUT THIS... I REMEMBER. ITS SIGNIFICANCE...
EH?
INCURSION.
WORLDS COLLIDING.
WORLDS END.
RUBBISH.
LOOK IN THE SKY... THERE IS NOTHING ON THE HORIZON EXCEPT THE SHORT SEASON OF THANOS.
STOP IMAGINING POOR ENDINGS FOR THE WORLD...A VERY REAL ONE IS COMING SOON.
NOW LEAVE, DOCTOR...
FAREWELL...
WE WILL NOT SEE ONE ANOTHER AGAIN.

THE TWELVE APOSTLES, AUSTRALIA.

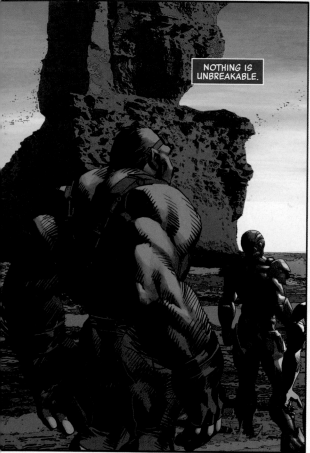

NOTHING IS UNBREAKABLE.

NOTHING LASTS FOREVER.

NOT THE BRAVEST. NOT THE STRONGEST.

NOT THE SMARTEST...

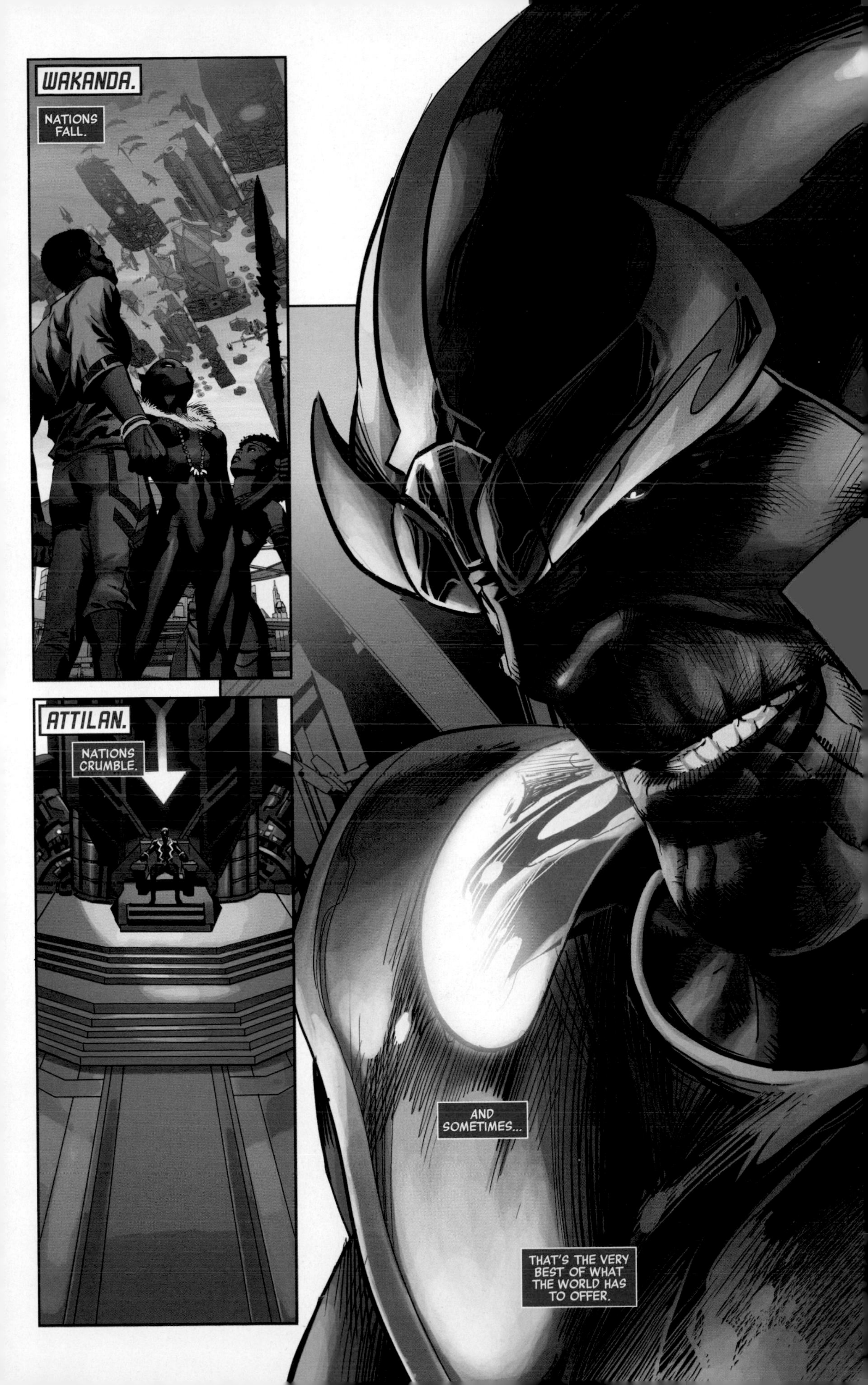
WAKANDA.
NATIONS FALL.
ATTILAN.
NATIONS CRUMBLE.
AND SOMETIMES...
THAT'S THE VERY BEST OF WHAT THE WORLD HAS TO OFFER.

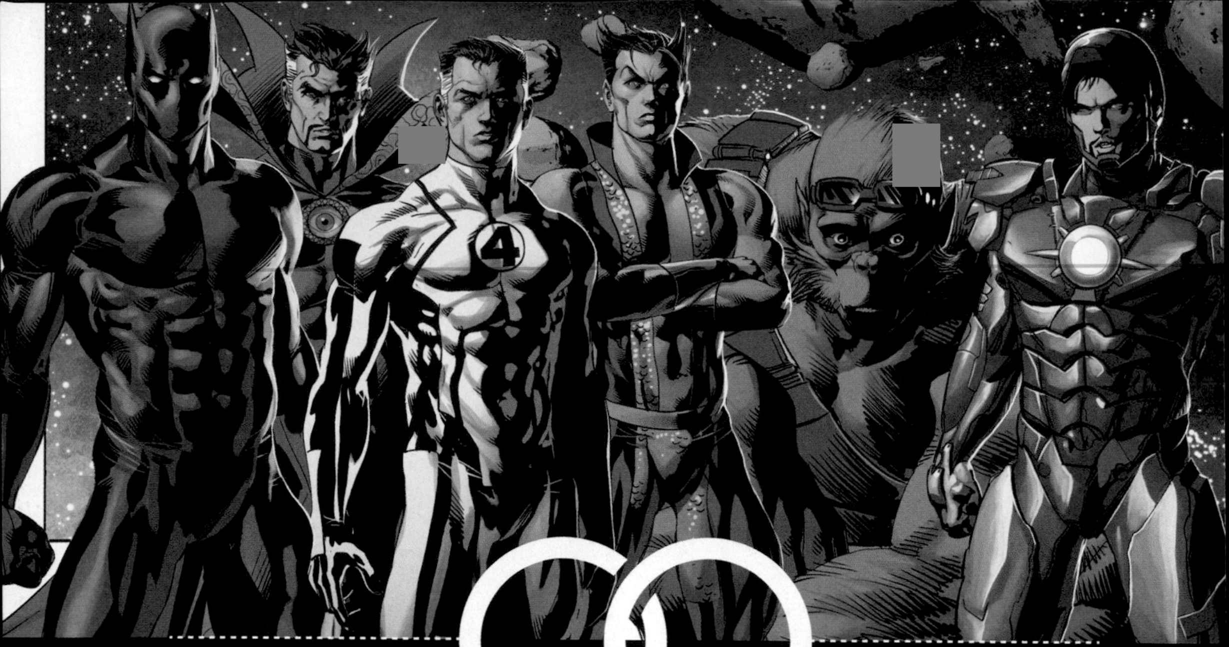

“BUILDERS”

PREVIOUSLY IN INFINITY

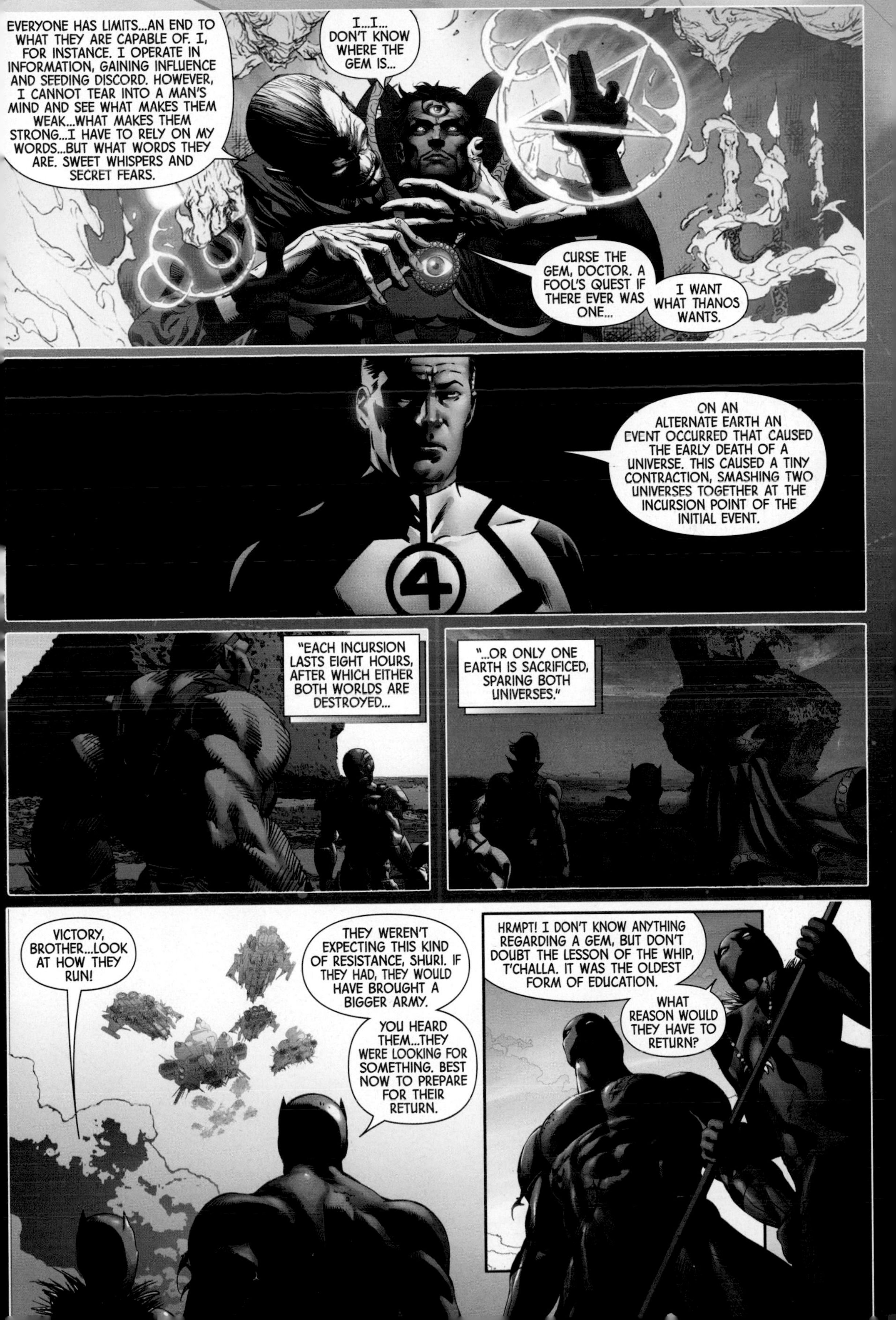
EVERYONE HAS LIMITS...AN END TO WHAT THEY ARE CAPABLE OF. I, FOR INSTANCE. I OPERATE IN INFORMATION, GAINING INFLUENCE AND SEEDING DISCORD. HOWEVER, I CANNOT TEAR INTO A MAN'S MIND AND SEE WHAT MAKES THEM WEAK...WHAT MAKES THEM STRONG...I HAVE TO RELY ON MY WORDS...BUT WHAT WORDS THEY ARE. SWEET WHISPERS AND SECRET FEARS.
I...I... DON'T KNOW WHERE THE GEM IS...
CURSE THE GEM, DOCTOR. A FOOL'S QUEST IF THERE EVER WAS ONE...
I WANT WHAT THANOS WANTS.
ON AN ALTERNATE EARTH AN EVENT OCCURRED THAT CAUSED THE EARLY DEATH OF A UNIVERSE. THIS CAUSED A TINY CONTRACTION, SMASHING TWO UNIVERSES TOGETHER AT THE INCURSION POINT OF THE INITIAL EVENT.
"EACH INCURSION LASTS EIGHT HOURS, AFTER WHICH EITHER BOTH WORLDS ARE DESTROYED...
"...OR ONLY ONE EARTH IS SACRIFICED, SPARING BOTH UNIVERSES."
VICTORY, BROTHER...LOOK AT HOW THEY RUN!
THEY WEREN'T EXPECTING THIS KIND OF RESISTANCE, SHURI. IF THEY HAD, THEY WOULD HAVE BROUGHT A BIGGER ARMY.
YOU HEARD THEM...THEY WERE LOOKING FOR SOMETHING. BEST NOW TO PREPARE FOR THEIR RETURN.
HRMPT! I DON'T KNOW ANYTHING REGARDING A GEM, BUT DON'T DOUBT THE LESSON OF THE WHIP, T'CHALLA. IT WAS THE OLDEST FORM OF EDUCATION.
WHAT REASON WOULD THEY HAVE TO RETURN?

ALL THESE WORLDS

◆

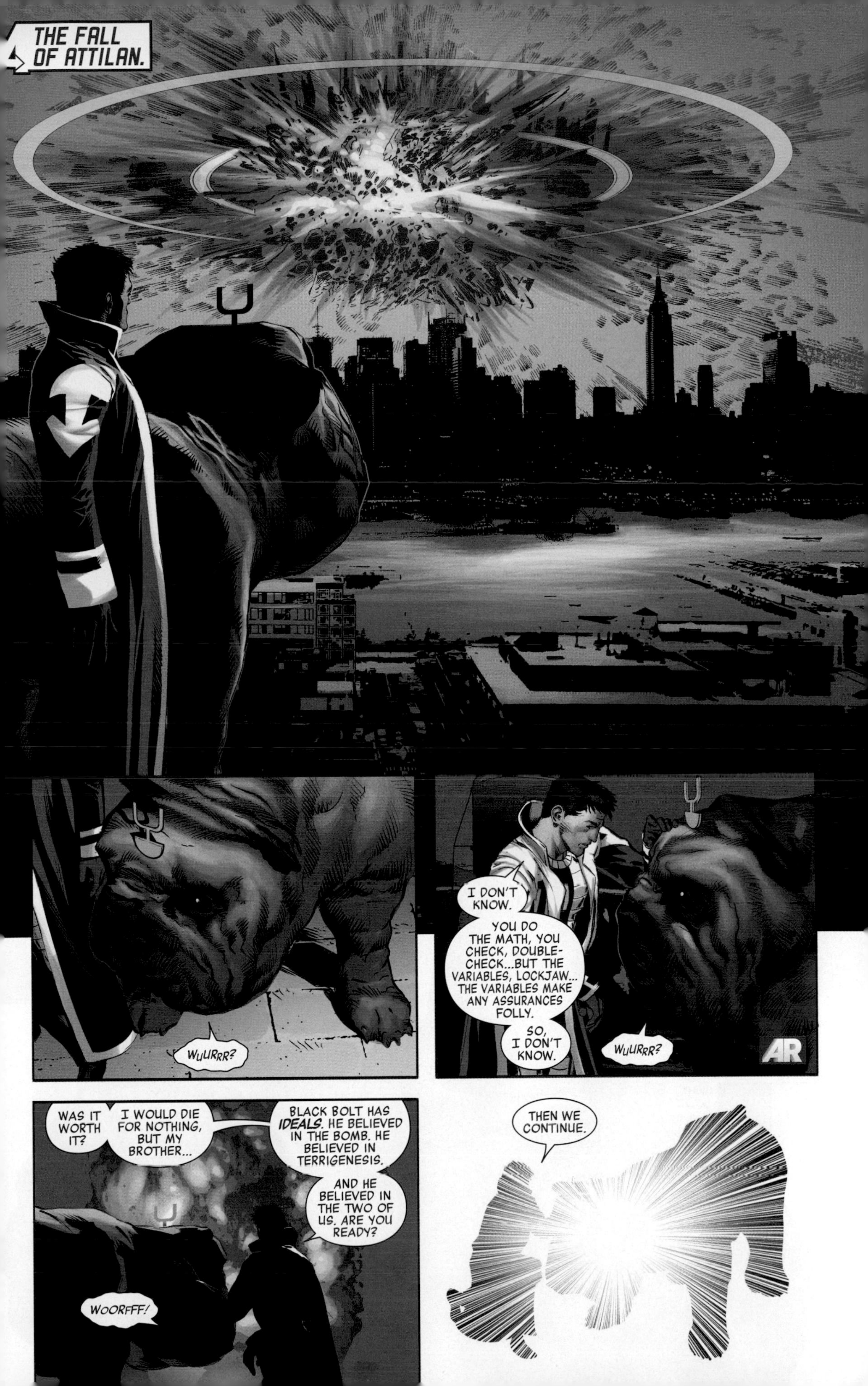
THE FALL OF ATTILAN.
WUURRR?
I DON'T KNOW.
YOU DO THE MATH, YOU CHECK, DOUBLE-CHECK...BUT THE VARIABLES, LOCKJAW... THE VARIABLES MAKE ANY ASSURANCES FOLLY.
SO, I DON'T KNOW.
WUURRR?
WAS IT WORTH IT?
I WOULD DIE FOR NOTHING, BUT MY BROTHER...
BLACK BOLT HAS *IDEALS*. HE BELIEVED IN THE BOMB. HE BELIEVED IN TERRIGENESIS.
AND HE BELIEVED IN THE TWO OF US. ARE YOU READY?
WOORFFF!
THEN WE CONTINUE.

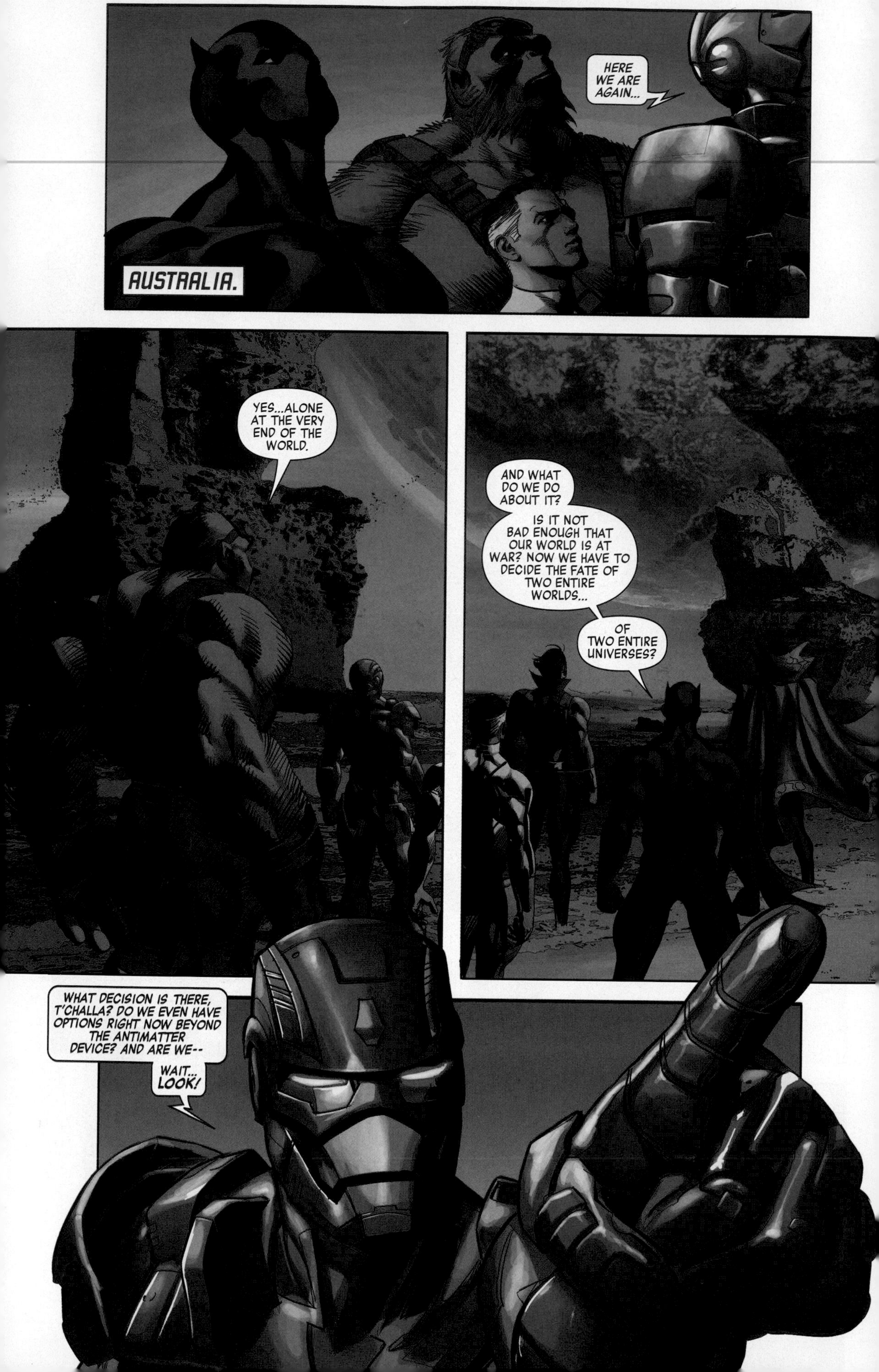
HERE WE ARE AGAIN...
AUSTRALIA.
YES...ALONE AT THE VERY END OF THE WORLD.
AND WHAT DO WE DO ABOUT IT?
IS IT NOT BAD ENOUGH THAT OUR WORLD IS AT WAR? NOW WE HAVE TO DECIDE THE FATE OF TWO ENTIRE WORLDS...
OF TWO ENTIRE UNIVERSES?
WHAT DECISION IS THERE, T'CHALLA? DO WE EVEN HAVE OPTIONS RIGHT NOW BEYOND THE ANTIMATTER DEVICE? AND ARE WE--
WAIT... LOOK!

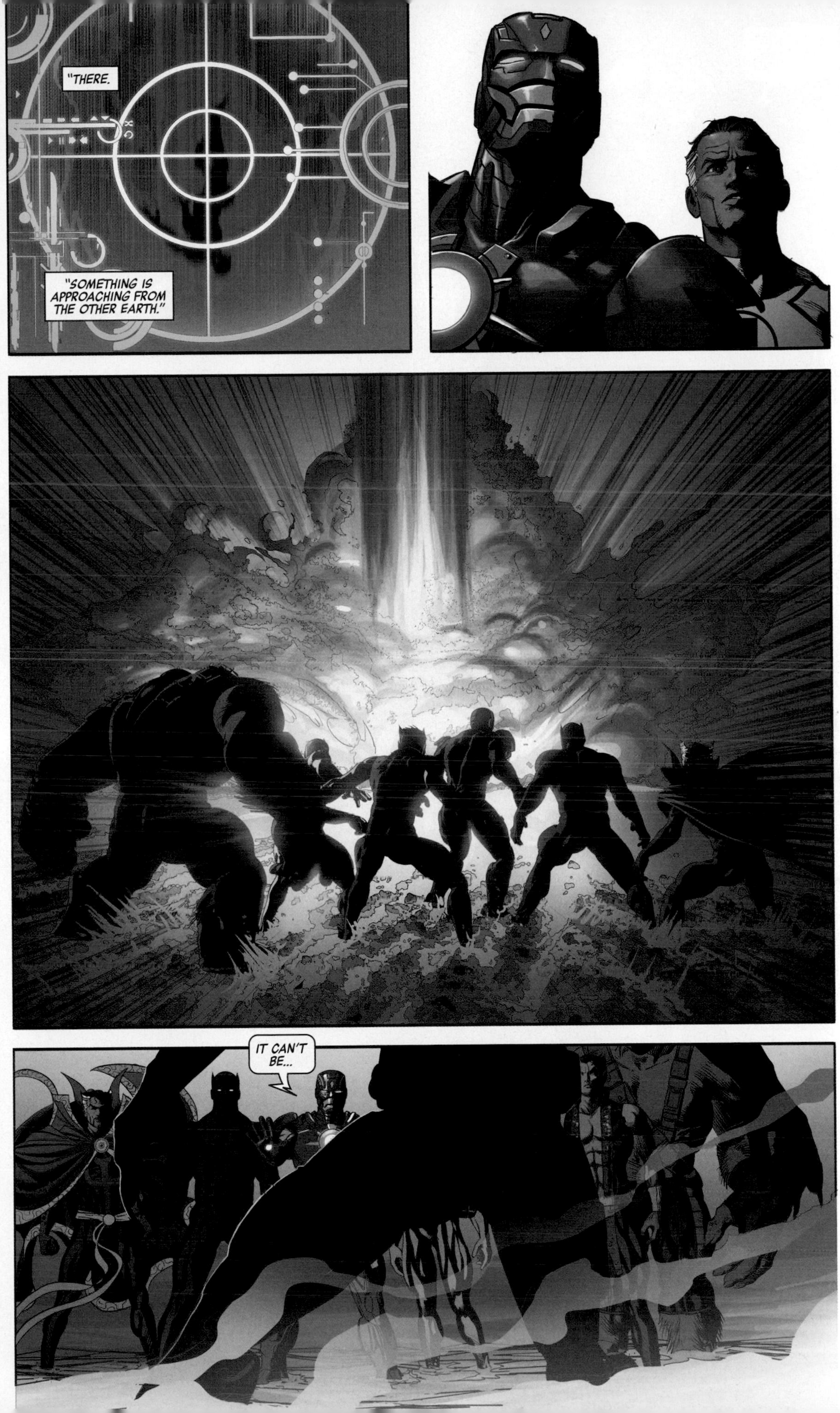
"THERE.
"SOMETHING IS APPROACHING FROM THE OTHER EARTH."
IT CAN'T BE...

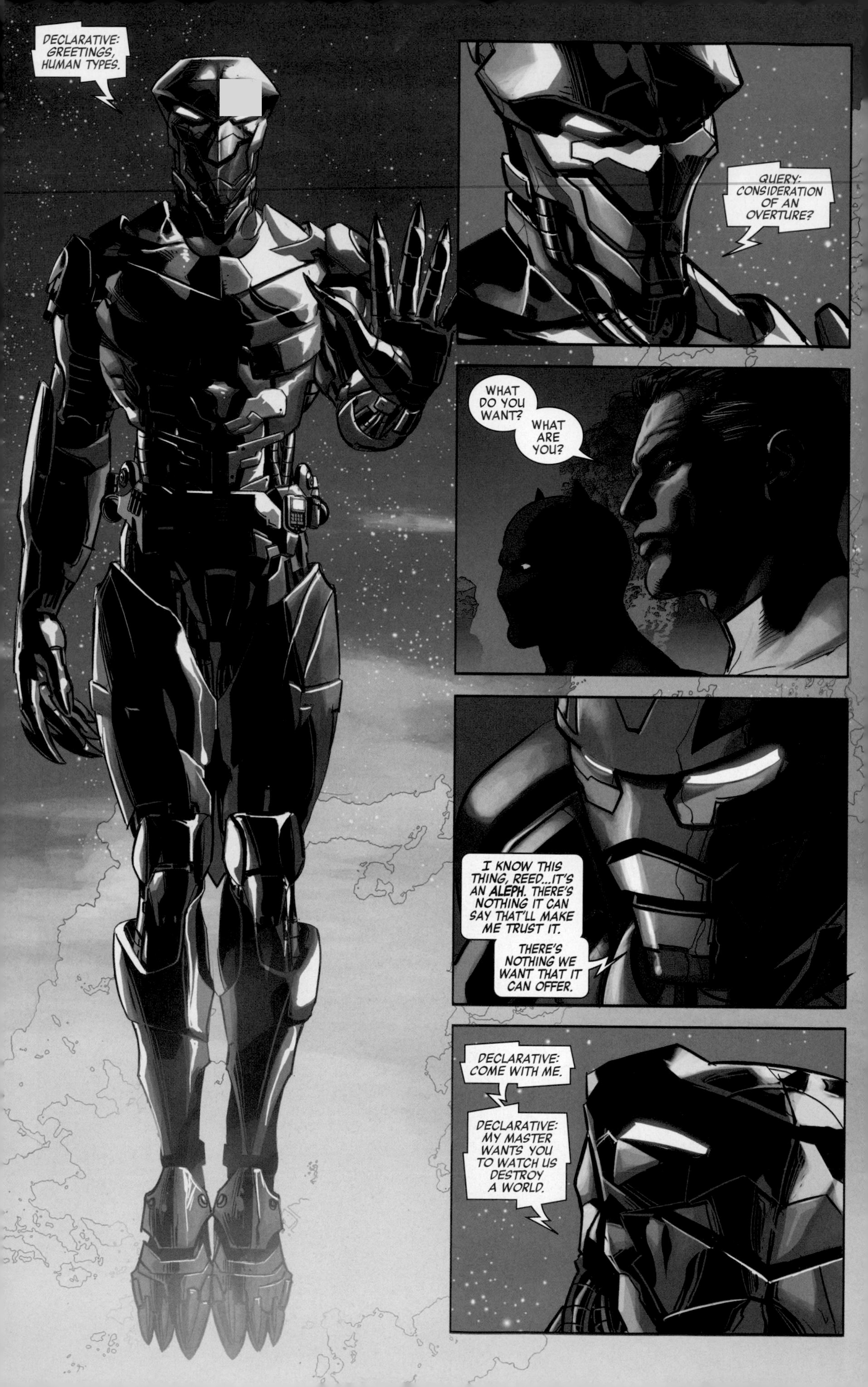
DECLARATIVE: GREETINGS, HUMAN TYPES.
QUERY: CONSIDERATION OF AN OVERTURE?
WHAT DO YOU WANT?
WHAT ARE YOU?
I KNOW THIS THING, REED...IT'S AN ALEPH. THERE'S NOTHING IT CAN SAY THAT'LL MAKE ME TRUST IT.
THERE'S NOTHING WE WANT THAT IT CAN OFFER.
DECLARATIVE: COME WITH ME.
DECLARATIVE: MY MASTER WANTS YOU TO WATCH US DESTROY A WORLD.

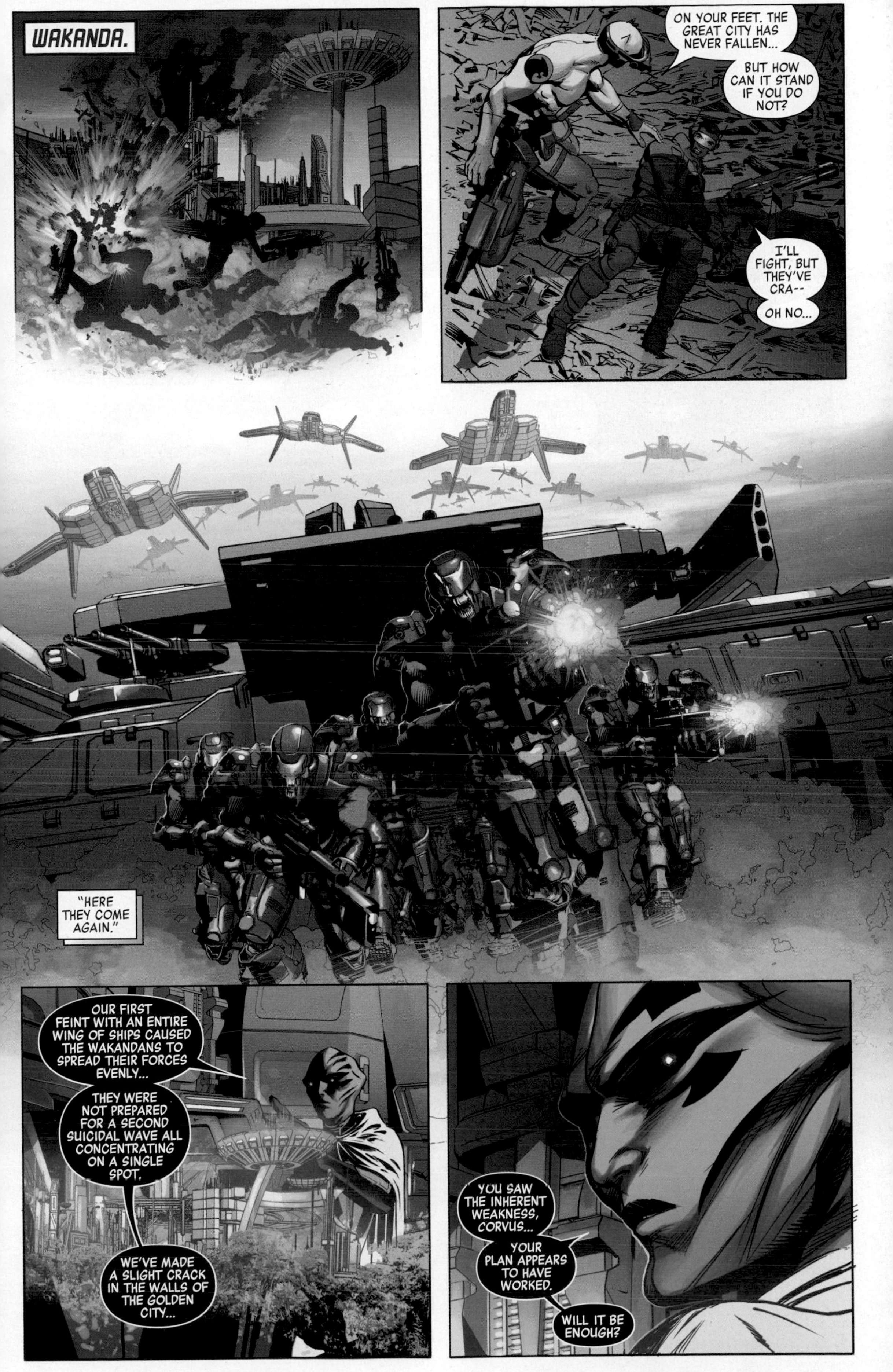
WAKANDA.
ON YOUR FEET. THE GREAT CITY HAS NEVER FALLEN...
BUT HOW CAN IT STAND IF YOU DO NOT?
I'LL FIGHT, BUT THEY'VE CRA--
OH NO...
"HERE THEY COME AGAIN."
OUR FIRST FEINT WITH AN ENTIRE WING OF SHIPS CAUSED THE WAKANDANS TO SPREAD THEIR FORCES EVENLY...
THEY WERE NOT PREPARED FOR A SECOND SUICIDAL WAVE ALL CONCENTRATING ON A SINGLE SPOT.
WE'VE MADE A SLIGHT CRACK IN THE WALLS OF THE GOLDEN CITY...
YOU SAW THE INHERENT WEAKNESS, CORVUS...
YOUR PLAN APPEARS TO HAVE WORKED.
WILL IT BE ENOUGH?

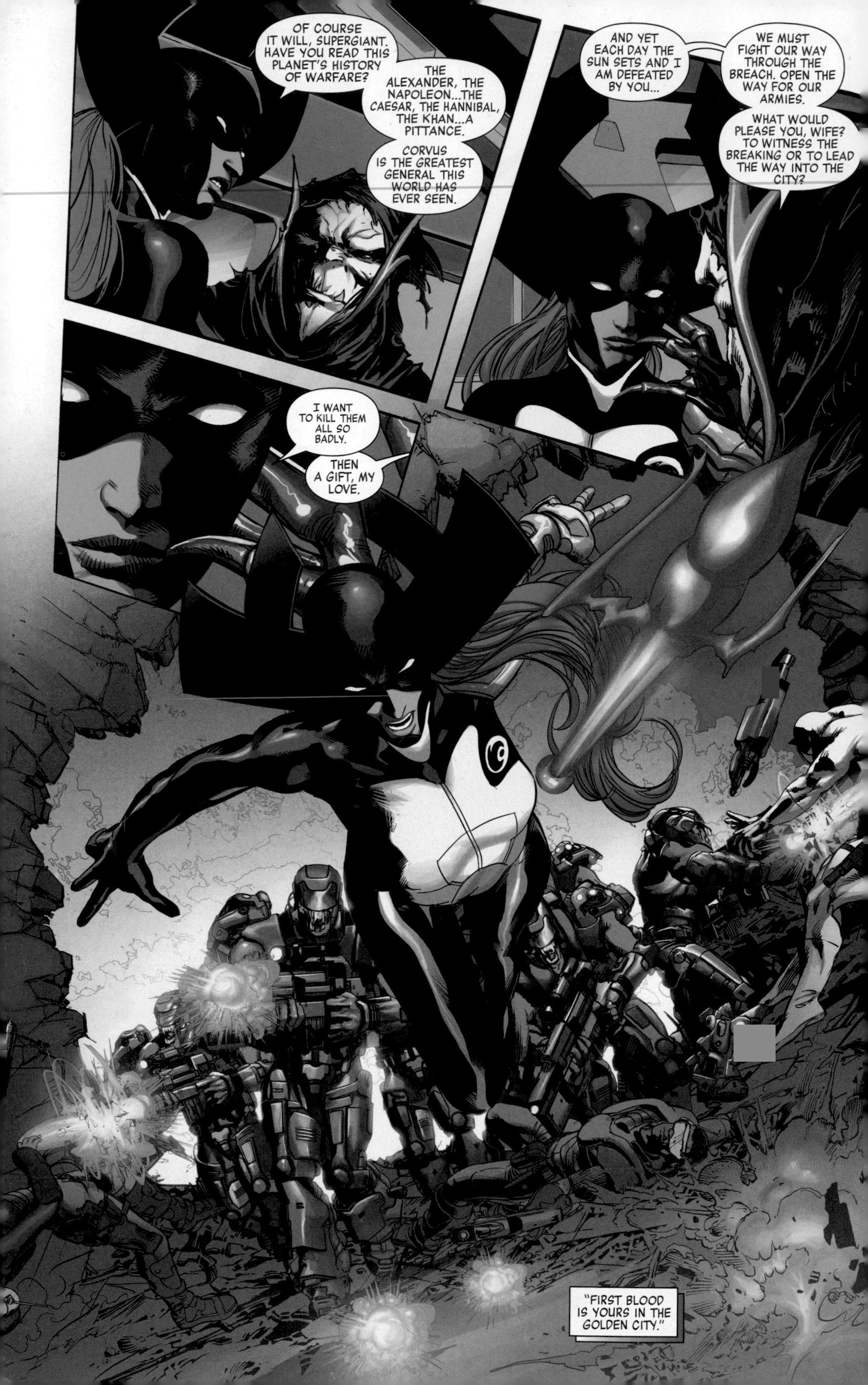
OF COURSE IT WILL, SUPERGIANT. HAVE YOU READ THIS PLANET'S HISTORY OF WARFARE?
THE ALEXANDER, THE NAPOLEON...THE CAESAR, THE HANNIBAL, THE KHAN...A PITTANCE.
CORVUS IS THE GREATEST GENERAL THIS WORLD HAS EVER SEEN.
AND YET EACH DAY THE SUN SETS AND I AM DEFEATED BY YOU...
WE MUST FIGHT OUR WAY THROUGH THE BREACH. OPEN THE WAY FOR OUR ARMIES.
WHAT WOULD PLEASE YOU, WIFE? TO WITNESS THE BREAKING OR TO LEAD THE WAY INTO THE CITY?
I WANT TO KILL THEM ALL SO BADLY.
THEN A GIFT, MY LOVE.
"FIRST BLOOD IS YOURS IN THE GOLDEN CITY."

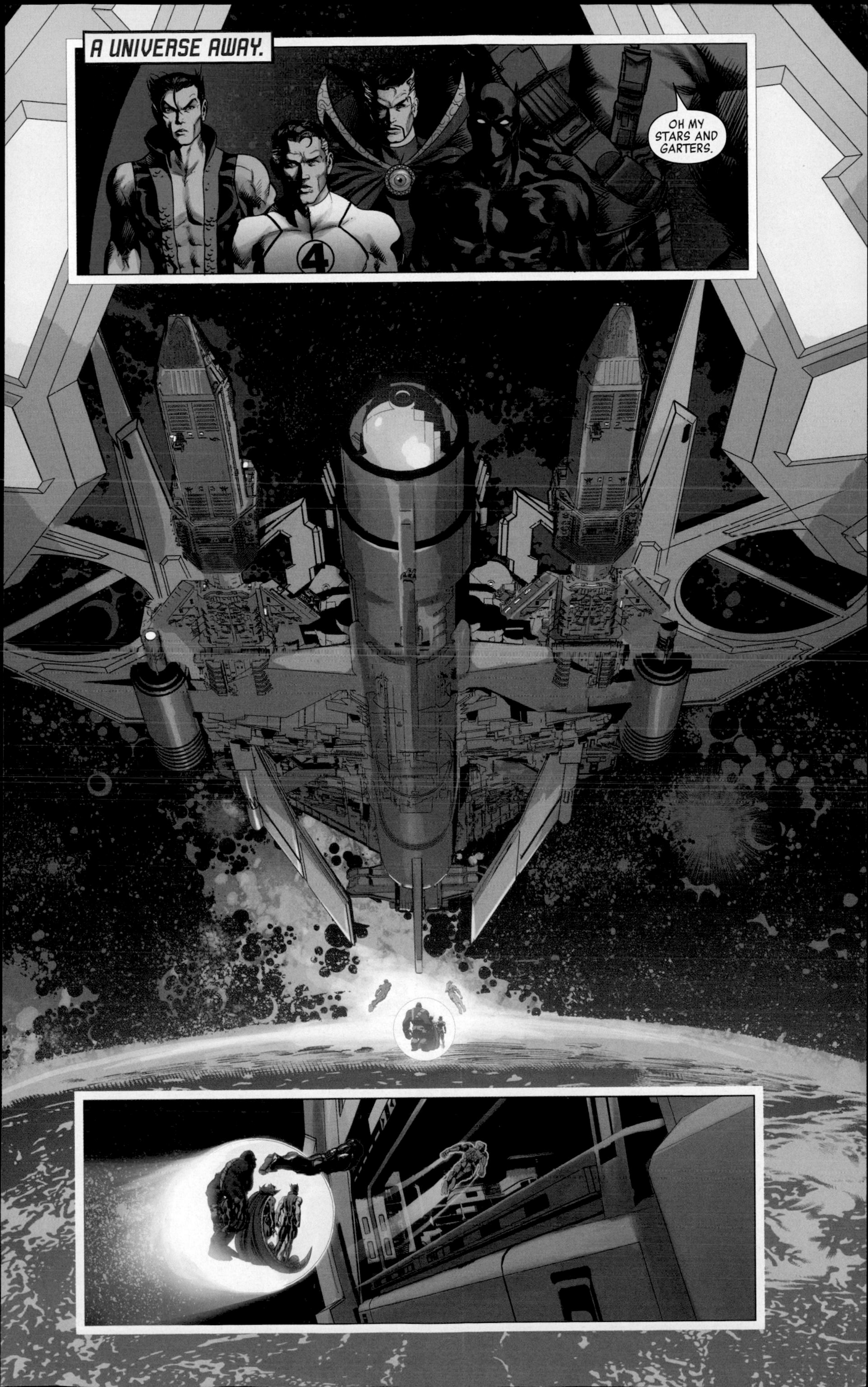
A UNIVERSE AWAY.
OH MY STARS AND GARTERS.

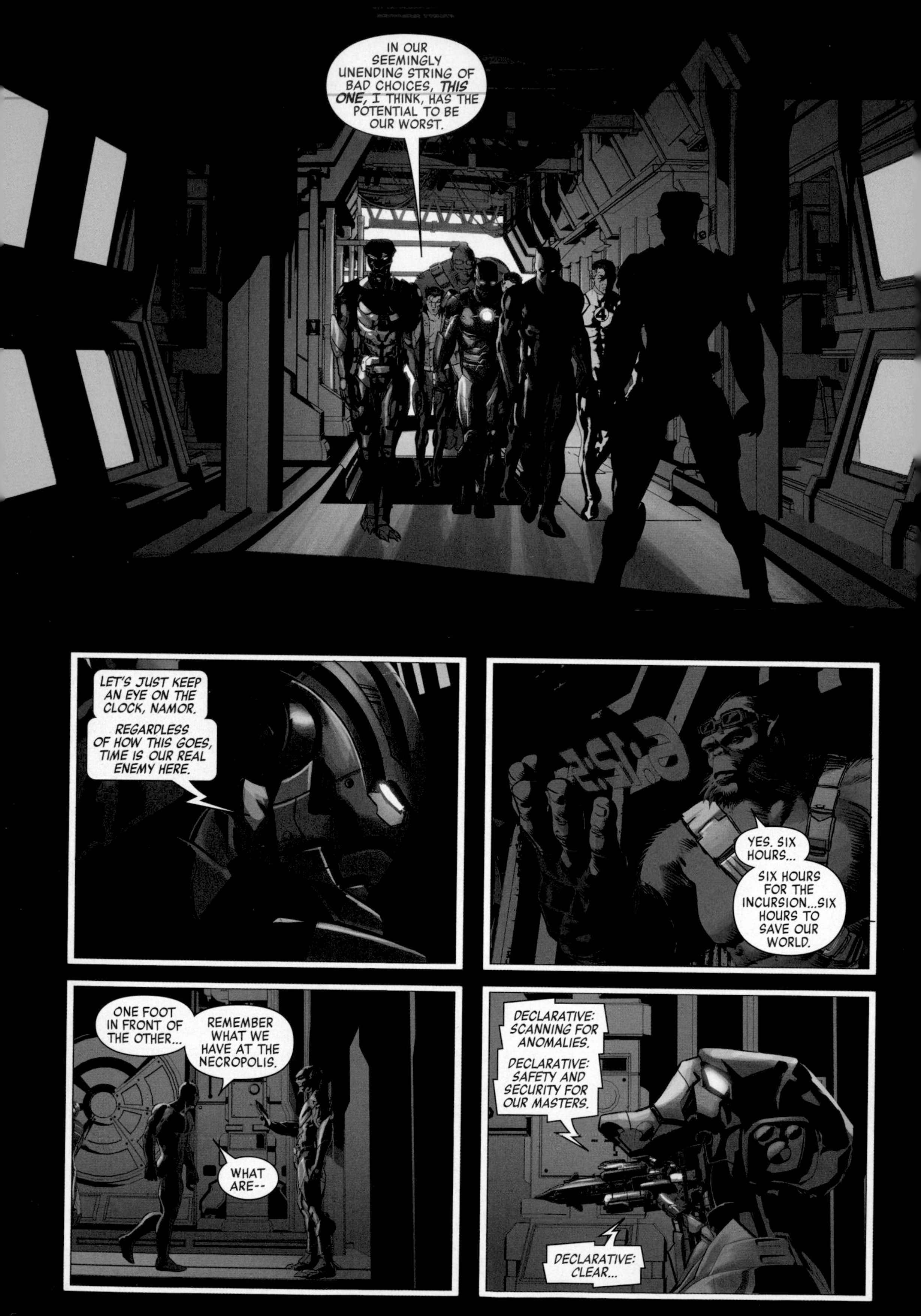
IN OUR SEEMINGLY UNENDING STRING OF BAD CHOICES, THIS ONE, I THINK, HAS THE POTENTIAL TO BE OUR WORST.
LET'S JUST KEEP AN EYE ON THE CLOCK, NAMOR.
REGARDLESS OF HOW THIS GOES, TIME IS OUR REAL ENEMY HERE.
YES. SIX HOURS...
SIX HOURS FOR THE INCURSION...SIX HOURS TO SAVE OUR WORLD.
ONE FOOT IN FRONT OF THE OTHER...
REMEMBER WHAT WE HAVE AT THE NECROPOLIS.
WHAT ARE--
DECLARATIVE: SCANNING FOR ANOMALIES.
DECLARATIVE: SAFETY AND SECURITY FOR OUR MASTERS.
DECLARATIVE: CLEAR...

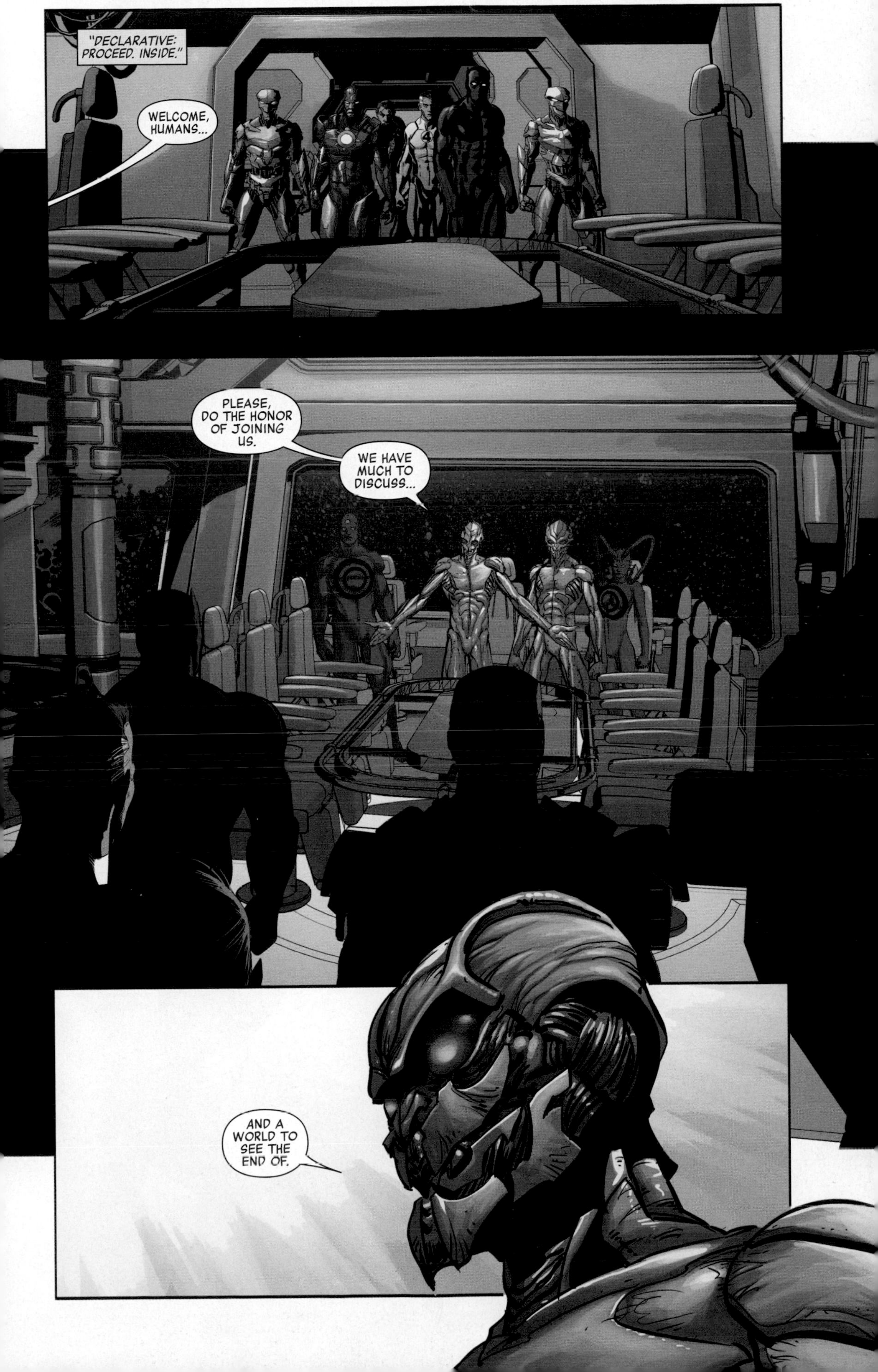
"DECLARATIVE: PROCEED. INSIDE."
WELCOME, HUMANS...
PLEASE, DO THE HONOR OF JOINING US.
WE HAVE MUCH TO DISCUSS...
AND A WORLD TO SEE THE END OF.

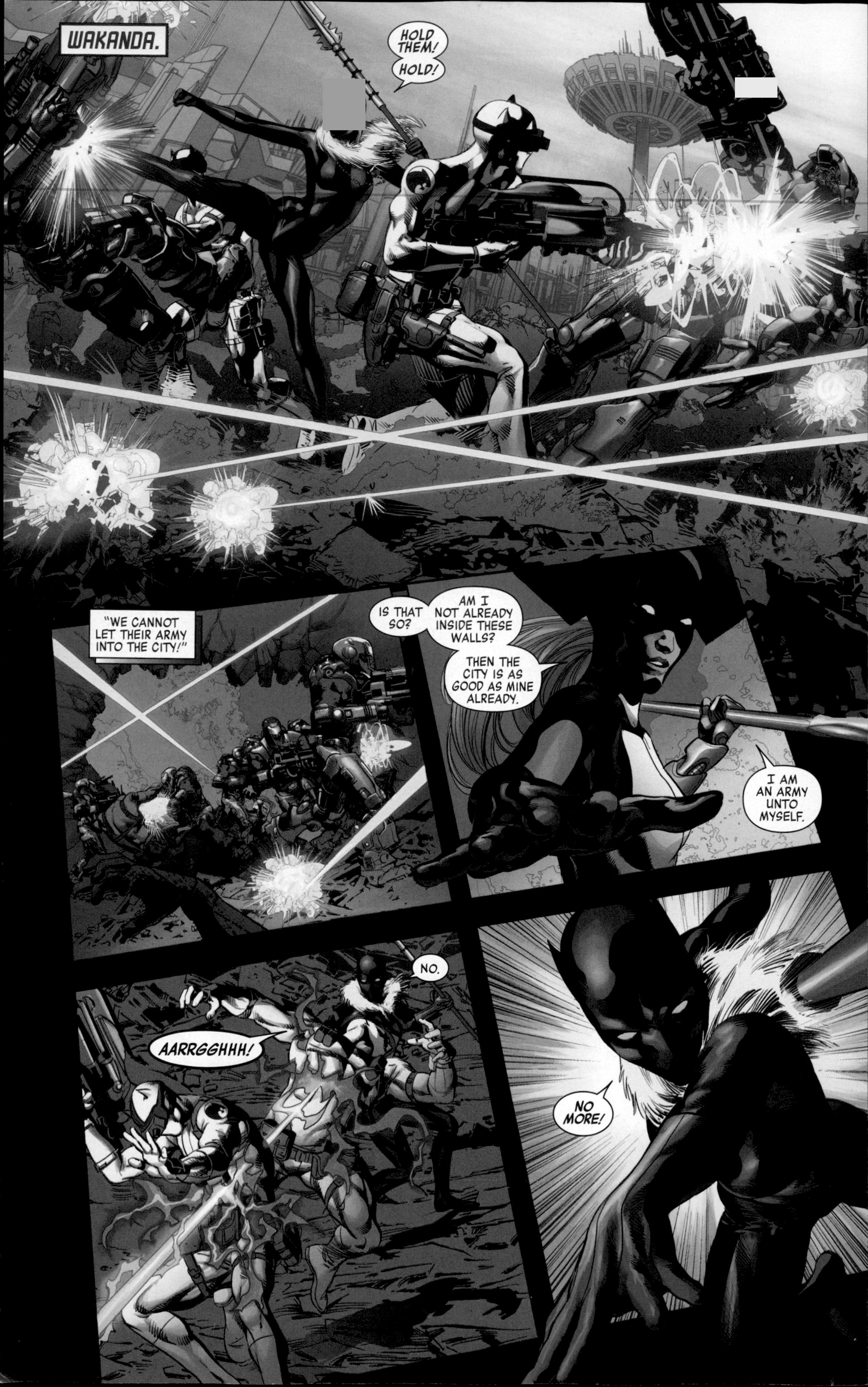
WAKANDA.
HOLD THEM!
HOLD!
"WE CANNOT LET THEIR ARMY INTO THE CITY!"
IS THAT SO?
AM I NOT ALREADY INSIDE THESE WALLS?
THEN THE CITY IS AS GOOD AS MINE ALREADY.
I AM AN ARMY UNTO MYSELF.
NO.
AARRGGHHH!
NO MORE!

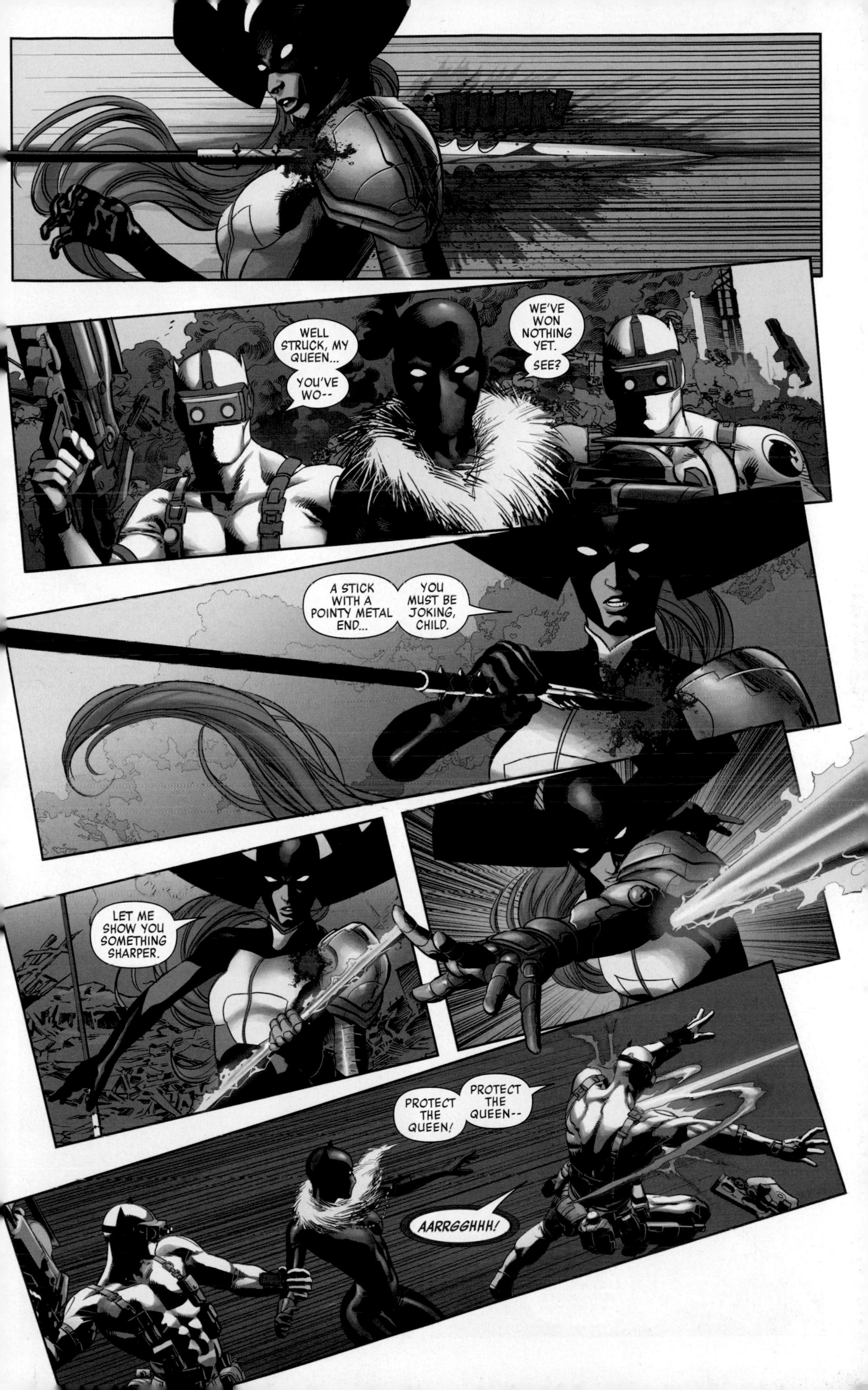
THUNK!
WELL STRUCK, MY QUEEN...
YOU'VE WO--
WE'VE WON NOTHING YET.
SEE?
A STICK WITH A POINTY METAL END...
YOU MUST BE JOKING, CHILD.
LET ME SHOW YOU SOMETHING SHARPER.
PROTECT THE QUEEN--
PROTECT THE QUEEN!
AARRGGHHH!

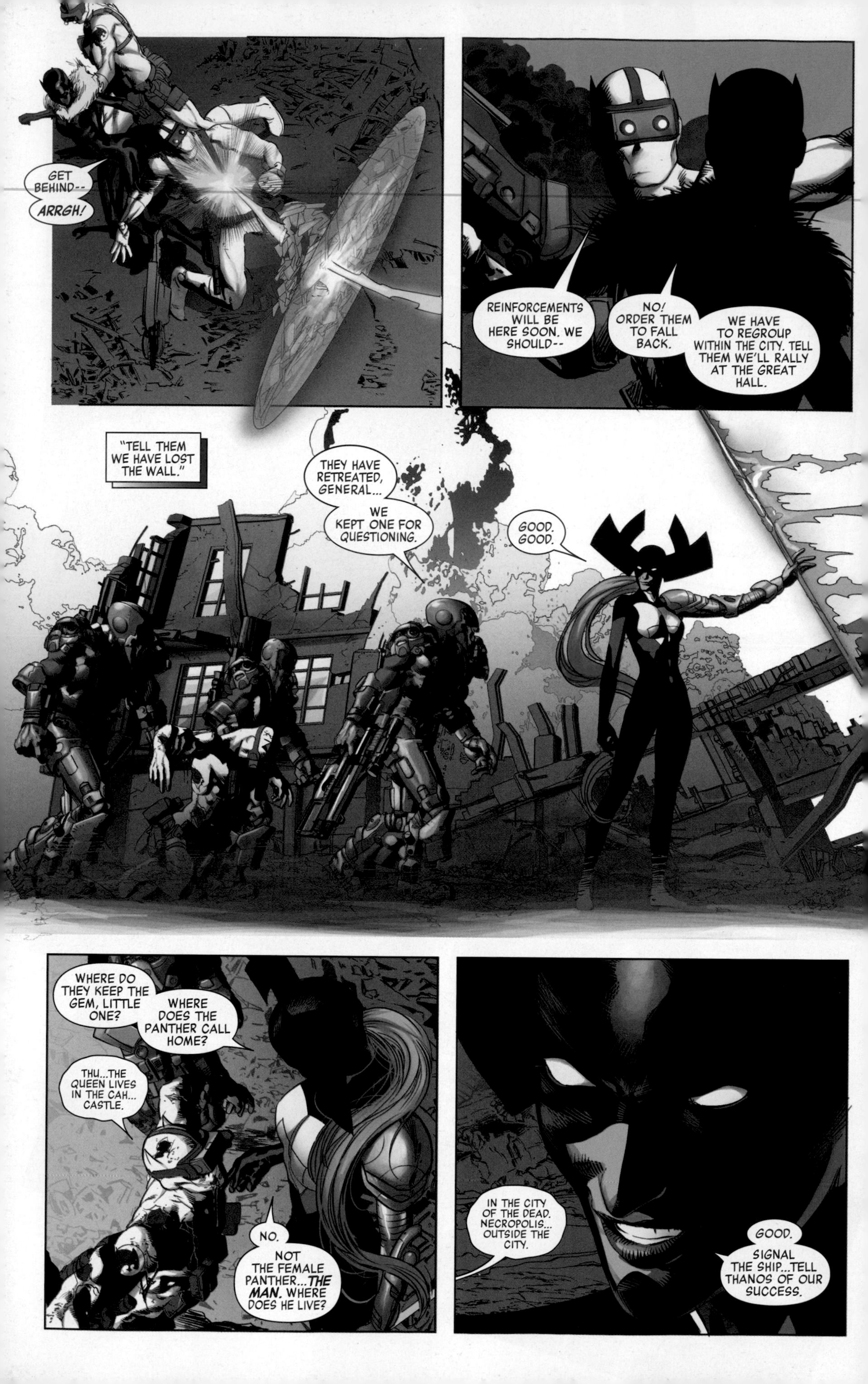
GET BEHIND--
ARRGH!
REINFORCEMENTS WILL BE HERE SOON. WE SHOULD--
NO! ORDER THEM TO FALL BACK.
WE HAVE TO REGROUP WITHIN THE CITY. TELL THEM WE'LL RALLY AT THE GREAT HALL.
"TELL THEM WE HAVE LOST THE WALL."
THEY HAVE RETREATED, GENERAL...
WE KEPT ONE FOR QUESTIONING.
GOOD. GOOD.
WHERE DO THEY KEEP THE GEM, LITTLE ONE?
WHERE DOES THE PANTHER CALL HOME?
THU...THE QUEEN LIVES IN THE CAH... CASTLE.
NO.
NOT THE FEMALE PANTHER...THE MAN. WHERE DOES HE LIVE?
IN THE CITY OF THE DEAD. NECROPOLIS... OUTSIDE THE CITY.
GOOD.
SIGNAL THE SHIP...TELL THANOS OF OUR SUCCESS.

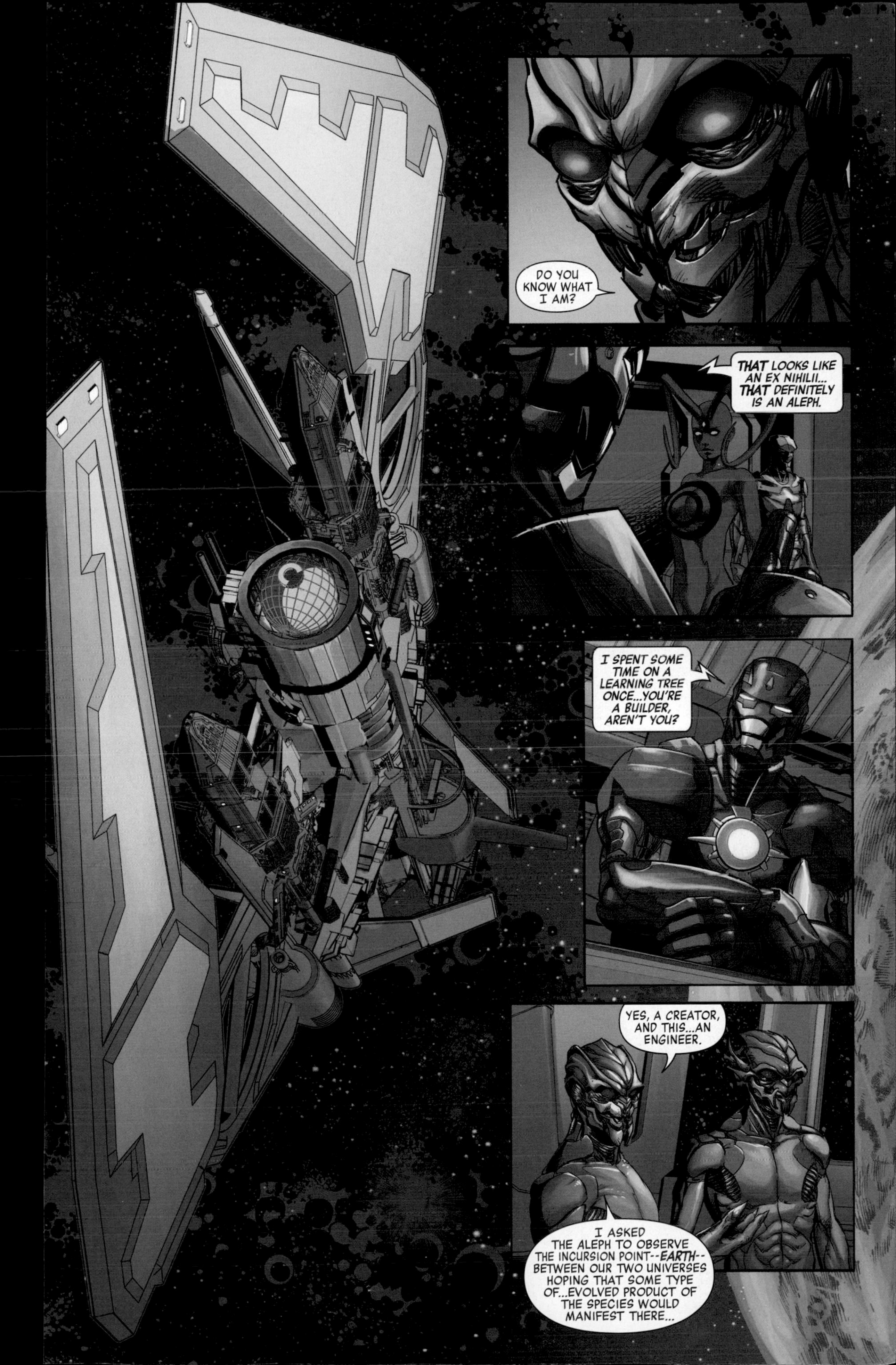
DO YOU KNOW WHAT I AM?
THAT LOOKS LIKE AN EX NIHILII... THAT DEFINITELY IS AN ALEPH.
I SPENT SOME TIME ON A LEARNING TREE ONCE...YOU'RE A BUILDER, AREN'T YOU?
YES, A CREATOR, AND THIS...AN ENGINEER.
I ASKED THE ALEPH TO OBSERVE THE INCURSION POINT--EARTH--BETWEEN OUR TWO UNIVERSES HOPING THAT SOME TYPE OF...EVOLVED PRODUCT OF THE SPECIES WOULD MANIFEST THERE...

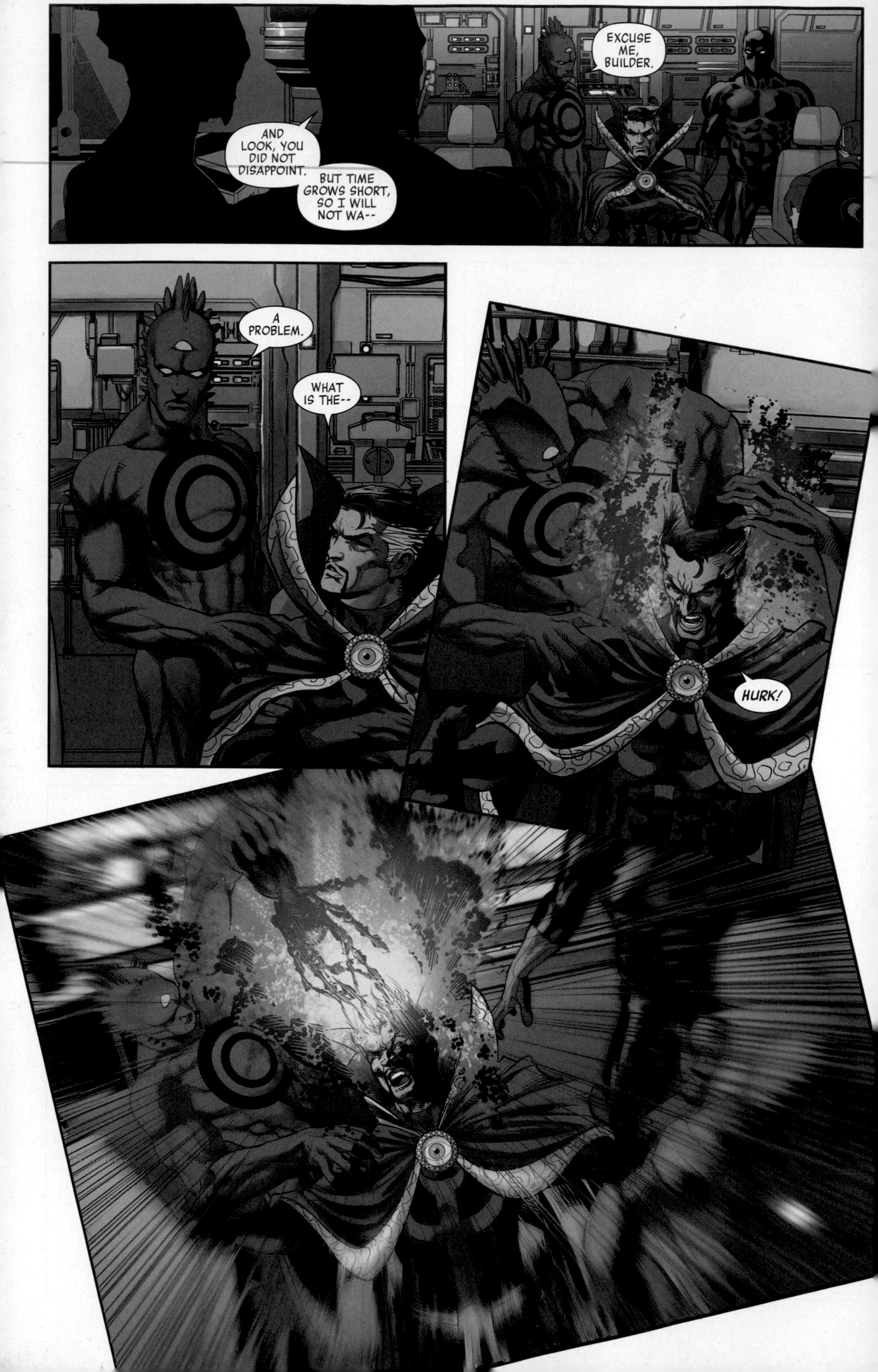
AND LOOK, YOU DID NOT DISAPPOINT.
BUT TIME GROWS SHORT, SO I WILL NOT WA--
EXCUSE ME, BUILDER.
A PROBLEM.
WHAT IS THE--
HURK!

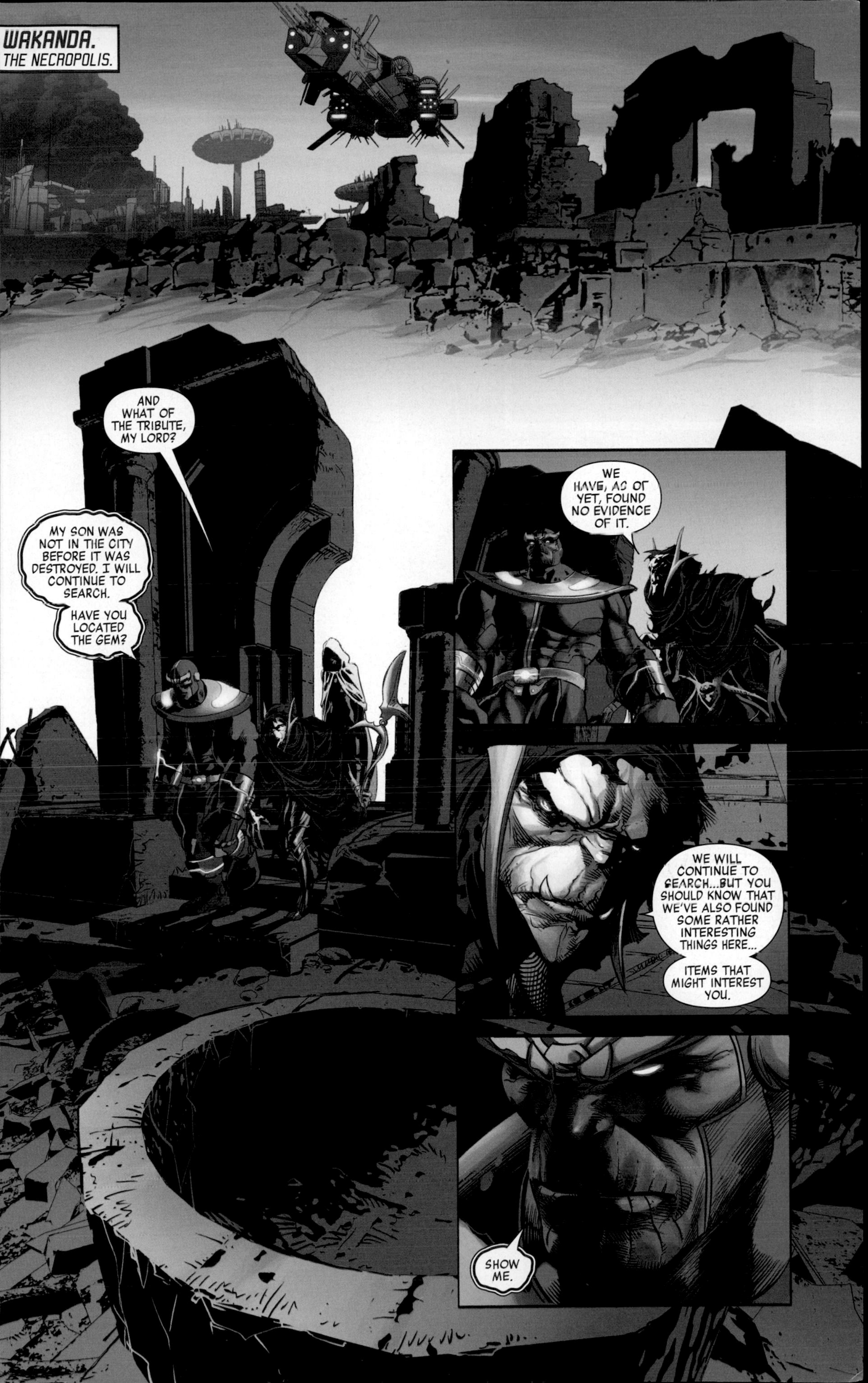
WAKANDA. THE NECROPOLIS.
AND WHAT OF THE TRIBUTE, MY LORD?
MY SON WAS NOT IN THE CITY BEFORE IT WAS DESTROYED. I WILL CONTINUE TO SEARCH.
HAVE YOU LOCATED THE GEM?
WE HAVE, AS OF YET, FOUND NO EVIDENCE OF IT.
WE WILL CONTINUE TO SEARCH...BUT YOU SHOULD KNOW THAT WE'VE ALSO FOUND SOME RATHER INTERESTING THINGS HERE...
ITEMS THAT MIGHT INTEREST YOU.
SHOW ME.

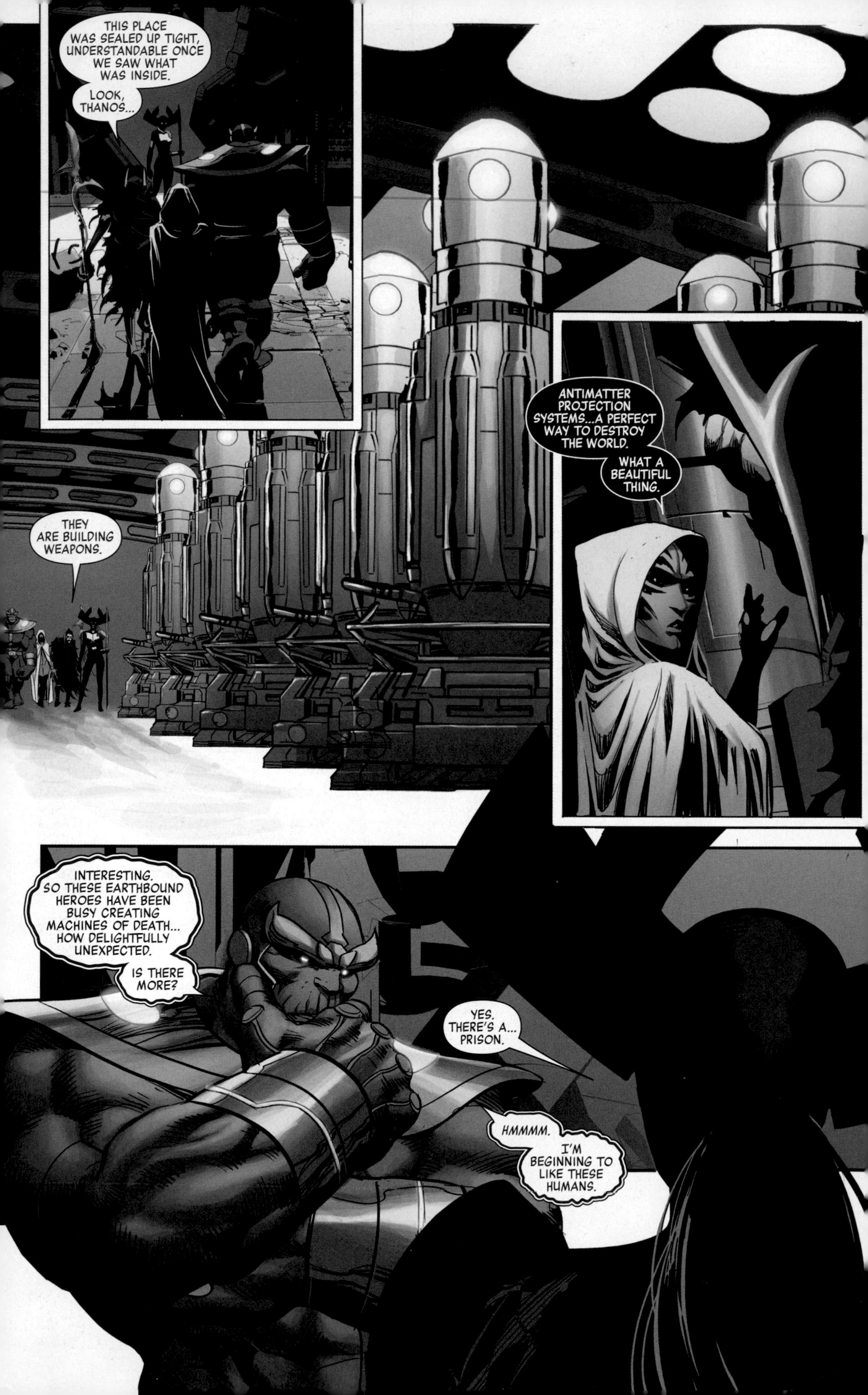

THIS PLACE WAS SEALED UP TIGHT, UNDERSTANDABLE ONCE WE SAW WHAT WAS INSIDE.
LOOK, THANOS...
THEY ARE BUILDING WEAPONS.
ANTIMATTER PROJECTION SYSTEMS...A PERFECT WAY TO DESTROY THE WORLD.
WHAT A BEAUTIFUL THING.
INTERESTING. SO THESE EARTHBOUND HEROES HAVE BEEN BUSY CREATING MACHINES OF DEATH... HOW DELIGHTFULLY UNEXPECTED.
IS THERE MORE?
YES. THERE'S A... PRISON.
HMMMM.
I'M BEGINNING TO LIKE THESE HUMANS.

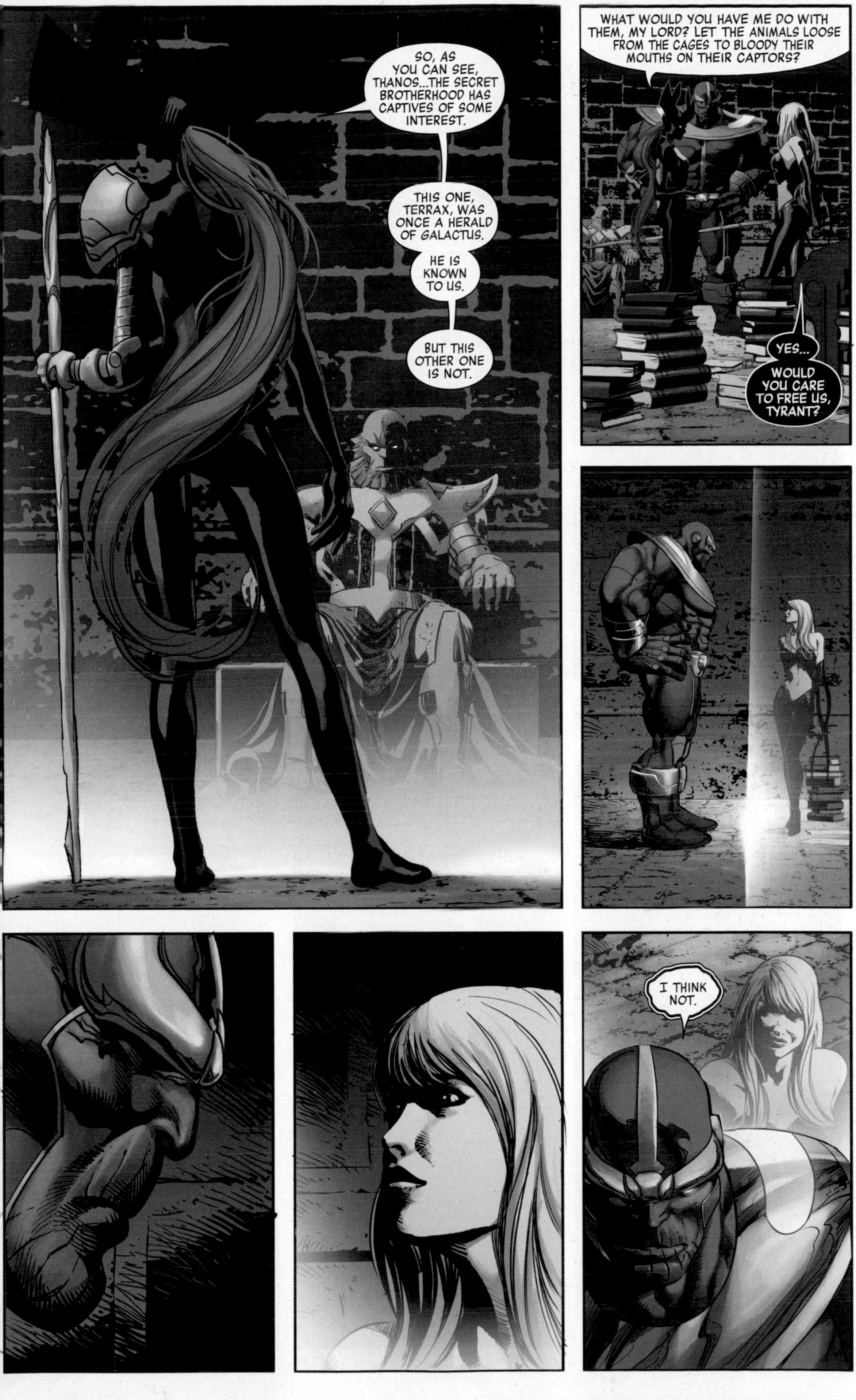
SO, AS YOU CAN SEE, THANOS...THE SECRET BROTHERHOOD HAS CAPTIVES OF SOME INTEREST.
THIS ONE, TERRAX, WAS ONCE A HERALD OF GALACTUS.
HE IS KNOWN TO US.
BUT THIS OTHER ONE IS NOT.
WHAT WOULD YOU HAVE ME DO WITH THEM, MY LORD? LET THE ANIMALS LOOSE FROM THE CAGES TO BLOODY THEIR MOUTHS ON THEIR CAPTORS?
YES...
WOULD YOU CARE TO FREE US, TYRANT?
I THINK NOT.

A HIDDEN INHUMAN TRIBE. THE GEM IS LOST. LOCATED IN THE GREAT SOUTHERN CREVICE OF GREENLAND. ALL THESE MEN ARE LIARS AND KINGS. THE SON IS THERE. THE SON OF THANOS IS IN LOR.

AH, A MIND WEB, THE INFECTIOUS NETWORKED REMNANTS OF A WHISPERER--*ARTIFACTING* LEFTOVER FROM A *POSSESSION*.

I CAN TELL YOU THE EFFECTS WILL PASS. THERE ARE NO WHISPERERS IN THIS UNIVERSE, BUT IN THE PAST, WE HAVE STUDIED THEM IN YOURS.

EXCUSE ME... I HAVE TO ASK, WHERE ARE YOU FROM? YOU KNOW ABOUT THIS THING, SO DID YOUR SPECIES BEGIN IN OUR UNIVERSE?

WHERE ANYONE BEGINS IS INCONSEQUENTIAL, HUMAN...IT'S WHERE YOU END UP THAT MATTERS.

FOR US, IT WAS THE ENTIRE MULTIVERSE.

WAS?

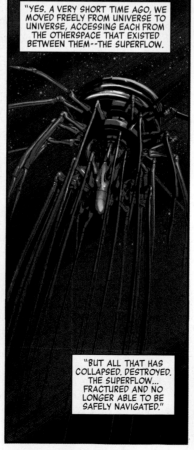

"YES. A VERY SHORT TIME AGO, WE MOVED FREELY FROM UNIVERSE TO UNIVERSE, ACCESSING EACH FROM THE OTHERSPACE THAT EXISTED BETWEEN THEM--THE SUPERFLOW.

"BUT ALL THAT HAS COLLAPSED. DESTROYED. THE SUPERFLOW... FRACTURED AND NO LONGER ABLE TO BE SAFELY NAVIGATED."

THE HARBINGER OF THE END OF EVERYTHING.

WHICH MY PEOPLE HAVE PLEDGED TO PREVENT. *WHICH IS WHY WE ARE SPEAKING...*

...AS RIGHT NOW, A GROUP OF...ENTITIES, SUCH AS YOURSELF, HAVE JUST DEFEATED THE BUILDERS EXISTING IN YOUR UNIVERSE.

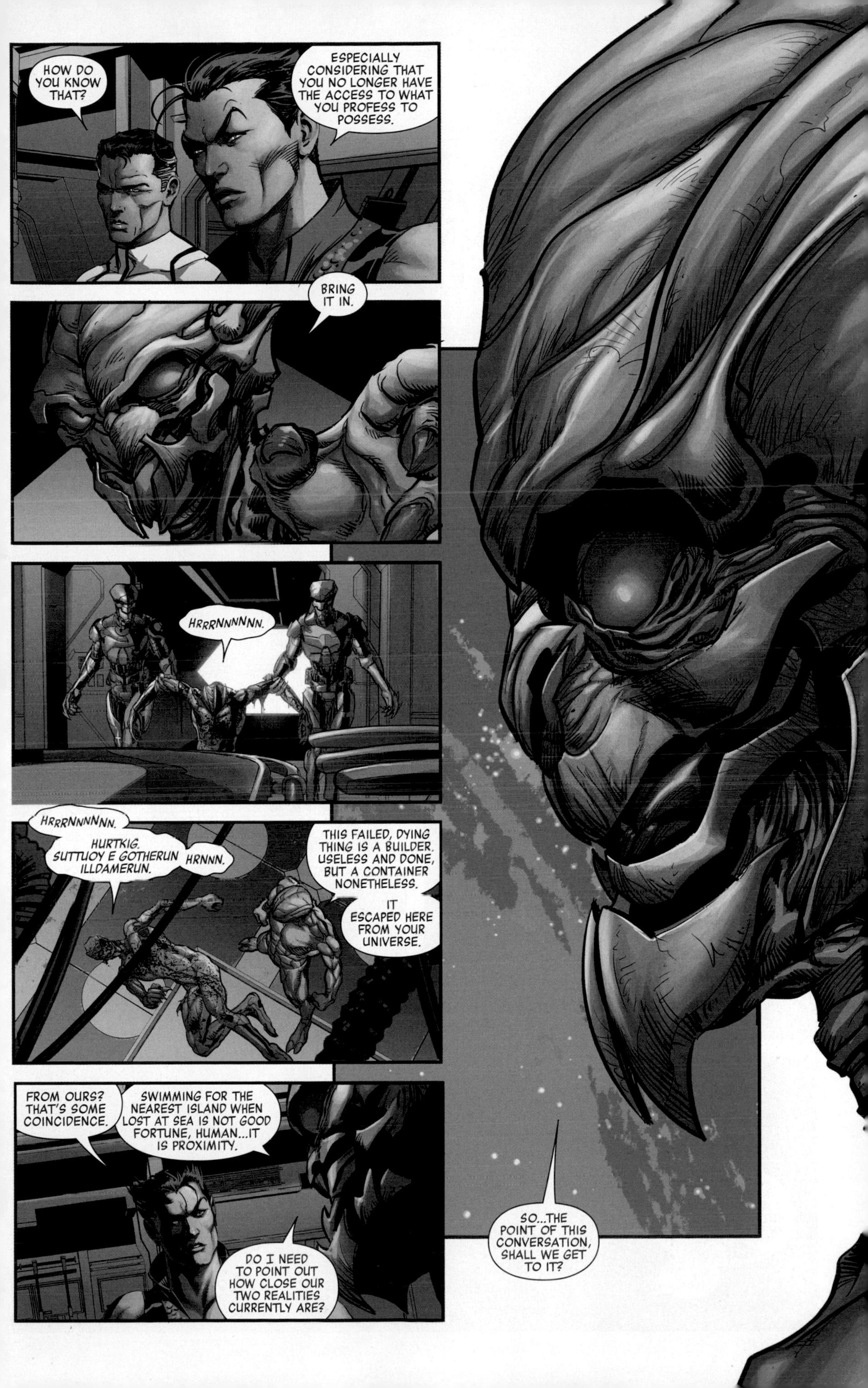
HOW DO YOU KNOW THAT?
ESPECIALLY CONSIDERING THAT YOU NO LONGER HAVE THE ACCESS TO WHAT YOU PROFESS TO POSSESS.
BRING IT IN.
HRRRNNNNNN.
HRRRNNNNNN.
HURTKIG. SUTTUOY E GOTHERUN ILLDAMERUN.
HRNNN.
THIS FAILED, DYING THING IS A BUILDER. USELESS AND DONE, BUT A CONTAINER NONETHELESS.
IT ESCAPED HERE FROM YOUR UNIVERSE.
FROM OURS? THAT'S SOME COINCIDENCE.
SWIMMING FOR THE NEAREST ISLAND WHEN LOST AT SEA IS NOT GOOD FORTUNE, HUMAN...IT IS PROXIMITY.
DO I NEED TO POINT OUT HOW CLOSE OUR TWO REALITIES CURRENTLY ARE?
SO...THE POINT OF THIS CONVERSATION, SHALL WE GET TO IT?

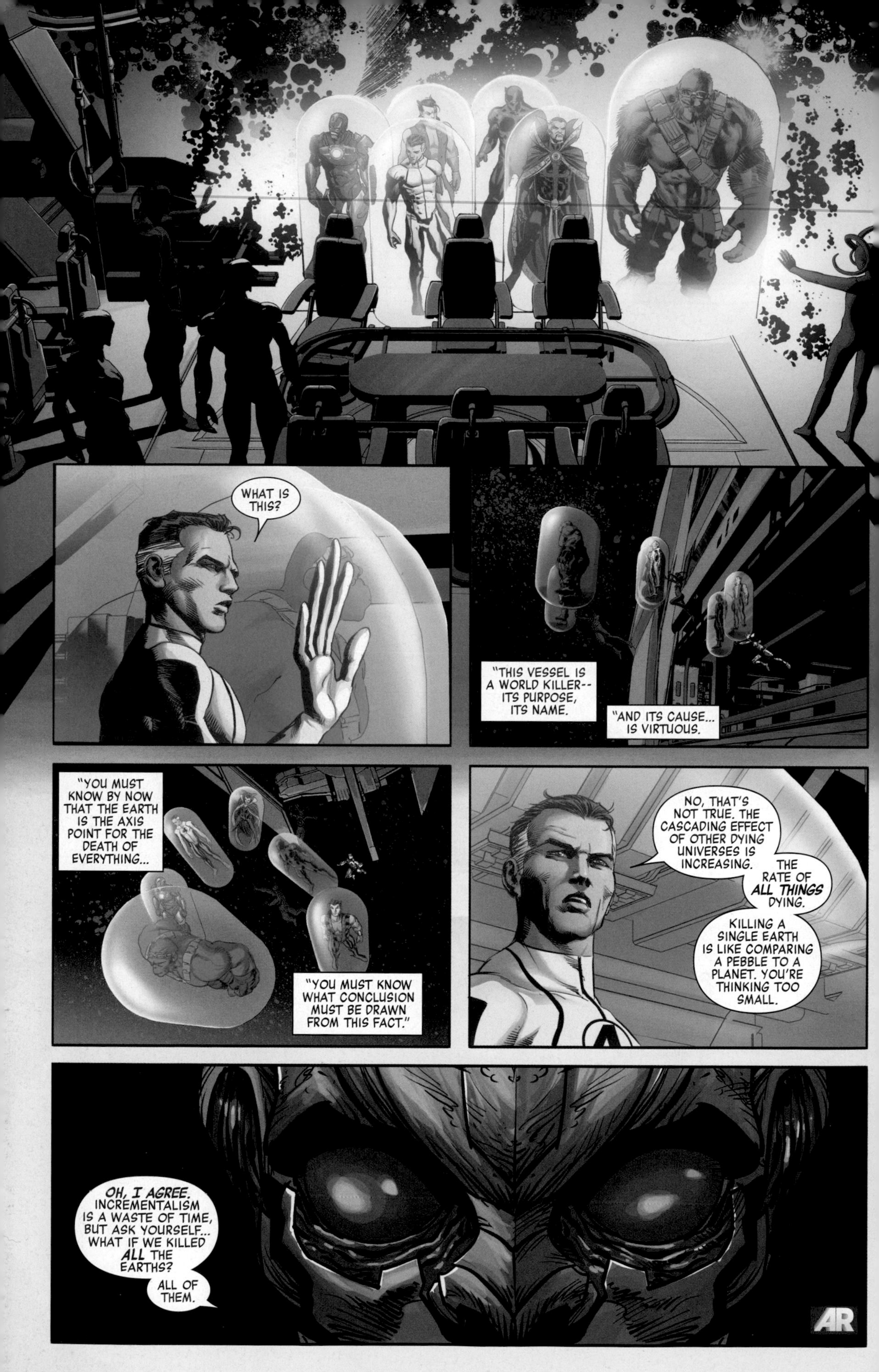

WHAT IS THIS?
"THIS VESSEL IS A WORLD KILLER-- ITS PURPOSE, ITS NAME.
"AND ITS CAUSE... IS VIRTUOUS.
"YOU MUST KNOW BY NOW THAT THE EARTH IS THE AXIS POINT FOR THE DEATH OF EVERYTHING...
"YOU MUST KNOW WHAT CONCLUSION MUST BE DRAWN FROM THIS FACT."
NO, THAT'S NOT TRUE. THE CASCADING EFFECT OF OTHER DYING UNIVERSES IS INCREASING.
THE RATE OF ALL THINGS DYING.
KILLING A SINGLE EARTH IS LIKE COMPARING A PEBBLE TO A PLANET. YOU'RE THINKING TOO SMALL.
OH, I AGREE. INCREMENTALISM IS A WASTE OF TIME, BUT ASK YOURSELF... WHAT IF WE KILLED ALL THE EARTHS?
ALL OF THEM.
AR

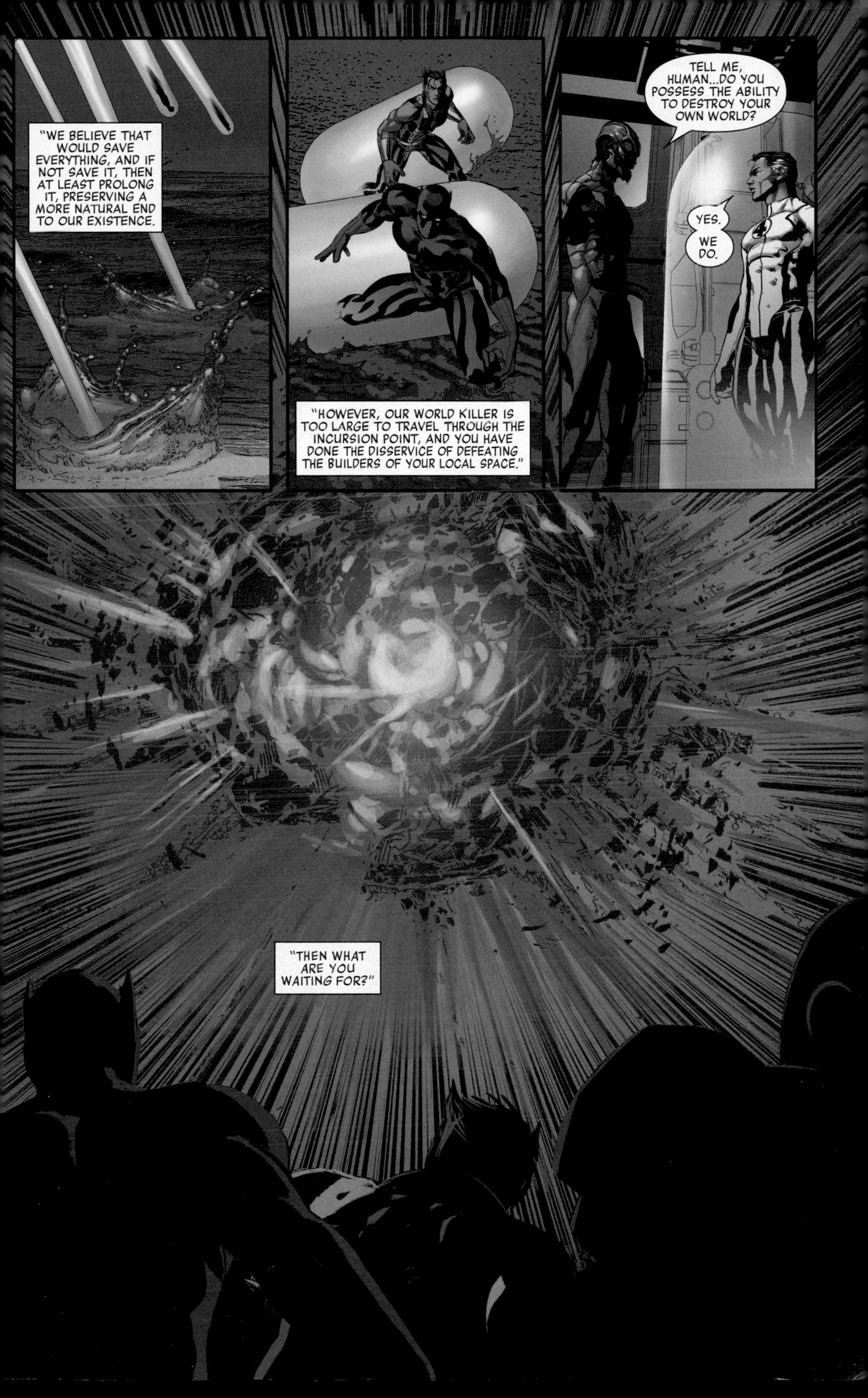
"WE BELIEVE THAT WOULD SAVE EVERYTHING, AND IF NOT SAVE IT, THEN AT LEAST PROLONG IT, PRESERVING A MORE NATURAL END TO OUR EXISTENCE.
"HOWEVER, OUR WORLD KILLER IS TOO LARGE TO TRAVEL THROUGH THE INCURSION POINT, AND YOU HAVE DONE THE DISSERVICE OF DEFEATING THE BUILDERS OF YOUR LOCAL SPACE."
TELL ME, HUMAN...DO YOU POSSESS THE ABILITY TO DESTROY YOUR OWN WORLD?
YES.
WE DO.
"THEN WHAT ARE YOU WAITING FOR?"

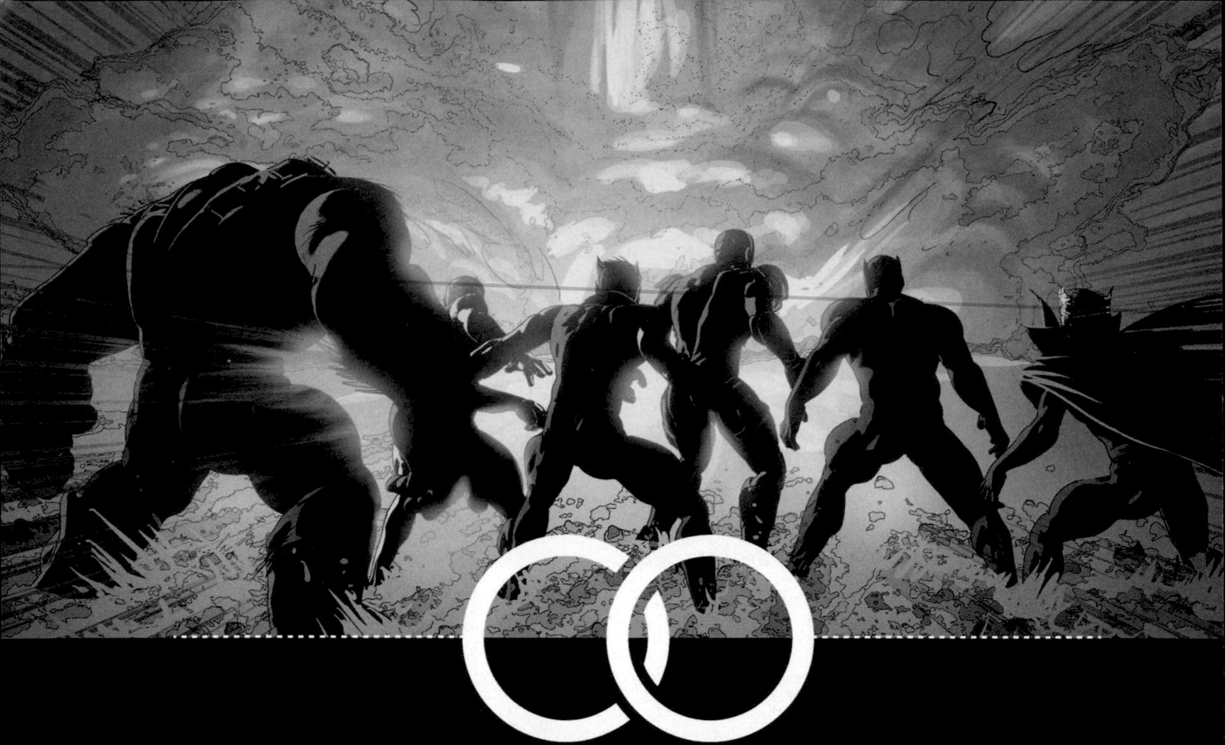

PREVIOUSLY IN INFINITY

ON AN ALTERNATE EARTH AN EVENT OCCURRED THAT CAUSED THE EARLY DEATH OF A UNIVERSE. THIS CAUSED A TINY CONTRACTION, SMASHING TWO UNIVERSES TOGETHER AT THE INCURSION POINT OF THE INITIAL EVENT.
EACH INCURSION POINT LASTS EIGHT HOURS, AFTER WHICH EITHER BOTH WORLDS ARE DESTROYED, OR ONLY ONE EARTH IS SACRIFICED, SPARING BOTH UNIVERSES.
BLACK SWAN, YOU JUMPED HERE FROM ANOTHER WORLD...YOU HAD SOME KIND OF DEVICE, AND YOU DESTROYED THE PLANET YOU CAME FROM.
THE TURN OF THE WHEEL BREAKS HOPE, CRUSHES WHAT MAKES US DECENT AND STEALS WHAT HONOR REMAINS.
WE WILL TRY EVERY GOOD AND RIGHTEOUS SOLUTION WE CAN.
AND IF THOSE DON'T WORK?
THEN WE WILL HAVE TO LEARN HOW TO DESTROY A WORLD.
LOOK AT WHAT THE WORLD HAS MADE OF US BOTH. ANTI-MATTER INJECTION SYSTEMS MEANT TO DESTROY WORLDS. IS IT GOING TO BE ENOUGH?
INFINITE WORLDS, T'CHALLA. YOU KNOW IT ISN'T.
WAKANDA CANNOT WIN A WAR WITH ATLANTIS. THE QUEEN--YOUR SISTER--HAS ENEMIES. I WILL OFFER FAVORABLE TERMS, AND IN EXCHANGE I ASK ONLY FOR A CESSATION OF HOSTILITIES.
MAKE YOUR OFFER THROUGH THE NORMAL CHANNELS. IF I CHOOSE TO FIGHT FOR IT IN THE COUNCIL, IT'S BEST IF THE IDEA DOESN'T ORIGINATE WITH ME.
I LIKE THIS PLAN. AND WHAT FOLLOWS SUCH DEVIOUS ACTIONS, BROTHER?
AH! VERY GOOD...
"...I'LL MAKE READY THE BOMB!"

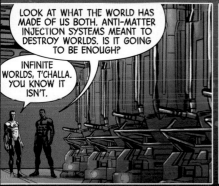

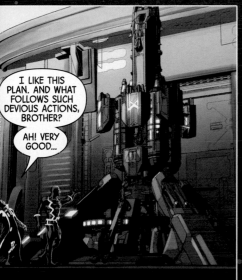

ENDGAME

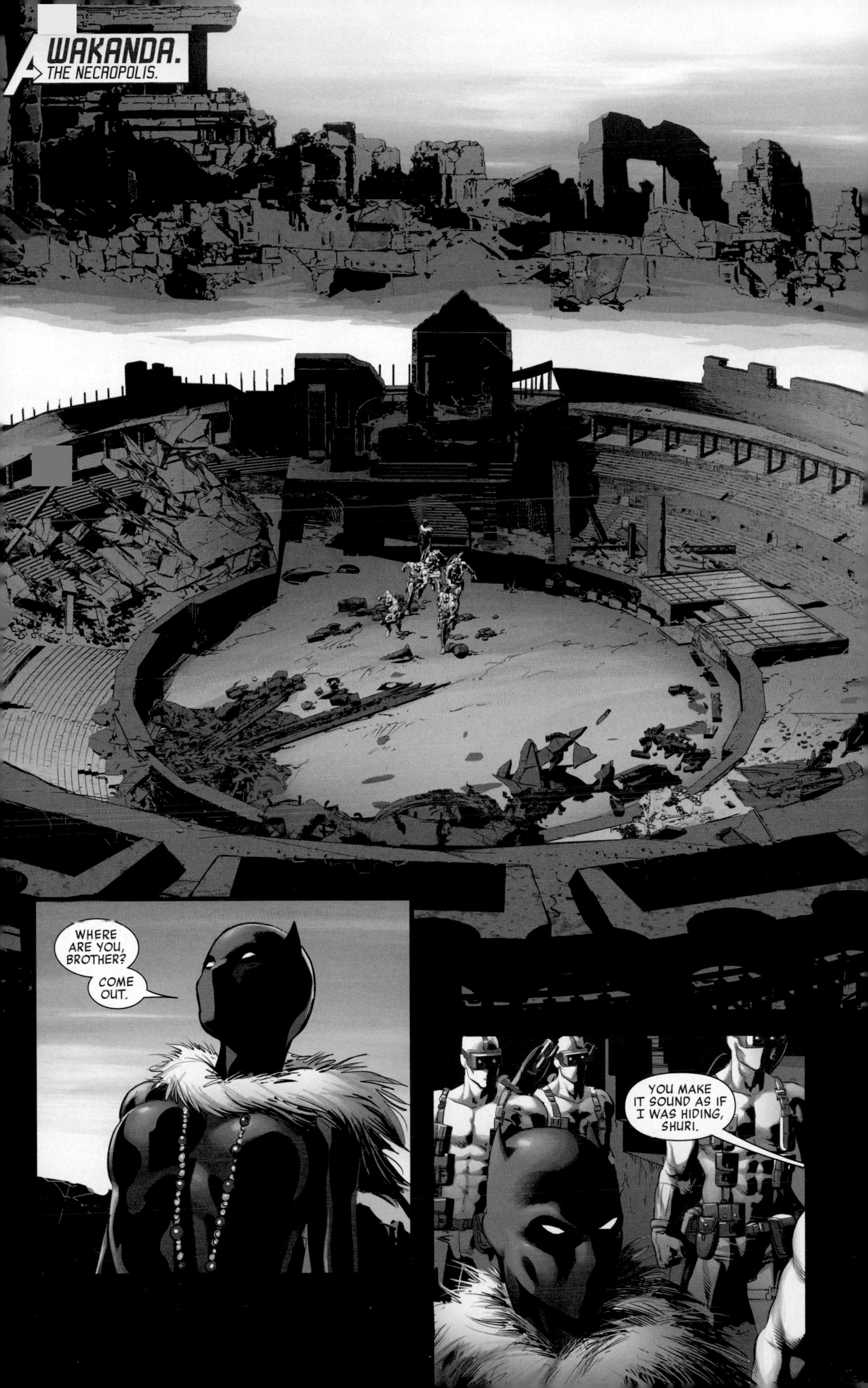
WAKANDA.
THE NECROPOLIS.
WHERE ARE YOU, BROTHER?
COME OUT.
YOU MAKE IT SOUND AS IF I WAS HIDING, SHURI.

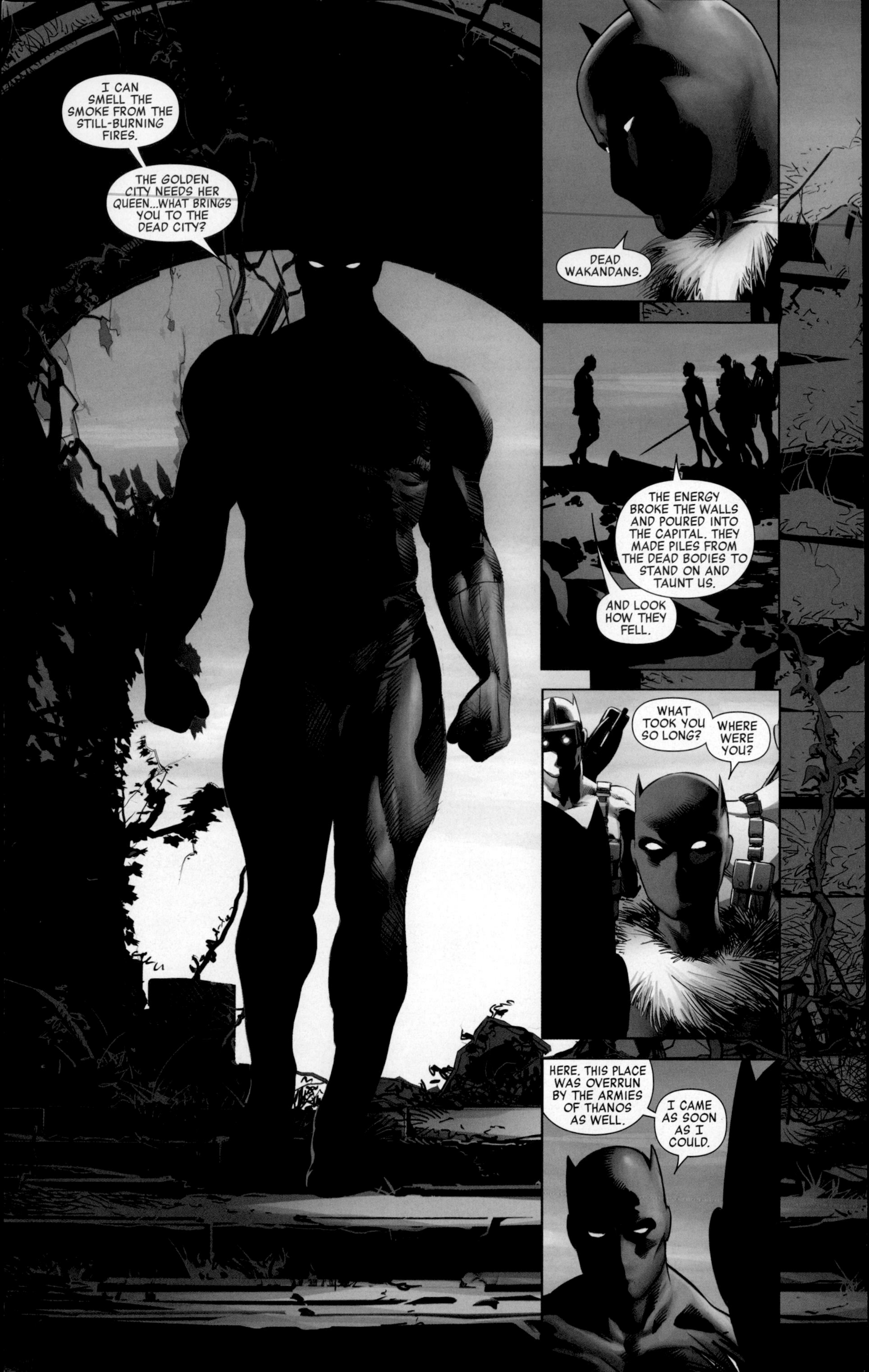
I CAN SMELL THE SMOKE FROM THE STILL-BURNING FIRES.
THE GOLDEN CITY NEEDS HER QUEEN...WHAT BRINGS YOU TO THE DEAD CITY?
DEAD WAKANDANS.
THE ENERGY BROKE THE WALLS AND POURED INTO THE CAPITAL. THEY MADE PILES FROM THE DEAD BODIES TO STAND ON AND TAUNT US.
AND LOOK HOW THEY FELL.
WHAT TOOK YOU SO LONG?
WHERE WERE YOU?
HERE. THIS PLACE WAS OVERRUN BY THE ARMIES OF THANOS AS WELL.
I CAME AS SOON AS I COULD.

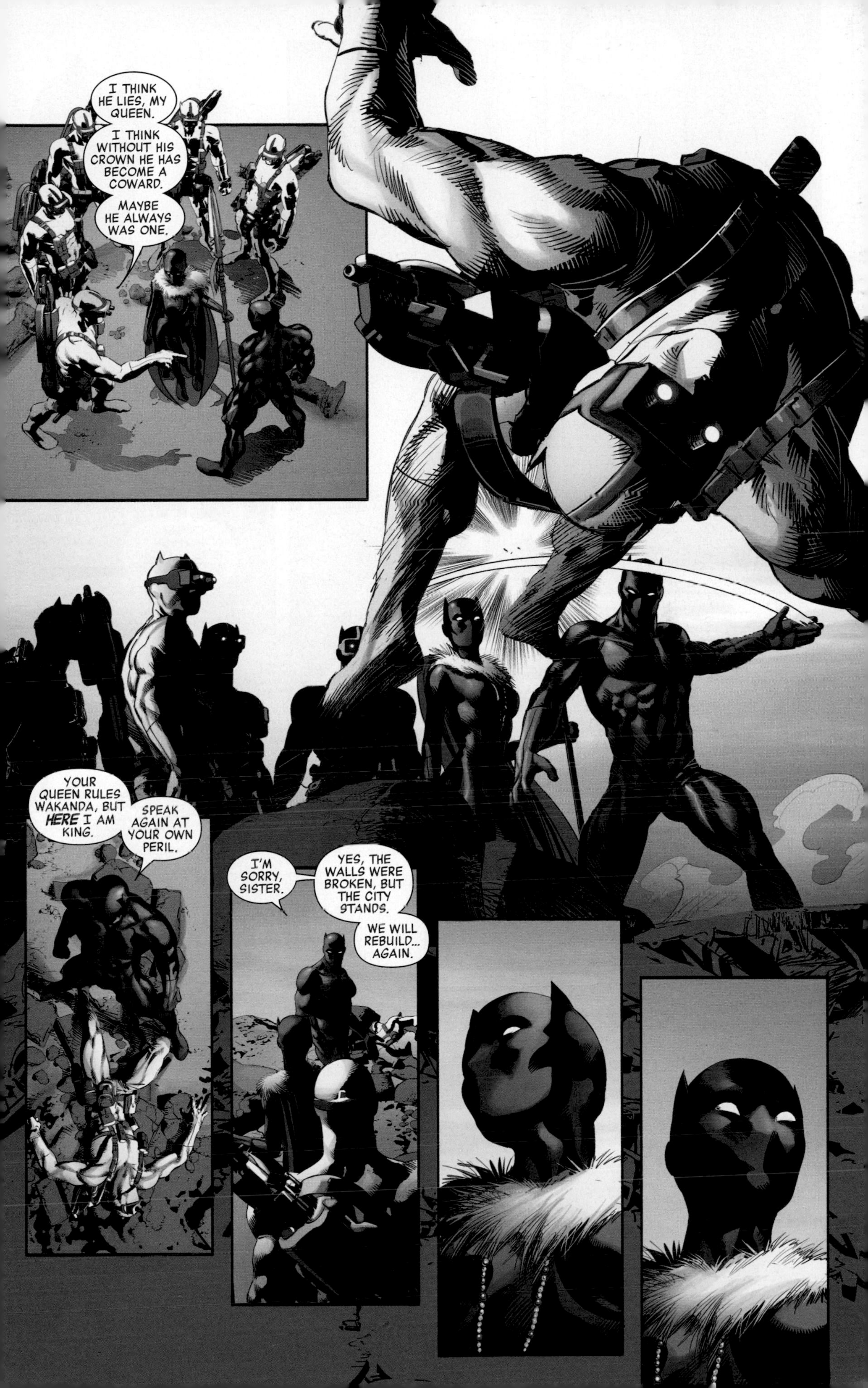
I THINK HE LIES, MY QUEEN.
I THINK WITHOUT HIS CROWN HE HAS BECOME A COWARD.
MAYBE HE ALWAYS WAS ONE.
YOUR QUEEN RULES WAKANDA, BUT HERE I AM KING.
SPEAK AGAIN AT YOUR OWN PERIL.
I'M SORRY, SISTER.
YES, THE WALLS WERE BROKEN, BUT THE CITY STANDS.
WE WILL REBUILD... AGAIN.

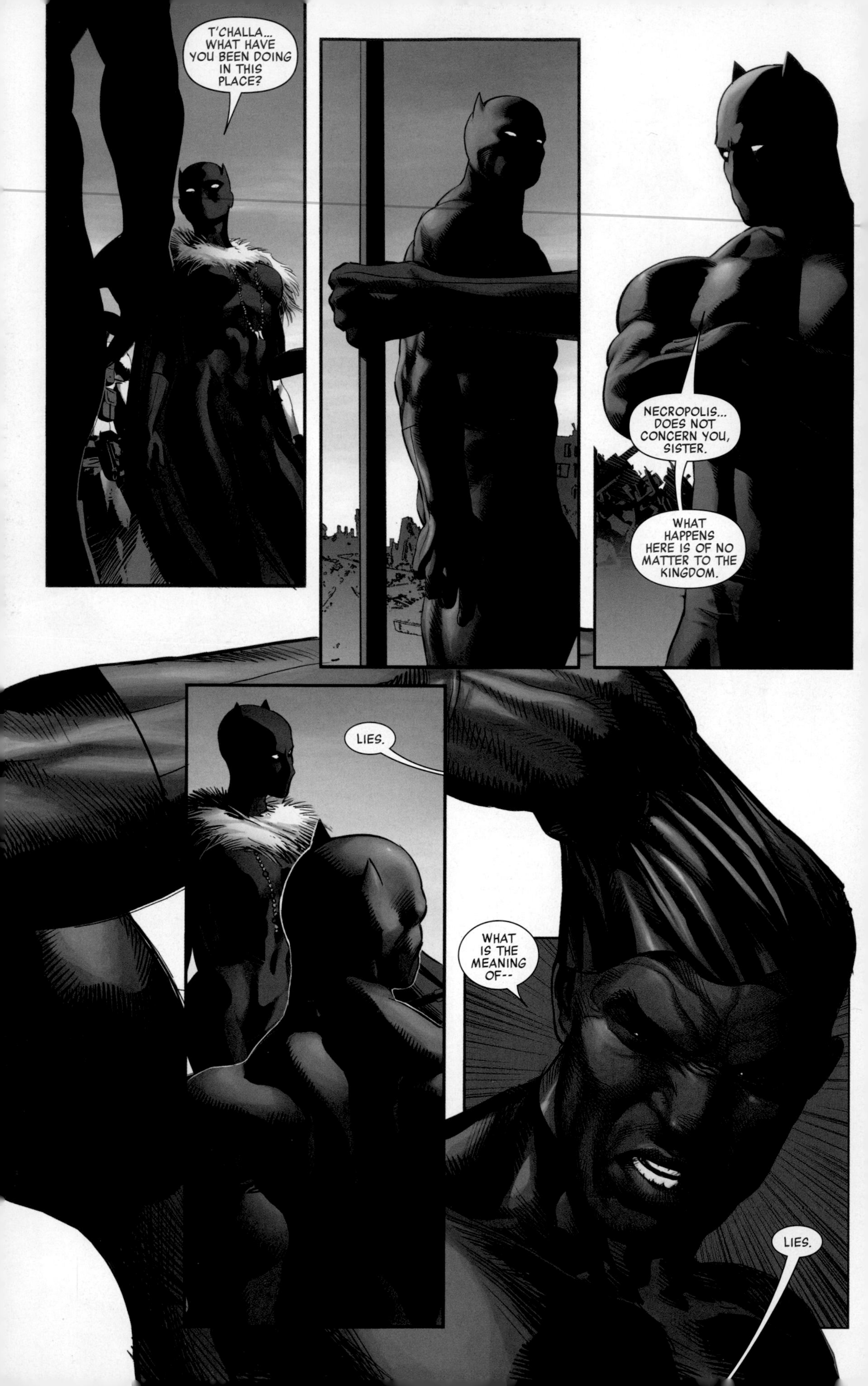
T'CHALLA... WHAT HAVE YOU BEEN DOING IN THIS PLACE?
NECROPOLIS... DOES NOT CONCERN YOU, SISTER.
WHAT HAPPENS HERE IS OF NO MATTER TO THE KINGDOM.
LIES.
WHAT IS THE MEANING OF--
LIES.

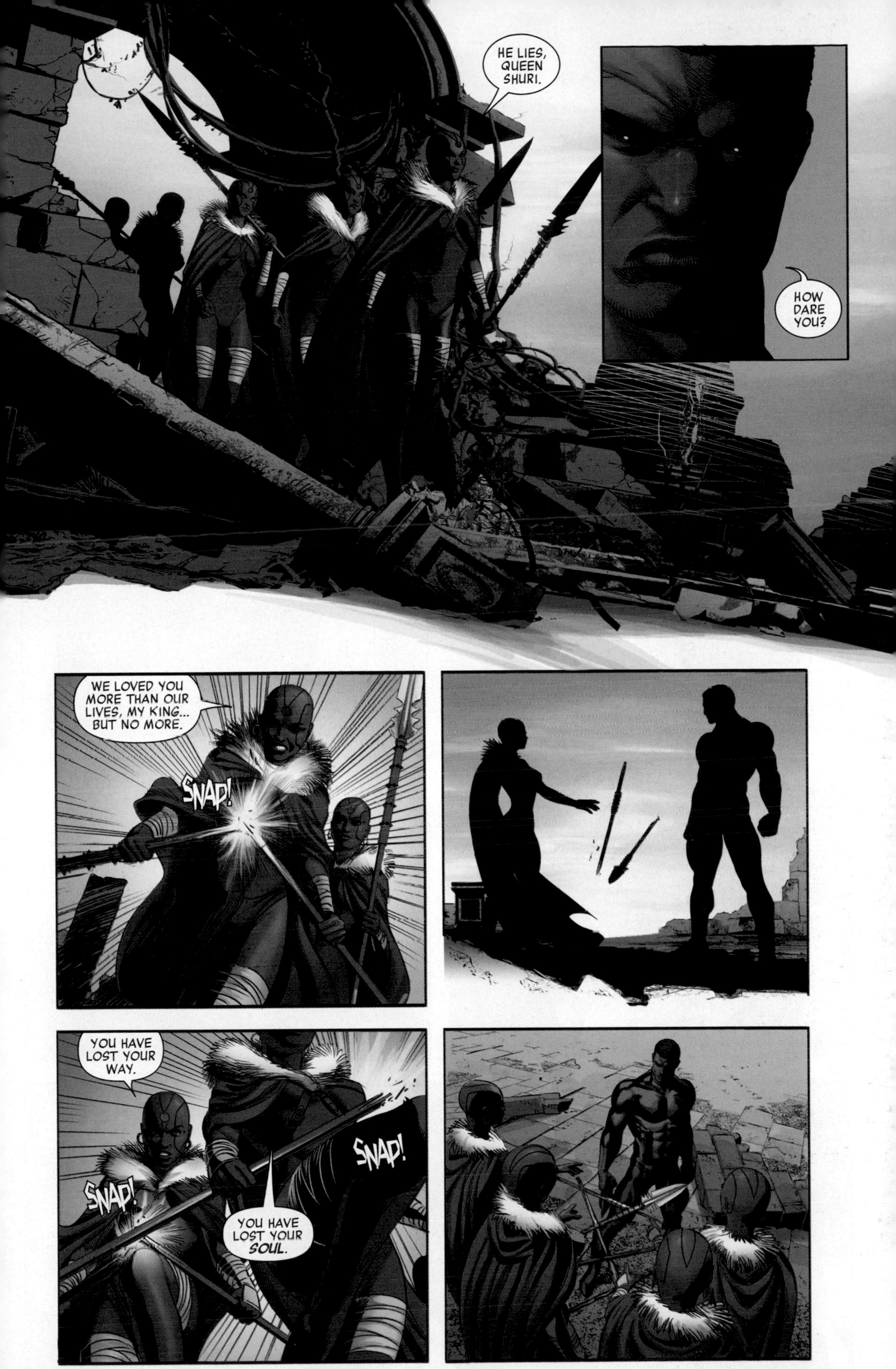
HE LIES, QUEEN SHURI.
HOW DARE YOU?
WE LOVED YOU MORE THAN OUR LIVES, MY KING... BUT NO MORE.
SNAP!
YOU HAVE LOST YOUR WAY.
SNAP!
SNAP!
YOU HAVE LOST YOUR SOUL.

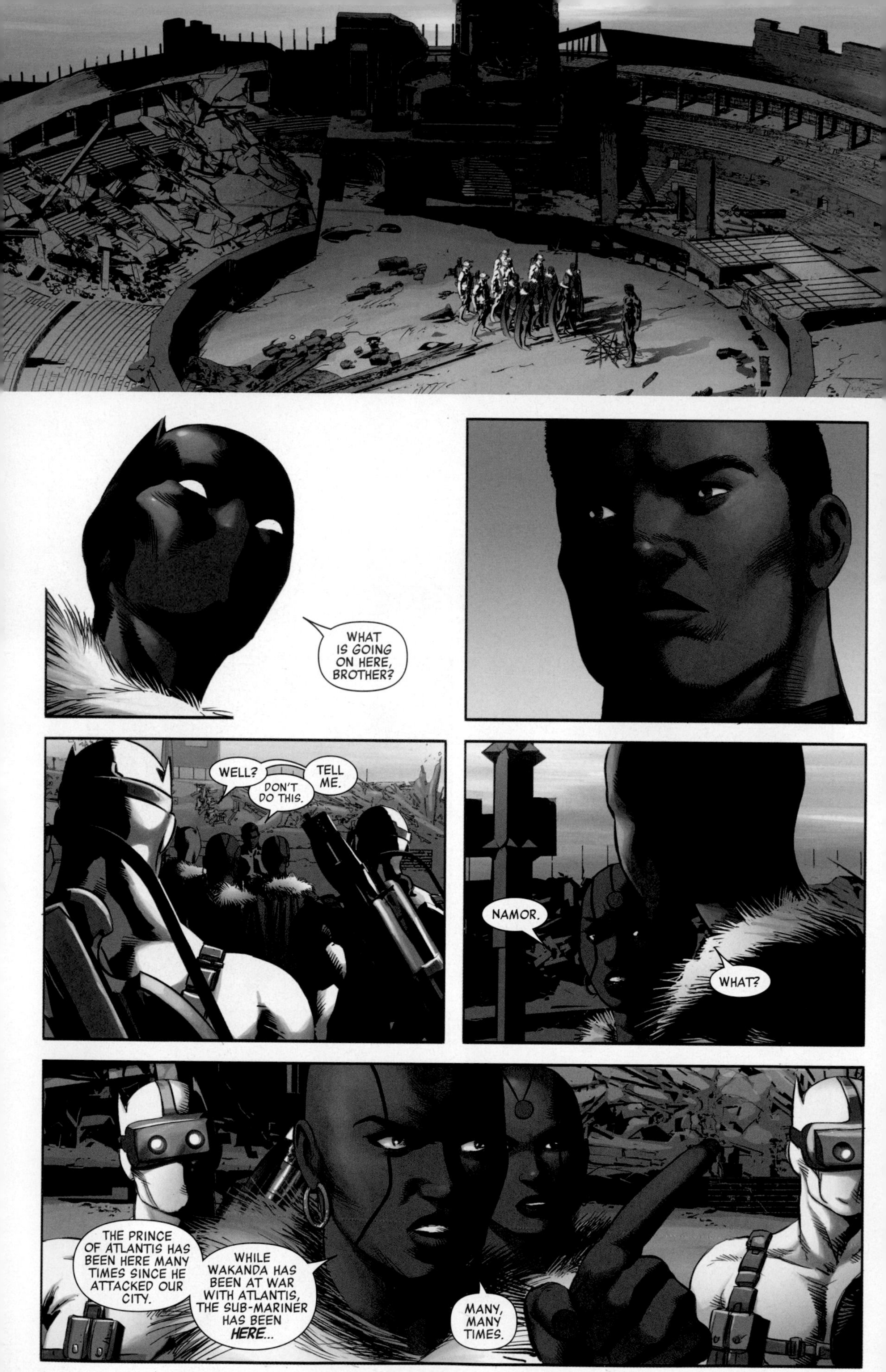

WHAT IS GOING ON HERE, BROTHER?
WELL?
DON'T DO THIS.
TELL ME.
NAMOR.
WHAT?
THE PRINCE OF ATLANTIS HAS BEEN HERE MANY TIMES SINCE HE ATTACKED OUR CITY.
WHILE WAKANDA HAS BEEN AT WAR WITH ATLANTIS, THE SUB-MARINER HAS BEEN HERE...
MANY, MANY TIMES.

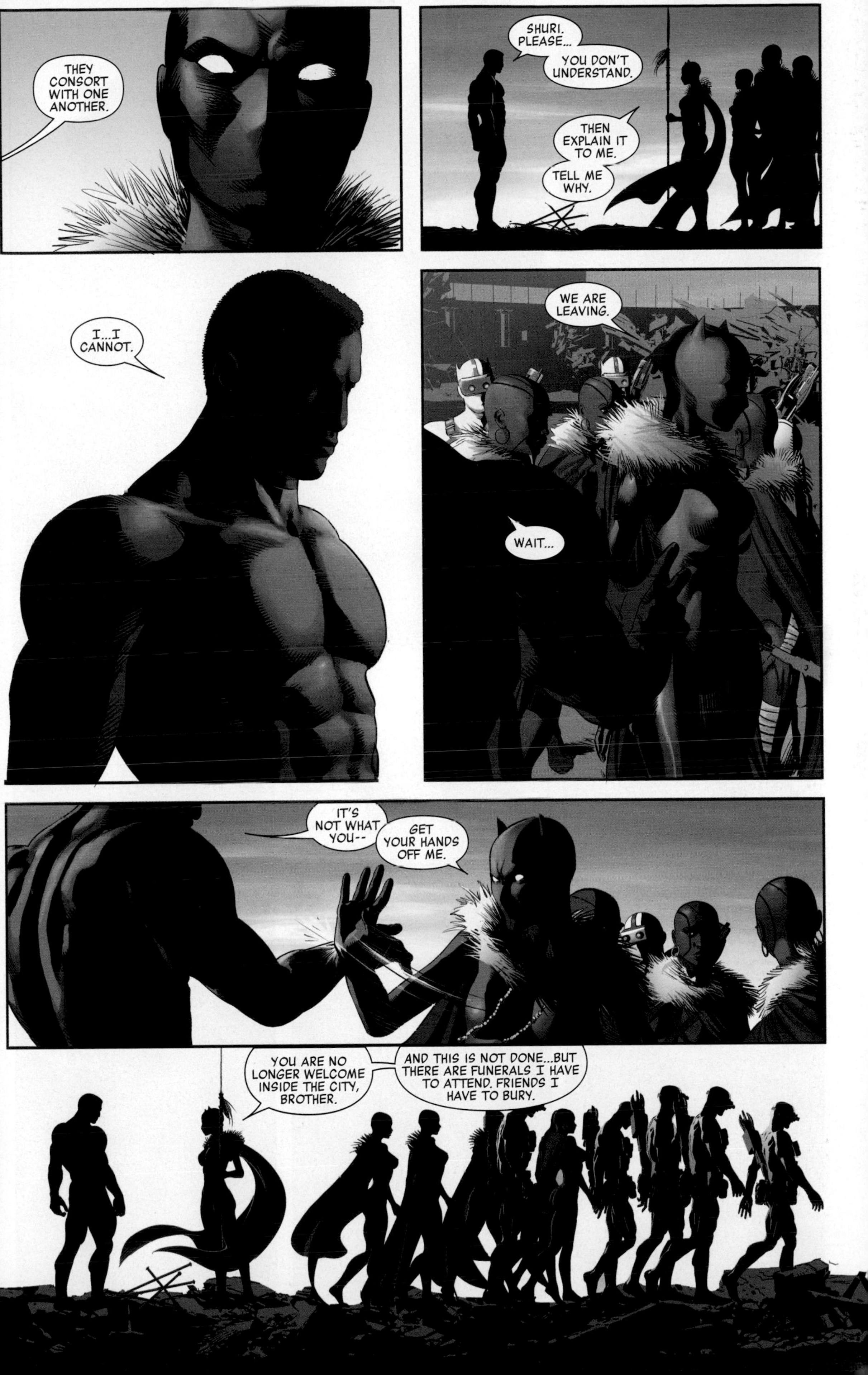
THEY CONSORT WITH ONE ANOTHER.
SHURI. PLEASE...
YOU DON'T UNDERSTAND.
THEN EXPLAIN IT TO ME.
TELL ME WHY.
I...I CANNOT.
WE ARE LEAVING.
WAIT...
IT'S NOT WHAT YOU--
GET YOUR HANDS OFF ME.
YOU ARE NO LONGER WELCOME INSIDE THE CITY, BROTHER.
AND THIS IS NOT DONE...BUT THERE ARE FUNERALS I HAVE TO ATTEND. FRIENDS I HAVE TO BURY.

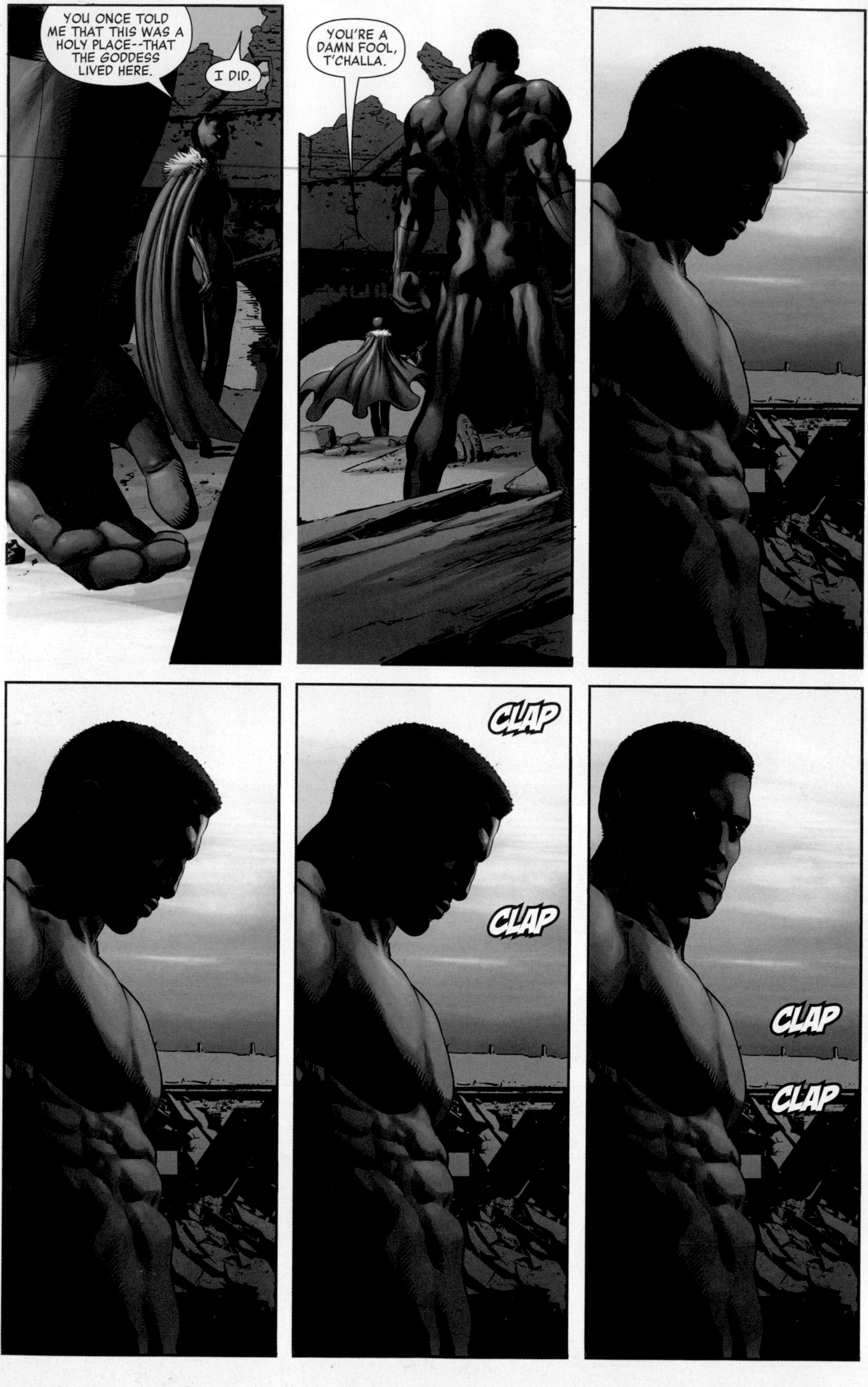
YOU ONCE TOLD ME THAT THIS WAS A HOLY PLACE--THAT THE GODDESS LIVED HERE.
I DID.
YOU'RE A DAMN FOOL, T'CHALLA.
CLAP
CLAP
CLAP
CLAP

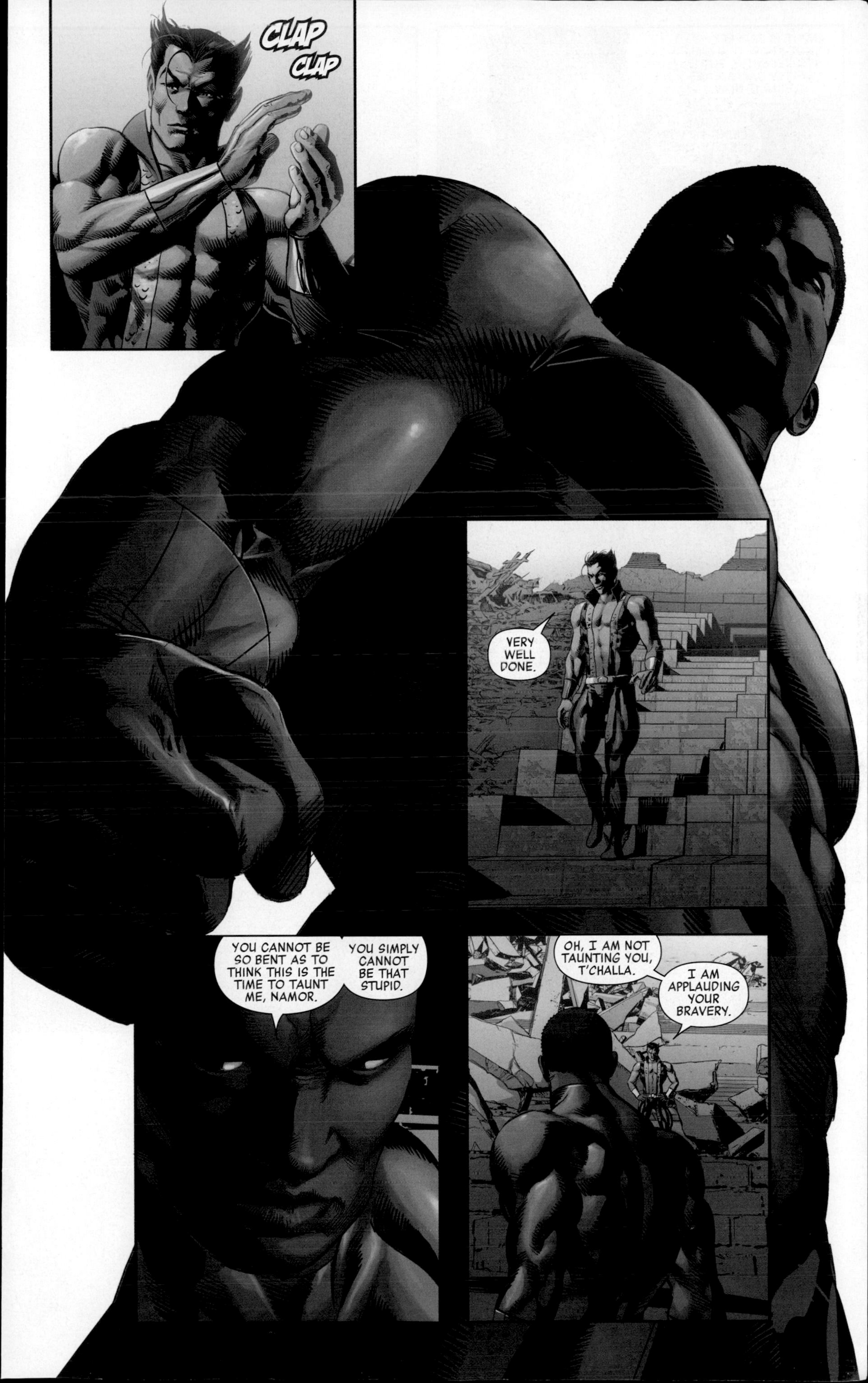
CLAP
CLAP
VERY WELL DONE.
YOU CANNOT BE SO BENT AS TO THINK THIS IS THE TIME TO TAUNT ME, NAMOR.
YOU SIMPLY CANNOT BE THAT STUPID.
OH, I AM NOT TAUNTING YOU, T'CHALLA.
I AM APPLAUDING YOUR BRAVERY.

AND IT IS BRAVERY--I DID NOT KNOW IT MYSELF UNTIL RECENTLY, BUT I AM FULLY CAPABLE OF SEEING IT NOW.

I AM SEEING SO VERY CLEARLY THESE DAYS.

SEE, NOW YOU KNOW WHAT I KNOW.

AND WHAT IS THAT?

WHAT IT'S LIKE TO FACE DEATH HAVING ALREADY LOST EVERYTHING THAT YOU HOLD DEAR.

YOU SPENT YOUR ENTIRE LIFE BUILDING A PERFECT KINGDOM, AND NOW YOU'VE BEEN CAST OUT.

YOU COULD HAVE TOLD HER MANY THINGS--WHAT WE ARE DOING. THE NATURE OF YOU AND I. YOU COULD HAVE SAID, "NAMOR IS HERE NOW...I CAN GIVE HIM TO YOU!"

BUT YOU DID NOT. BECAUSE YOU KNOW...WHAT WE USED TO CALL *LIFE* HAS VERY LITTLE WORTH THESE DAYS.

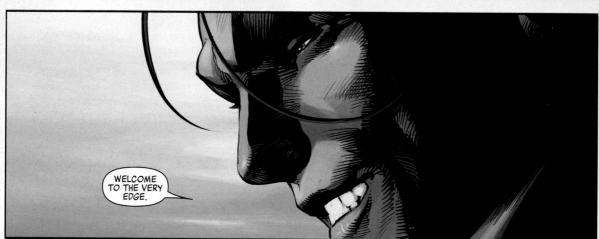

WELCOME TO THE VERY EDGE.

"FOR IT IS THE PERFECT PLACE...

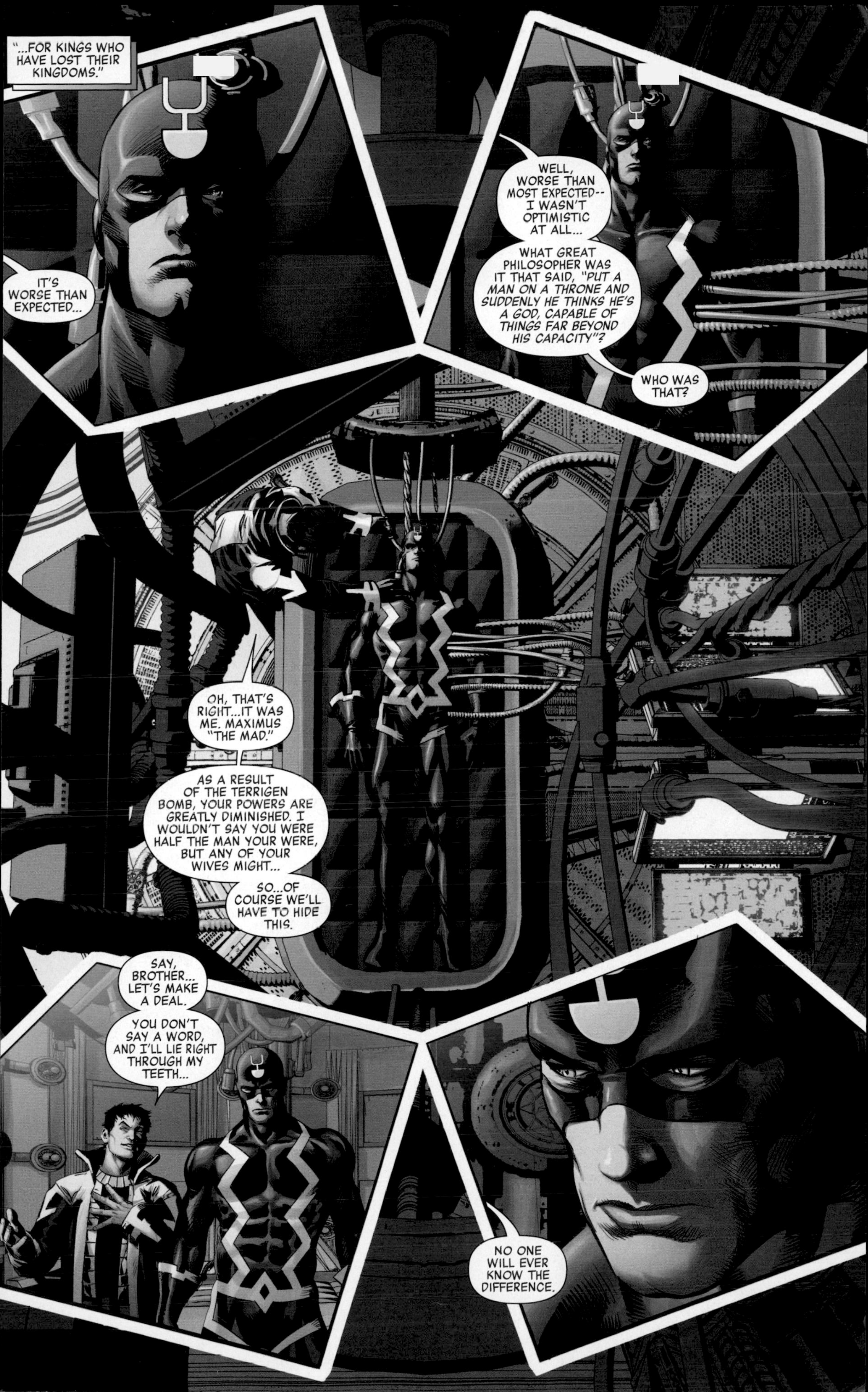
"...FOR KINGS WHO HAVE LOST THEIR KINGDOMS."
IT'S WORSE THAN EXPECTED...
WELL, WORSE THAN MOST EXPECTED-- I WASN'T OPTIMISTIC AT ALL...
WHAT GREAT PHILOSOPHER WAS IT THAT SAID, "PUT A MAN ON A THRONE AND SUDDENLY HE THINKS HE'S A GOD, CAPABLE OF THINGS FAR BEYOND HIS CAPACITY"?
WHO WAS THAT?
OH, THAT'S RIGHT...IT WAS ME. MAXIMUS "THE MAD."
AS A RESULT OF THE TERRIGEN BOMB, YOUR POWERS ARE GREATLY DIMINISHED. I WOULDN'T SAY YOU WERE HALF THE MAN YOUR WERE, BUT ANY OF YOUR WIVES MIGHT...
SO...OF COURSE WE'LL HAVE TO HIDE THIS.
SAY, BROTHER... LET'S MAKE A DEAL.
YOU DON'T SAY A WORD, AND I'LL LIE RIGHT THROUGH MY TEETH...
NO ONE WILL EVER KNOW THE DIFFERENCE.

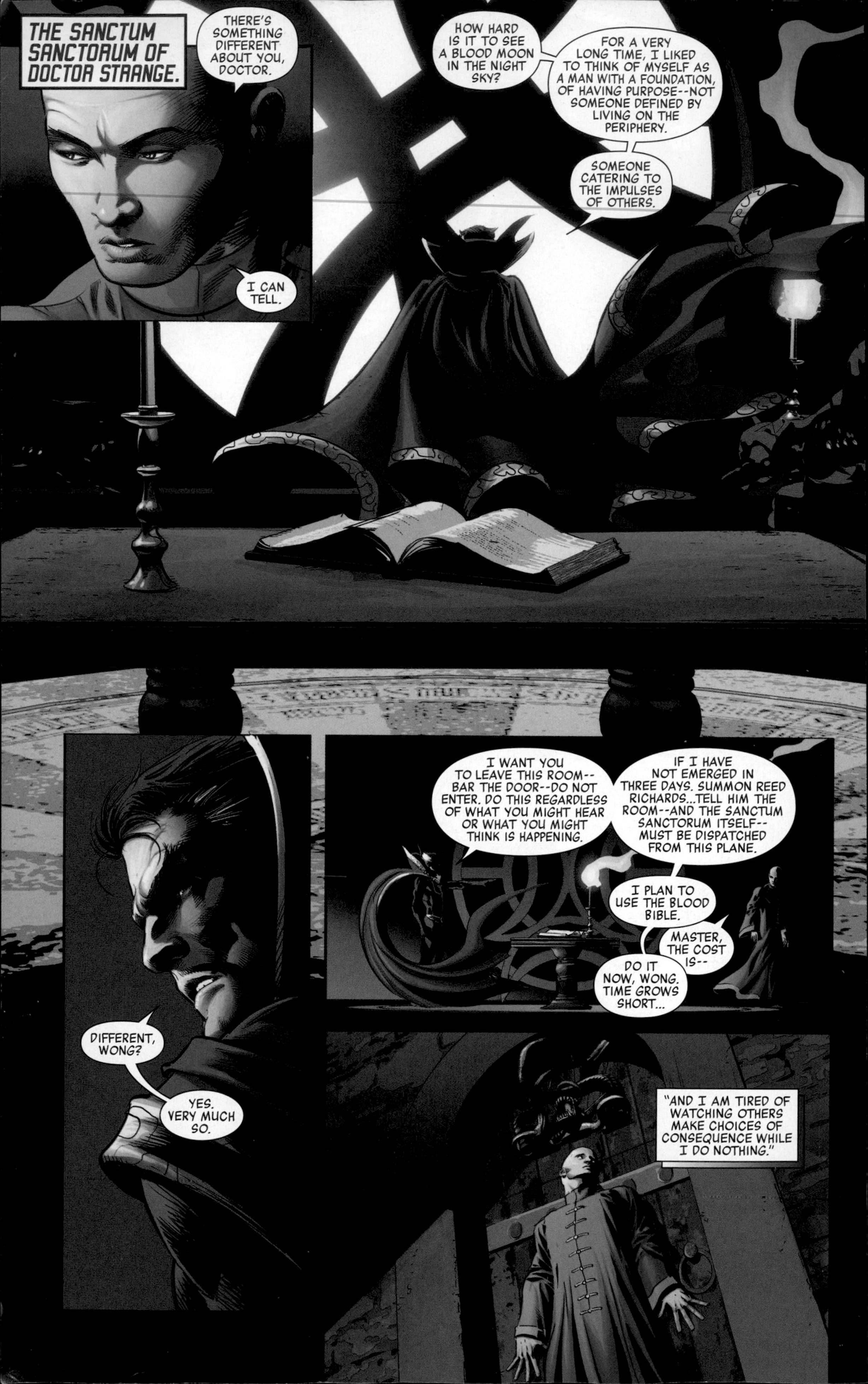
THE SANCTUM SANCTORUM OF DOCTOR STRANGE.
THERE'S SOMETHING DIFFERENT ABOUT YOU, DOCTOR.
I CAN TELL.
HOW HARD IS IT TO SEE A BLOOD MOON IN THE NIGHT SKY?
FOR A VERY LONG TIME, I LIKED TO THINK OF MYSELF AS A MAN WITH A FOUNDATION, OF HAVING PURPOSE--NOT SOMEONE DEFINED BY LIVING ON THE PERIPHERY.
SOMEONE CATERING TO THE IMPULSES OF OTHERS.
DIFFERENT, WONG?
YES. VERY MUCH SO.
I WANT YOU TO LEAVE THIS ROOM--BAR THE DOOR--DO NOT ENTER. DO THIS REGARDLESS OF WHAT YOU MIGHT HEAR OR WHAT YOU MIGHT THINK IS HAPPENING.
IF I HAVE NOT EMERGED IN THREE DAYS. SUMMON REED RICHARDS...TELL HIM THE ROOM--AND THE SANCTUM SANCTORUM ITSELF--MUST BE DISPATCHED FROM THIS PLANE.
I PLAN TO USE THE BLOOD BIBLE.
MASTER, THE COST IS--
DO IT NOW, WONG. TIME GROWS SHORT...
"AND I AM TIRED OF WATCHING OTHERS MAKE CHOICES OF CONSEQUENCE WHILE I DO NOTHING."

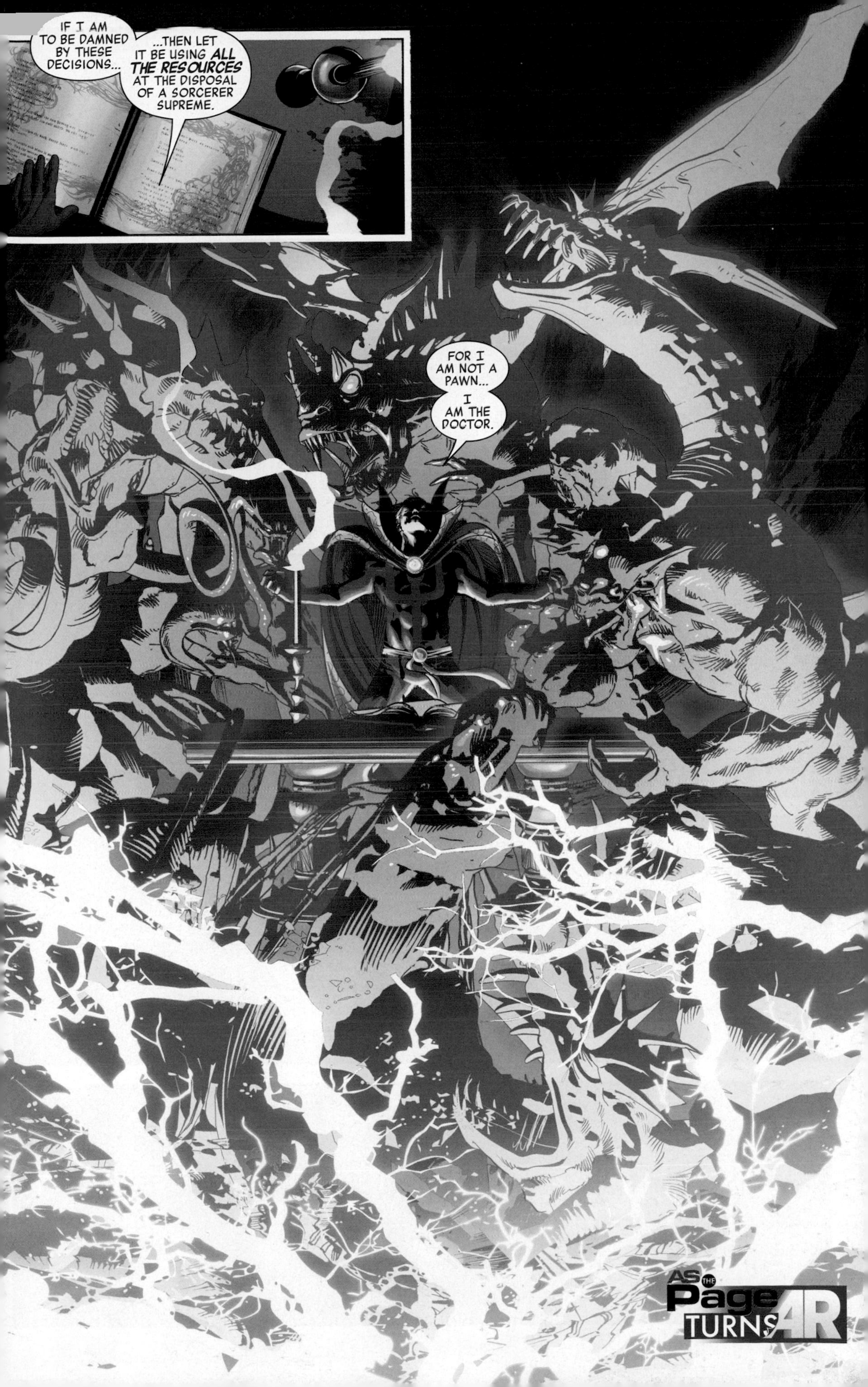
IF I AM TO BE DAMNED BY THESE DECISIONS...
...THEN LET IT BE USING ALL THE RESOURCES AT THE DISPOSAL OF A SORCERER SUPREME.
FOR I AM NOT A PAWN...
I AM THE DOCTOR.
AS THE Page TURNS AR

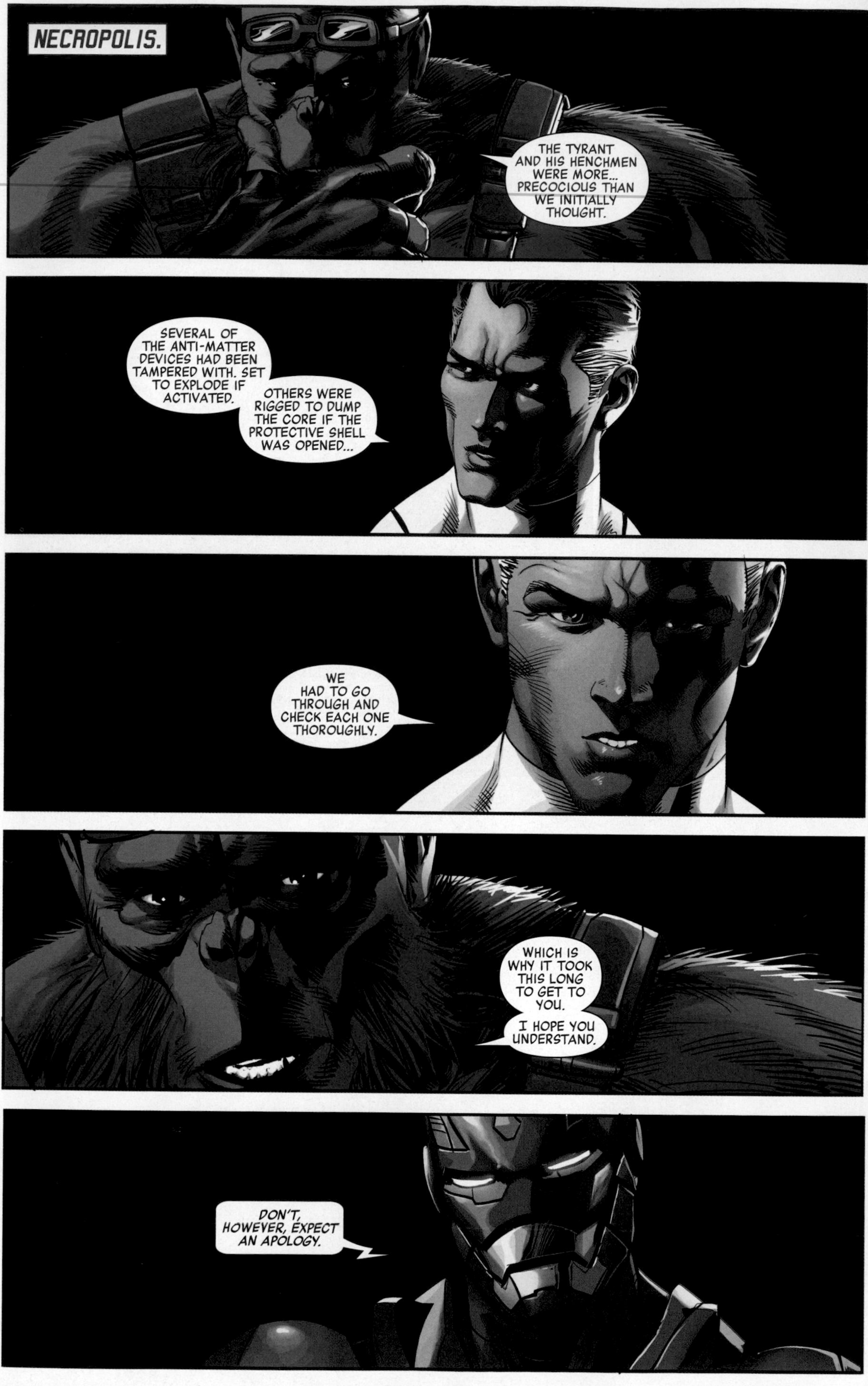
NECROPOLIS.
THE TYRANT AND HIS HENCHMEN WERE MORE... PRECOCIOUS THAN WE INITIALLY THOUGHT.
SEVERAL OF THE ANTI-MATTER DEVICES HAD BEEN TAMPERED WITH. SET TO EXPLODE IF ACTIVATED.
OTHERS WERE RIGGED TO DUMP THE CORE IF THE PROTECTIVE SHELL WAS OPENED...
WE HAD TO GO THROUGH AND CHECK EACH ONE THOROUGHLY.
WHICH IS WHY IT TOOK THIS LONG TO GET TO YOU.
I HOPE YOU UNDERSTAND.
DON'T, HOWEVER, EXPECT AN APOLOGY.

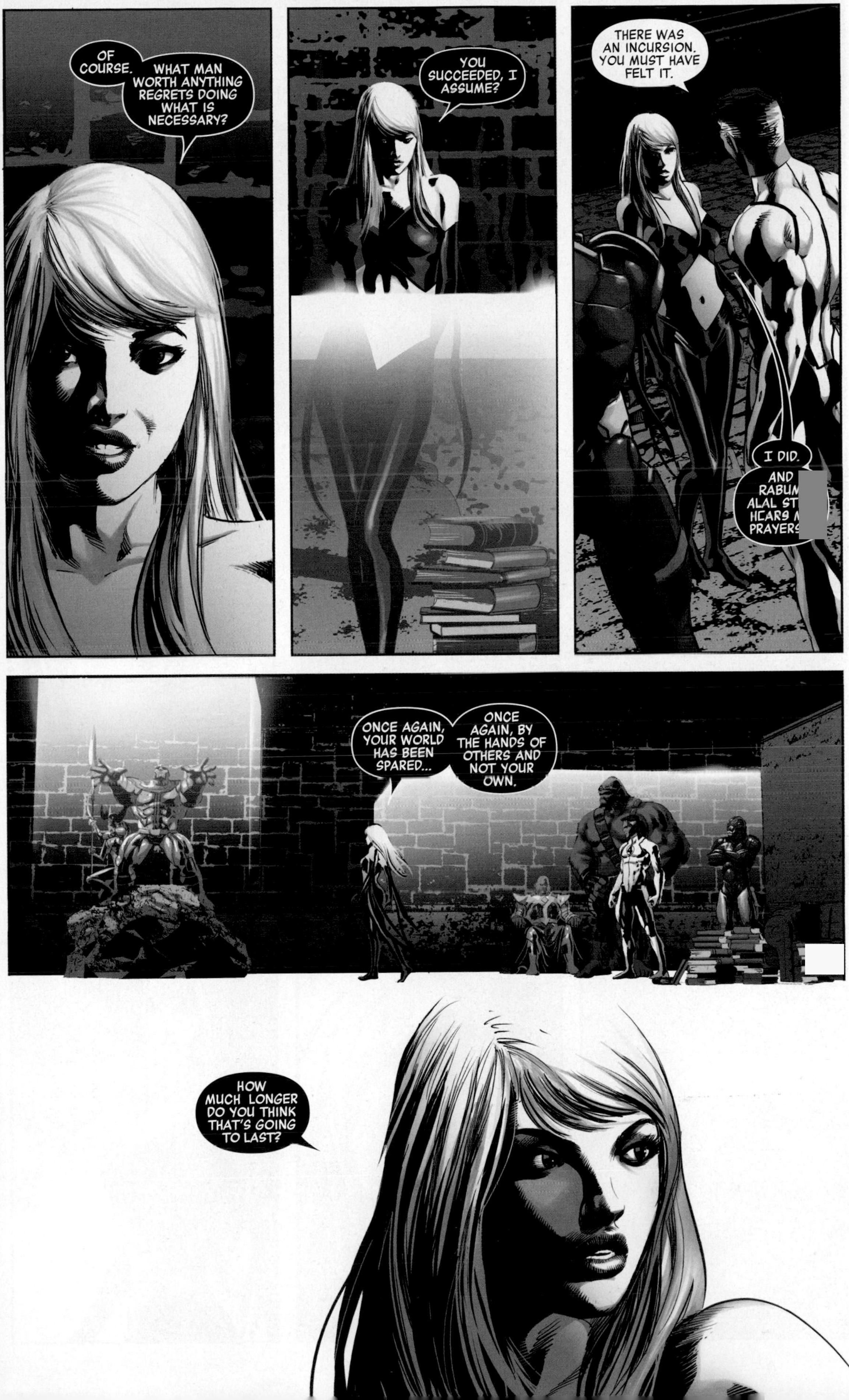
OF COURSE.
WHAT MAN WORTH ANYTHING REGRETS DOING WHAT IS NECESSARY?
YOU SUCCEEDED, I ASSUME?
THERE WAS AN INCURSION. YOU MUST HAVE FELT IT.
I DID.
AND RABUM ALAL ST HEARS M PRAYERS
ONCE AGAIN, YOUR WORLD HAS BEEN SPARED...
ONCE AGAIN, BY THE HANDS OF OTHERS AND NOT YOUR OWN.
HOW MUCH LONGER DO YOU THINK THAT'S GOING TO LAST?

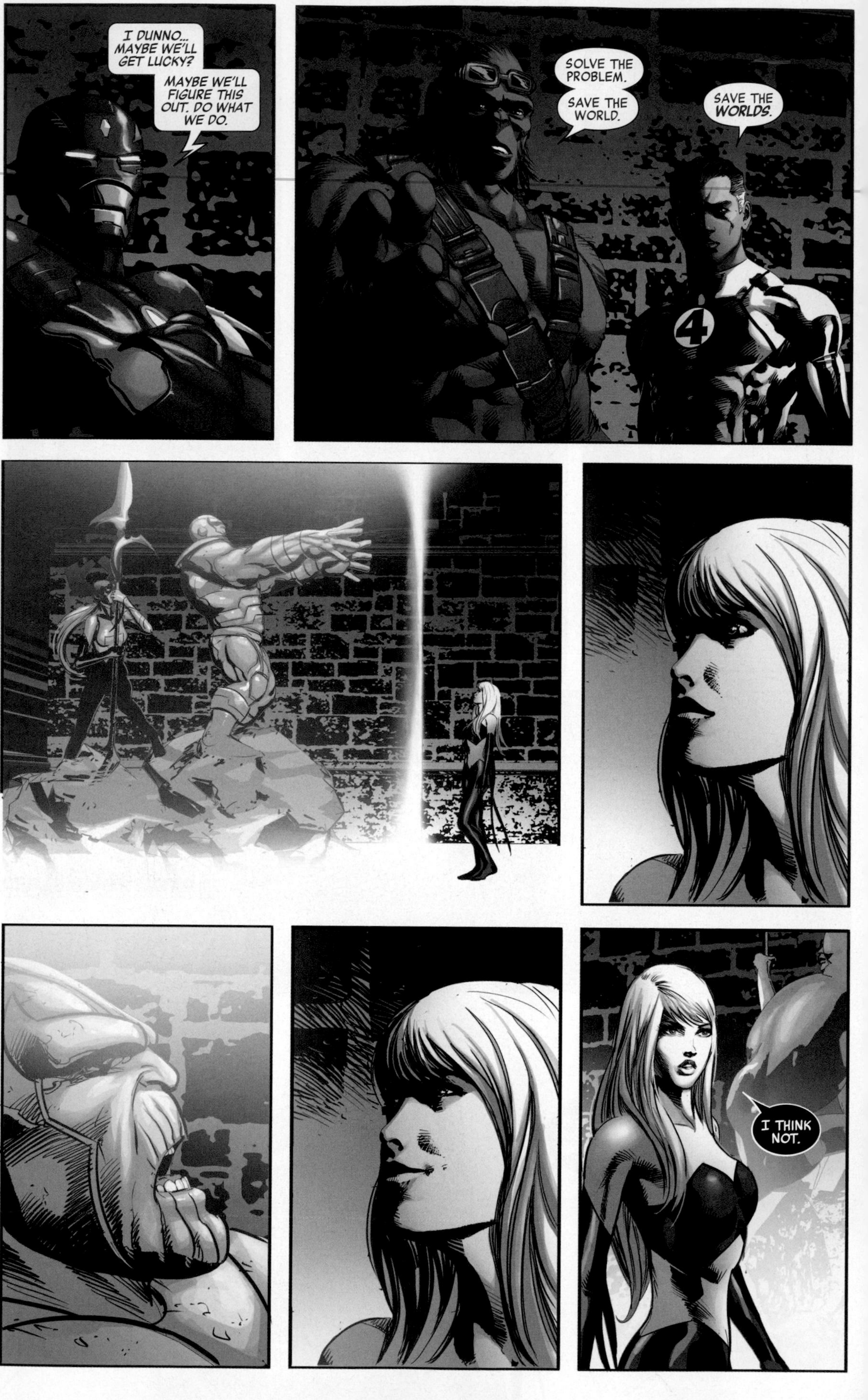
I DUNNO... MAYBE WE'LL GET LUCKY?
MAYBE WE'LL FIGURE THIS OUT. DO WHAT WE DO.
SOLVE THE PROBLEM.
SAVE THE WORLD.
SAVE THE WORLDS.
4
I THINK NOT.

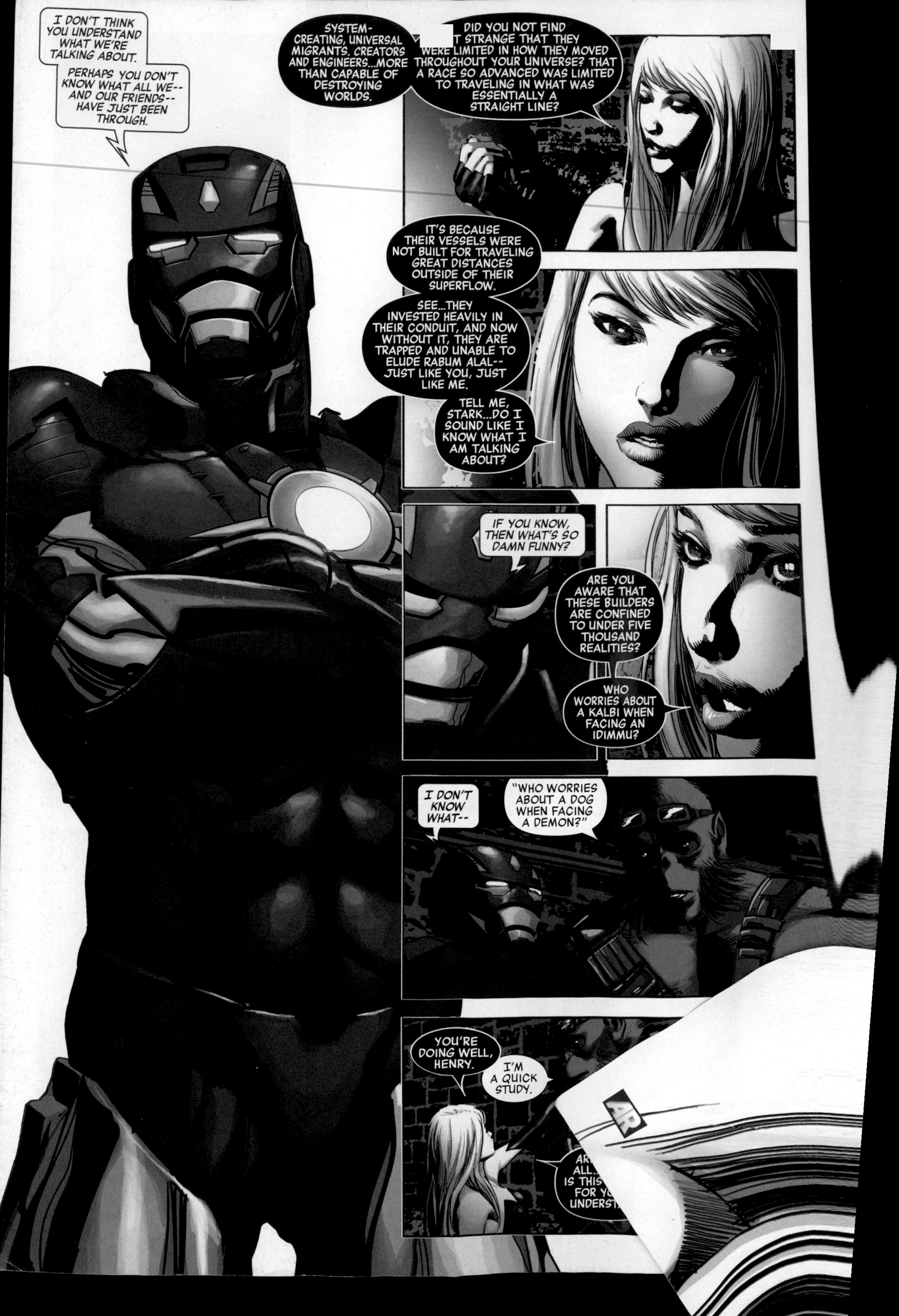
I DON'T THINK YOU UNDERSTAND WHAT WE'RE TALKING ABOUT.
PERHAPS YOU DON'T KNOW WHAT ALL WE-- AND OUR FRIENDS-- HAVE JUST BEEN THROUGH.
SYSTEM-CREATING, UNIVERSAL MIGRANTS. CREATORS AND ENGINEERS...MORE THAN CAPABLE OF DESTROYING WORLDS.
DID YOU NOT FIND T STRANGE THAT THEY WERE LIMITED IN HOW THEY MOVED THROUGHOUT YOUR UNIVERSE? THAT A RACE SO ADVANCED WAS LIMITED TO TRAVELING IN WHAT WAS ESSENTIALLY A STRAIGHT LINE?
IT'S BECAUSE THEIR VESSELS WERE NOT BUILT FOR TRAVELING GREAT DISTANCES OUTSIDE OF THEIR SUPERFLOW.
SEE...THEY INVESTED HEAVILY IN THEIR CONDUIT, AND NOW WITHOUT IT, THEY ARE TRAPPED AND UNABLE TO ELUDE RABUM ALAL-- JUST LIKE YOU, JUST LIKE ME.
TELL ME, STARK...DO I SOUND LIKE I KNOW WHAT I AM TALKING ABOUT?
IF YOU KNOW, THEN WHAT'S SO DAMN FUNNY?
ARE YOU AWARE THAT THESE BUILDERS ARE CONFINED TO UNDER FIVE THOUSAND REALITIES?
WHO WORRIES ABOUT A KALBI WHEN FACING AN IDIMMU?
I DON'T KNOW WHAT--
"WHO WORRIES ABOUT A DOG WHEN FACING A DEMON?"
YOU'RE DOING WELL, HENRY.
I'M A QUICK STUDY.

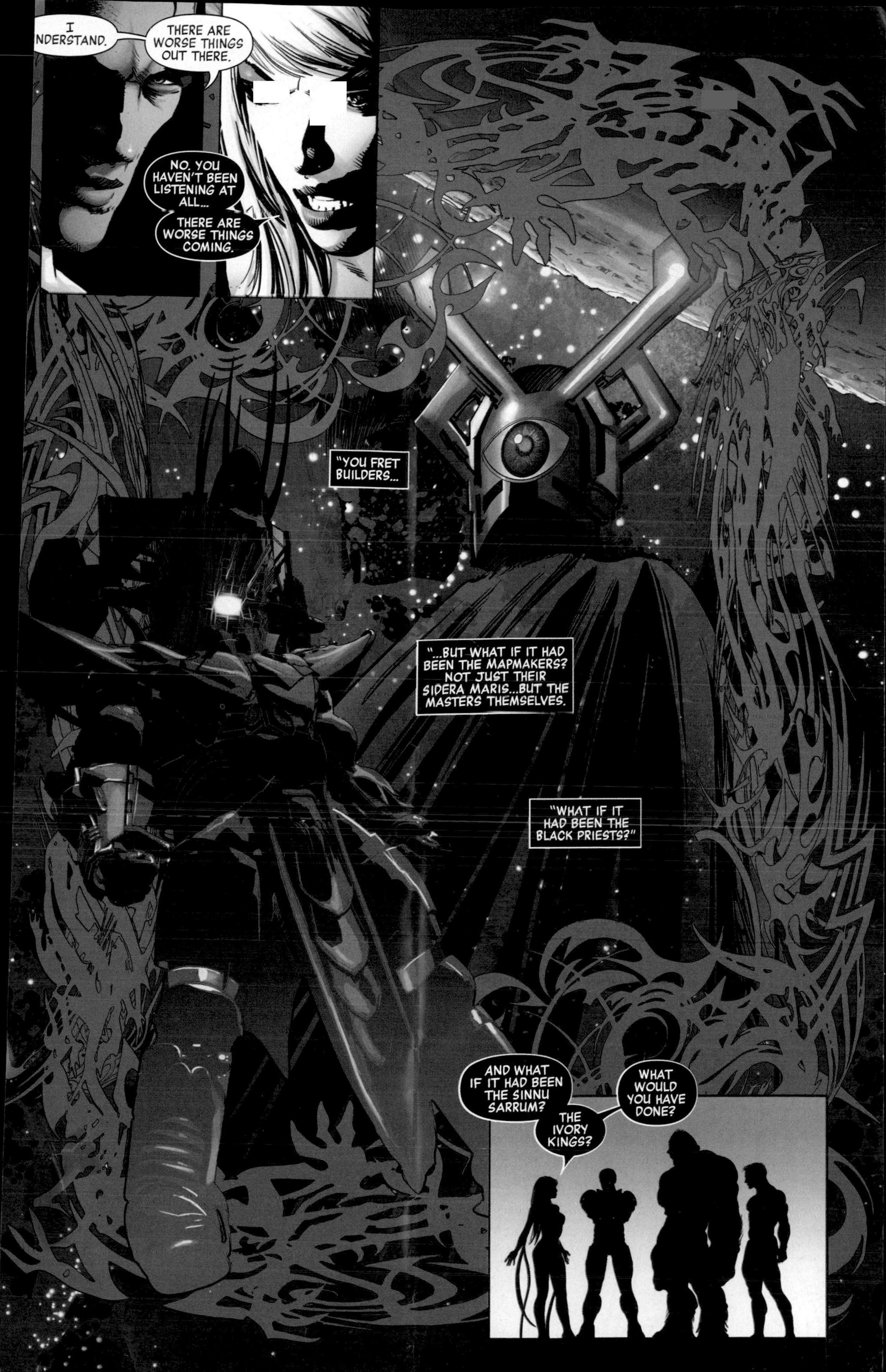
I NDERSTAND.
THERE ARE WORSE THINGS OUT THERE.
NO. YOU HAVEN'T BEEN LISTENING AT ALL...
THERE ARE WORSE THINGS COMING.
"YOU FRET BUILDERS...
"...BUT WHAT IF IT HAD BEEN THE MAPMAKERS? NOT JUST THEIR SIDERA MARIS...BUT THE MASTERS THEMSELVES.
"WHAT IF IT HAD BEEN THE BLACK PRIESTS?"
AND WHAT IF IT HAD BEEN THE SINNU SARRUM?
THE IVORY KINGS?
WHAT WOULD YOU HAVE DONE?

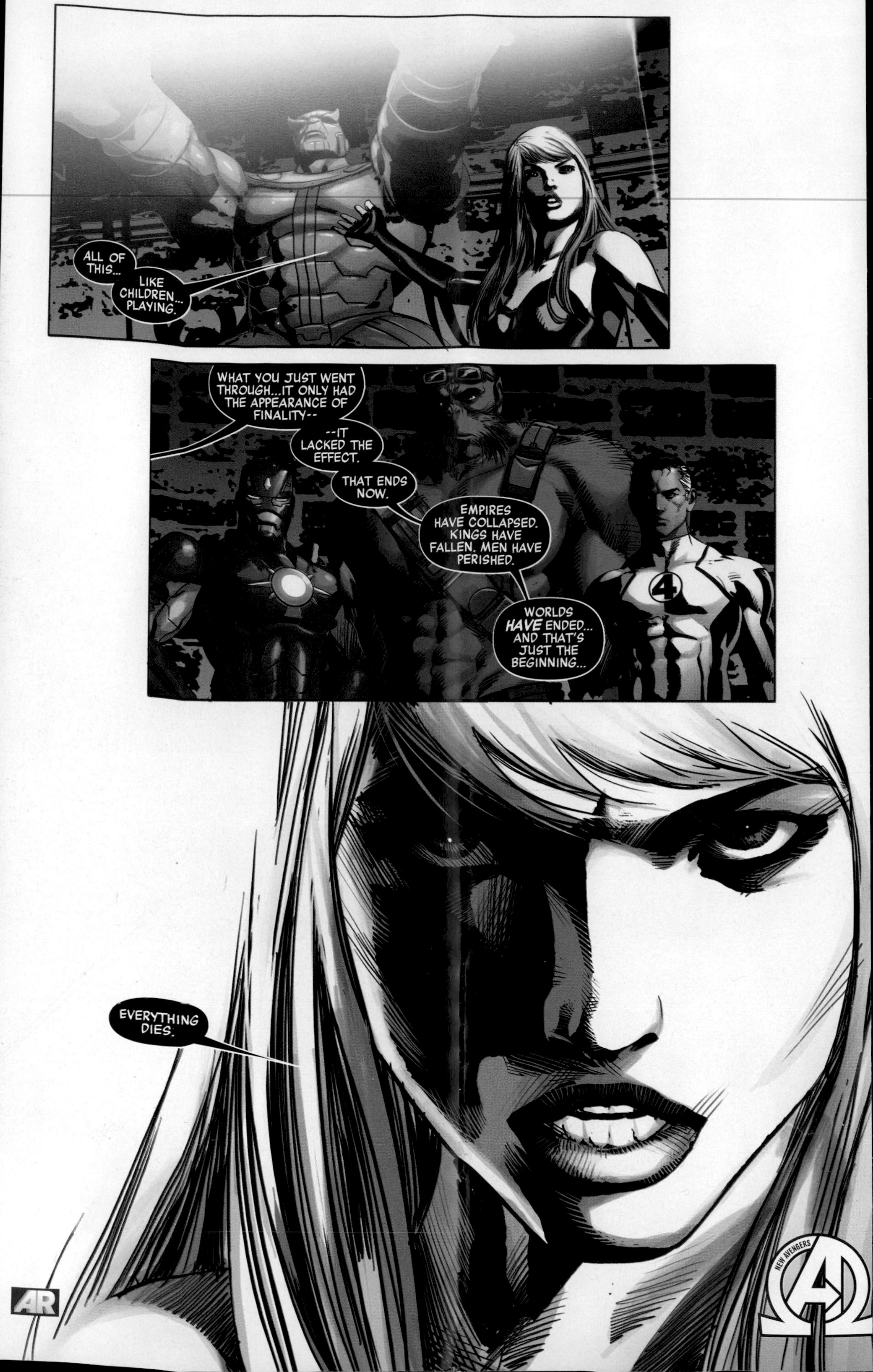
ALL OF THIS...
LIKE CHILDREN... PLAYING.
WHAT YOU JUST WENT THROUGH...IT ONLY HAD THE APPEARANCE OF FINALITY--
--IT LACKED THE EFFECT.
THAT ENDS NOW.
EMPIRES HAVE COLLAPSED. KINGS HAVE FALLEN. MEN HAVE PERISHED.
WORLDS HAVE ENDED... AND THAT'S JUST THE BEGINNING...
EVERYTHING DIES.

YOU'RE NEARING THE END OF BEING PASSIVE. THIS TIME OF TALKING ABOUT WHAT TO DO IS DRAWING TO A CLOSE...

YOU DON'T KNOW THAT, BLACK SWAN...

EVERYTHING HAS A SOLUTION.

EVERYTHING.

AND JUST HOW DID YOU SOLVE THIS INCURSION, REED RICHARDS?

WE DIDN'T HAVE TO.

YOU'RE MAKING MY POINT FOR ME.

ACTUALLY, IT'S INTERESTING...

THEY WERE A MULTI-UNIVERSAL, ANCIENT CIVILIZATION CALLED BUILDERS. WHO IT SEEMED--

HA! HA!

HA! HA! HA!

THE BUILDERS, YOU SAY...

HOW VERY OMINOUS. THAT IS INDEED SOME THREAT.

#7

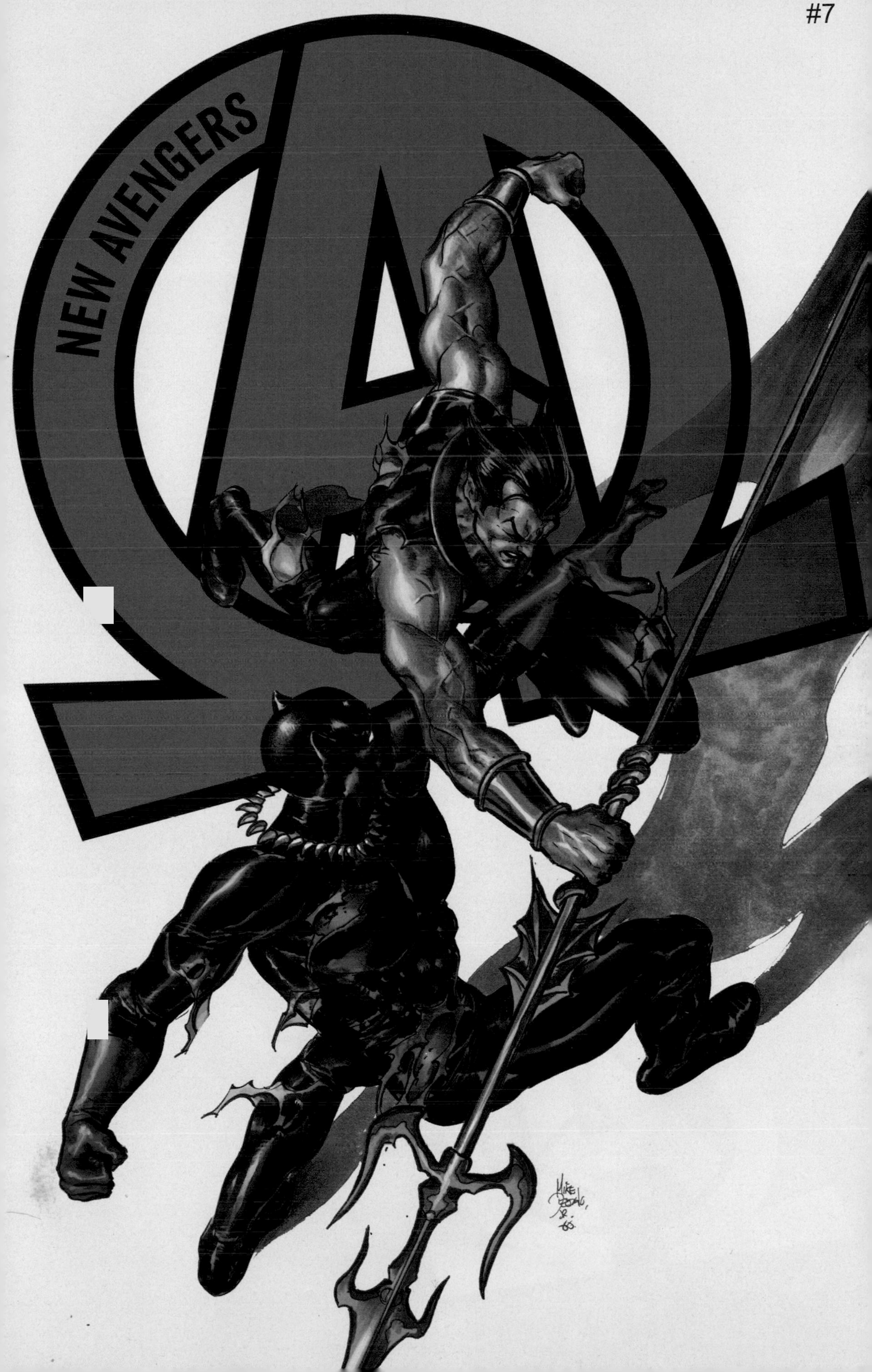
NEW AVENGERS

#8

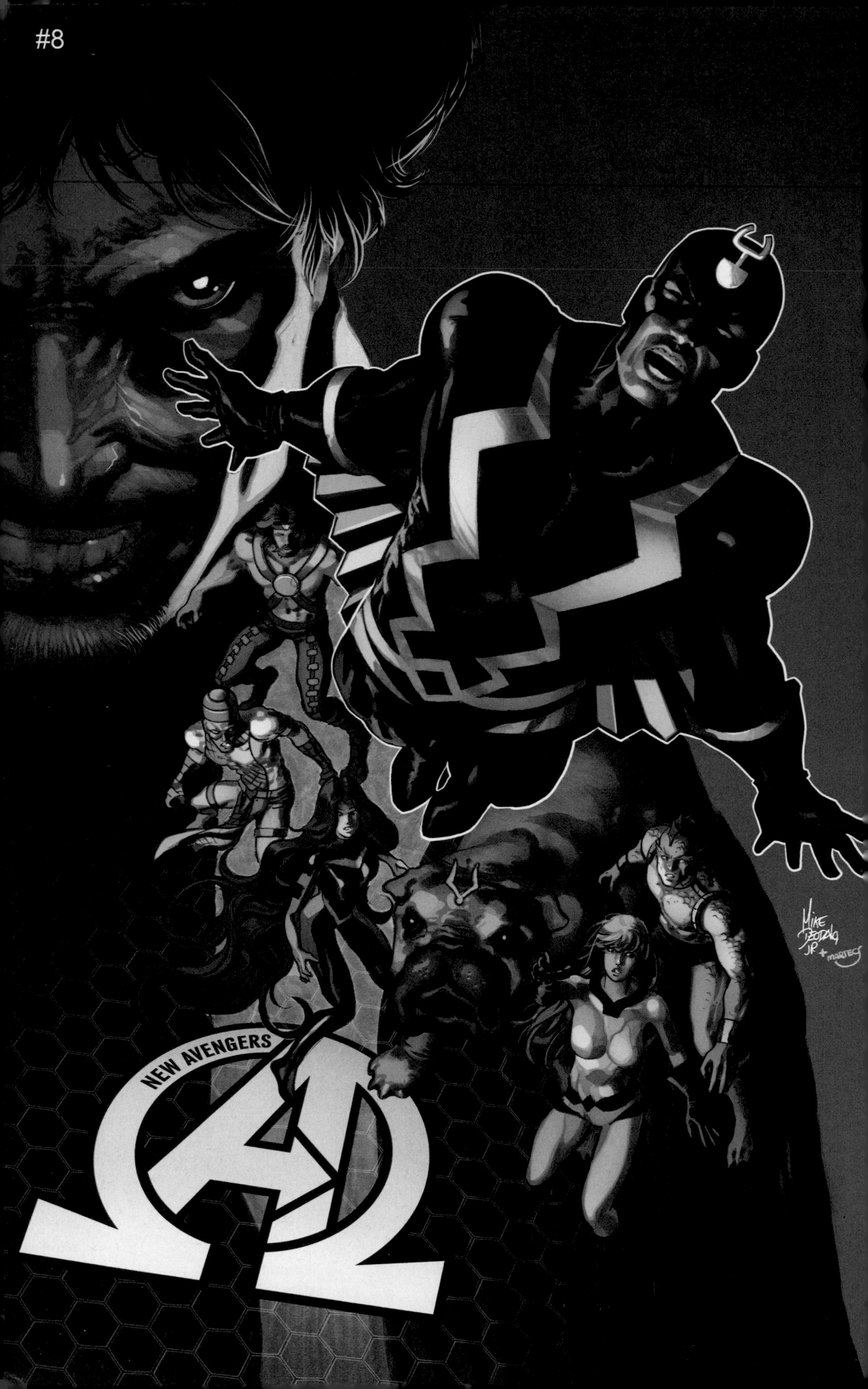
NEW AVENGERS

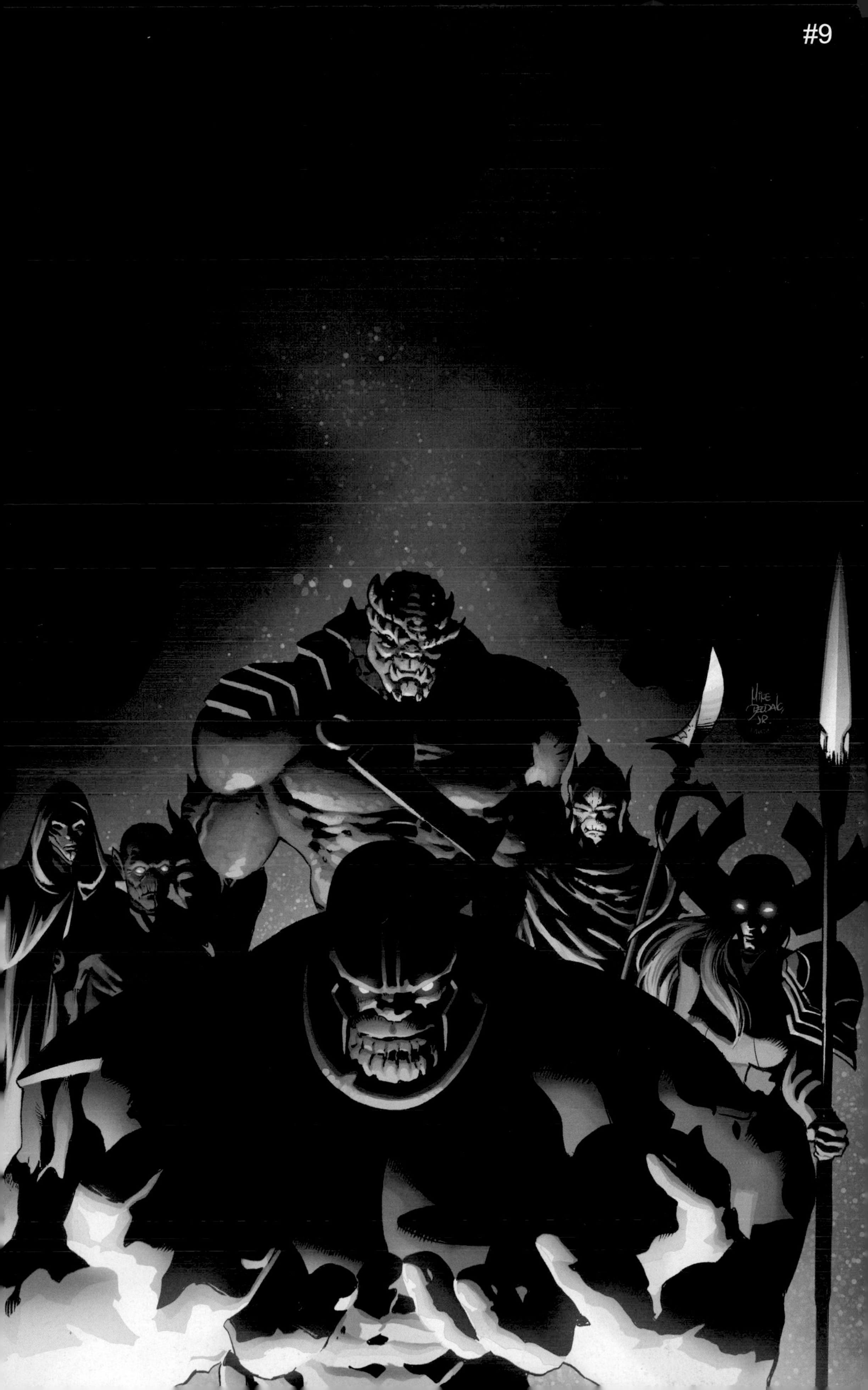
#9

#10

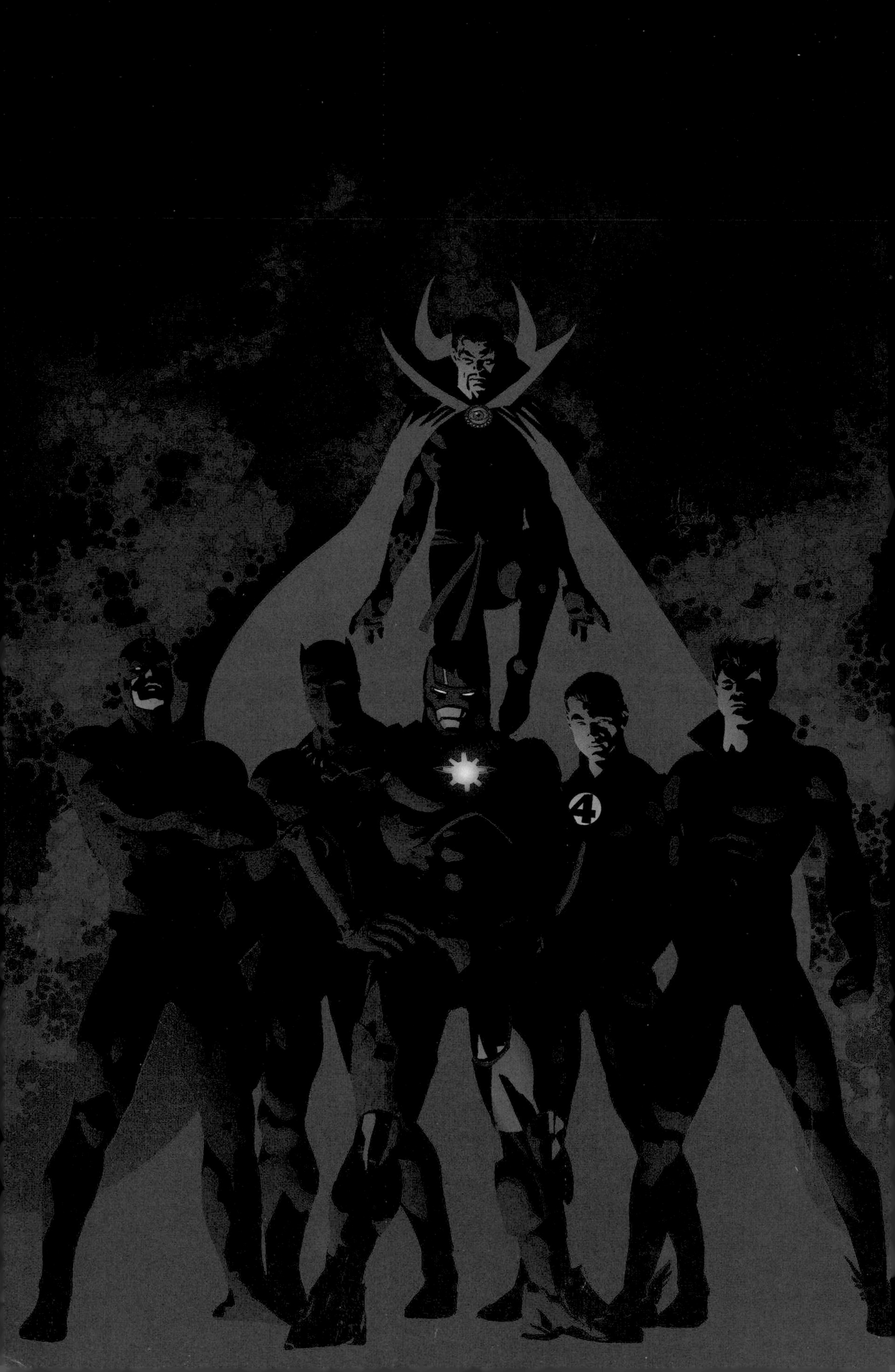

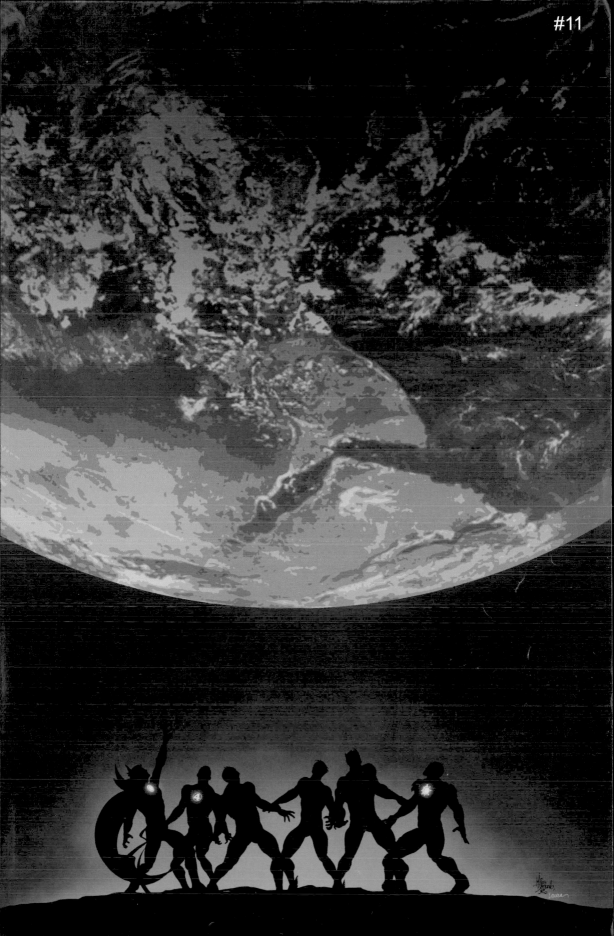

#12

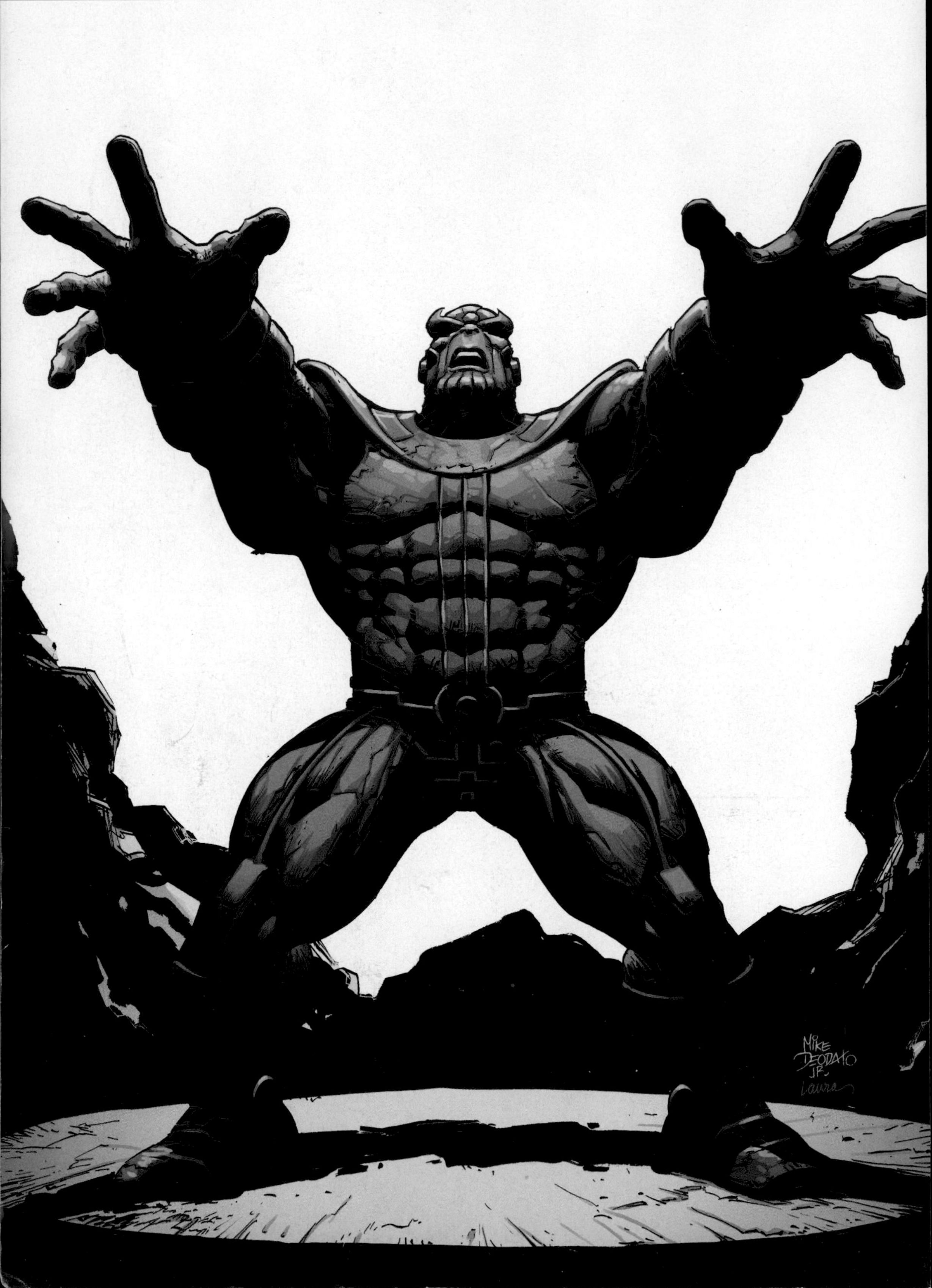
MIKE DEODATO JR.
Laura

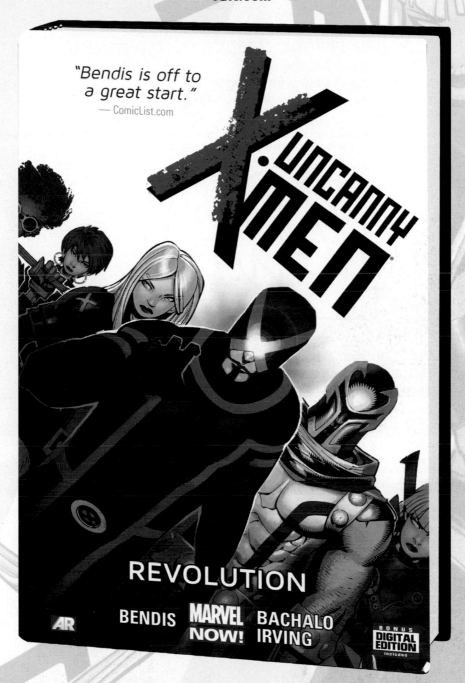

MARVEL AR AUGMENTED REALITY

MARVEL AUGMENTED REALITY (AR) ENHANCES AND CHANGES THE WAY YOU EXPERIENCE COMICS!

TO ACCESS THE FREE MARVEL AR CONTENT IN THIS BOOK*:

1. Locate the AR logo within the comic.
2. Go to Marvel.com/AR in your web browser.
3. Search by series title to find the corresponding AR.
4. Enjoy Marvel AR!

*All AR content that appears in this book has been archived and will be available only at Marvel.com/AR – no longer in the Marvel AR App. Content subject to change and availability.

NEW AVENGERS AR INDEX